JIMMY DELANEY

–THE STUFF OF LEGEND–

JIMMY DELANEY

– THE STUFF OF LEGEND –

David W. Potter

breedon **books**
PUBLISHING

First published in Great Britain in 2006 by
The Breedon Books Publishing Company Limited
Breedon House, 3 The Parker Centre,
Derby, DE21 4SZ.

ISBN 1 85983 496 5

Printed and bound by Biddles, King's Lynn, Norfolk.

Contents

Acknowledgements

I am very grateful for the help I have received from several sources in writing this book. First of all to the Delaney family, especially Pat, Kathleen, John (and his wife Trish) and Anne-Marie (whose son John Kennedy now wears the Hoops), who have given me a great deal of help and encouragement, as indeed have other members of the Cleland community.

In Ireland, Plunkett Carter was very helpful, as indeed was Willie Curran of Derry City. Sean Quinn of Shotts gave me some information about the provenance of the Delaneys. The Elgin historian Robert Weir was particularly helpful for his time at Elgin. My thanks are also due to my friends (who share with me the endogenous, terminal and irreversible condition called 'being Celtic daft') Tom Campbell, Craig McAughtrie and Eugene MacBride. They have given me loads of encouragement.

The library staff in the Wellgate Centre, Dundee, the National Library of Scotland and in Broxburn, Falkirk and Elgin were all very helpful and supportive.

Introduction

TO SAY that the story of Jimmy Delaney is the stuff of legend is a cliché. No one football player dominated the lives and thoughts of so many people for so long, or achieved so much for such a variety of football teams. To win three Cup-winners' medals in three separate countries must be unique, certainly in British football, but no less memorable was his goal which brought victory to the football-starved nation of Scotland in the Victory International of 1946.

He is also unusual, if not unique, in that he once had a street demonstration demanding his inclusion in the Scotland team to play England in the wartime international of 1944. But this was what the name Delaney meant to so many Scotsmen. In the same way that Patsy Gallacher was the most talked about name in the trenches of World War One, so too it was the name of Jimmy Delaney that lightened many a sore heart in North Africa, Italy and Burma, and on the High Seas.

This was a man born in a football-mad mining community in 1914, who learned his trade the hard way. He became a speedy right-winger with the ability to hit the dead-ball line (or the bye-line as it is called in Scotland) and cross with pinpoint accuracy, or more dramatically to cut inside and create havoc in the penalty area. He won honours – the Scottish Cup, Scottish League and Empire Exhibition Trophy – for his beloved Celtic until two severe blows cruelly disrupted his career. One was the shattering of his arm in a horrendous accident in a game against Arbroath in April 1939 and the other of course was the invasion of Poland by Adolf Hitler five months later. Yet he recovered, playing for Celtic in the unreal circumstances of World War Two until, with hostilities over, he asked for a pay rise and was soon on his way to Manchester United.

There he teamed up with fellow Scot and fellow Celtic supporter Matt Busby to win the English Cup for Manchester United, beating Stanley Matthews and Blackpool in the final of 1948. He formed an integral part of the first of several great Manchester United sides which were born under Busby.

Considered too old for the English League at the age of 35, he returned to Aberdeen in 1950 before moving to Falkirk. He then tried his luck in Ireland where he won the Irish Cup in 1954. Incredibly, he almost did the same in southern Ireland when his Cork Athletic side lost narrowly in the final.

The illustrious career of this soldier of fortune is already remarkable, but in addition he is also considered one of the best players of all time in the view of several Celtic historians. He won 13 caps for Scotland and, but for World War Two, would have won a great many more.

There were few more sporting players than Jimmy Delaney. He knew how the game should be played and he played it cleanly and fairly. On one occasion, when asked to present prizes at a school sports day, he uttered the immortal words, 'better to be a champion sport than a sports champion'. He should know – for he was both.

Chapter 1

The Early Years
1914–1933

IN VIEW of the fact that war indirectly played such a large part in Jimmy Delaney's life, it is perhaps ironic that he was born on 3 September 1914. He was therefore exactly 25 when World War Two broke out, but as we shall see, circumstances precluded him being called up for military service. For that at least he could be thankful.

As it was, Jimmy was born when the world was just a month into World War One. It was a terrible event, but the sad thing is that nobody knew, on 3 September 1914, as Jimmy Delaney came into the world, just quite how terrible it was going to be. It was still at the stage where everybody was frightened that they were going to miss out on the adventure. Already the British Expeditionary Force were in the field at Mons, defending gallant little Belgium over whom there was all the fuss, while the *poilus*, as the soldiers of the French army were called, were girding their loins for the defence of Paris. Paris would be saved, but Belgium would be lost. It would take a great deal of blood to get it back.

Jimmy Delaney was born in Cleland, a small mining village in Lanarkshire, close to Motherwell and Wishaw and not too far away from Glasgow, the massive second city of the empire and a city whose resources of manpower and industrial strength would soon be heavily relied upon in the struggle. Jimmy was of Irish descent, and when he was still young, his father willingly gave of his free time to help build the beautifully impressive Carfin Lourdes Grotto, Scotland's national shrine to Our Blessed Lady, which was finished in 1922.

Jimmy's birth certificate says that his father was called Patrick Delaney and that he was a coalminer, and that his mother was called Bridget. Her maiden surname was Nash, but the birth certificate also says that she was 'previously Delaney', as if she had been married to another gentleman, also called

Delaney, before she married Patrick on 28 February 1911. Jimmy was born at 159 Omoa Road, Cleland, at 7pm on 3 September 1914. It was a Thursday evening and 'home deliveries' were the norm in those days. Maternity hospitals did not exist as such, normal hospitals would only be used in times of emergency and nursing homes were the prerogative of the very rich. Very rich the Delaneys were certainly not.

Cleland owed its existence to two things. One was the Industrial Revolution and the other was the Irish Diaspora (dispersal). The Industrial Revolution had been going on all through the 19th century and the Irish Diaspora, which had been a trickle in the first half of the 19th century, soon became a flood after the potato famine of 1846. The fact that Cleland was virtually an Irish village (to this day one will struggle to find a Rangers supporter there!) does not make it unique. Croy, whence sprung Celtic's mighty Jimmy Quinn, is exactly the same and there are many areas of Scotland's cities which were and in some cases remain Irish dominated. One thinks of most of Glasgow's East End, for example, of Leith in Edinburgh and of Lochee in Dundee, which was happy to be commonly known from its earliest days as 'Little Tip' or 'Tipperary'!

The name 'Delaney' is explained in Dr MacLysaght's book *The Surnames of Ireland* as follows:

> *O Delaney or O Dubhshlainne (dubh – black, Slainne – perhaps the river Slaney). The prefix O has been almost completely discarded in the anglicised form of the name. It appears as Delane in Mayo. Both now and in the past it is of Leix and Kilkenny.*

The name itself has been spread throughout the world, and there is an obvious connection with 'Delano', the middle name of Franklin D. Roosevelt, President of the US from 1932 to 1945. Little is known about how this branch of the Delaney family came from Ireland to Scotland – other than it was sometime in the 19th century.

It is possible that the Delaneys came from Kilkenny. Sean Quinn tells the story of how some relatives of his were visiting Castlecomer in Kilkenny and raving about a player for Glasgow Celtic called Jimmy Delaney. A local of Castlecomer said that he knew the Delaney family, who came from 'over the hill', pointing to a place called Clough about a mile from Castlecomer.

The arrival of the Irish in Scotland is a study in itself. Many books have been written about their struggles, their hardships and their eventual triumph of being accepted into a Presbyterian country with no great history of tolerance. But the Irish were certainly needed for the factories and, in the case of Cleland, the mines of Scotland. Coal was required for almost everything in those days, even in peacetime and much more so in war. Fortunately there seemed to be a virtually inexhaustible supply of it. Old King Coal, as they said, was indeed a merry old soul.

The work of course was awful. Dirty, dangerous, damp – the conditions would hardly be much superior to those of the notorious silver mines at Laurion in Athens in the 5th century BC where slaves worked. Technically, of course, a miner in 19th and early 20th-century Scotland was a free man, but in practice little opportunity would be granted to him for any other job. It would be assumed that a miner's son would himself become a miner. A few would emigrate to Canada or Australia, some would disappear to London or Glasgow and a very fortunate few could become professional footballers. Certainly enough tried, but few actually made it.

The good thing about life in Cleland in the early years of the 20th century would have been the companionship. A siege mentality would very commonly develop in mining and in Irish areas. The feeling that the outside world was against them encouraged the inhabitants of Cleland to stick together. There would, for example, be a very good 'child protection' system of mothers looking after all the children, the local branch of the union would organise a 'social security' system and there would be a tremendous feeling of belonging. By the time that Jimmy was born in 1914, the Liberals of Henry Campbell-Bannerman and Herbert Asquith had slowly laid the foundations of the welfare state. At last there was now some sort of commitment from politicians that looking after the poorest of society was a good thing. A real welfare state, however, was a good 30 years (and two dreadful World Wars) away.

It would be expected that a boy living in Cleland would be interested in football and that he would have an emotional commitment to Glasgow Celtic Football Club. This institution had revolutionised the sport in Scotland since its foundation 25 years before Jimmy's birth. Its name was synonymous with good football and it was the representative of the Irish community. Under Willie Maley, and with men like Jimmy McMenemy, Jimmy Quinn and Patsy Gallacher, it had brought success to the Irish community, giving them a much-needed boost and support. McMenemy and Quinn, being native Scotsmen, had played successfully for the national team, which in those days beat England more often than not. Indeed, if there had been a World Cup in those days, Scotland would undeniably have won it.

Celtic had even, crucially, touched liberal opinion in Scotland and shown that there was at least one thing that the Irish could do, even if it was just playing football. As a result, love of Celtic had spread to areas other than the Catholic heartlands of West Central Scotland, and Maley had always been shrewd enough to realise that for Celtic to flourish, a few non-Catholics would have to be employed. This broadened the base of Celtic and allowed an increasing number of Presbyterians to admire and support the club, a phenomenon that was particularly marked in the east of Scotland.

This did not in any way alter the fact that the Irish community now had its team, and a successful team it was as well. In the year that World War One broke out, Celtic had won a League and Cup double (as they had in 1907 and 1908) and there were signs that the 1914 team was as great as the team had been between 1905 and 1910, when they won six League championships in a row. Sadly the war had now become the most important thing in Scottish life, even though football did continue and Celtic did continue winning.

Cleland, being a mining village, was comparatively less affected by the war than other parts of Scotland, as fewer men were involved in the Army. Of course, there was the early rush to join and Kitchener's infamous pointing finger in 1915 and 1916 would have persuaded some young men that life overseas in uniform was preferable to life down the pits in Cleland, but the country needed miners as much as it needed soldiers and the moral blackmail would have been correspondingly less. Near the railway station in Cleland, however, there is a memorial to those who died in World War One.

Little seems to be known about young Jimmy's early life, but times were hard. Jimmy would have started school in 1919 when World War One was over, but another war was going on between owners of mines and their workers. Glasgow had seen unrest and strife in the George Square riots and had rightly earned the name 'Red Clydeside'. Troops were deployed in Glasgow in 1919, and the Scottish Secretary of State, Robert Munro, talked openly about a 'Bolshevik rising'.

It was often stated that World War One was fought 'to make the world a safer place for Henry Ford and Pierrepont Morgan', the two great capitalists of the day. This was not exactly true of course, for many of the officer class gave their lives as well, but one of the legacies was that the ruling classes were ever edgy and fearful of what had happened in Russia in 1917. They frequently saw any concession to their workers, however justified or deserved, as a sign of weakness. This attitude did not lead to good industrial relations, especially as the workers felt that their sacrifices in World War One were worthier of a greater reward than seemed to be coming their way.

Mining unrest was ongoing throughout the early 1920s, culminating in the General Strike of 1926. This would have seen Cleland and the Delaney family very much involved. The resultant fiasco, which saw the Trade Union Congress give in after two weeks and leave the miners to be starved back to work a few months later, left a legacy of victimisation and bitterness. Poverty and starvation would have been no alien concept to the miners of Cleland in the late 1920s. Jimmy was less than 12 years old at the time of the General Strike. He was no stranger to hard times.

Perhaps this had an effect on him 20 years later when he left his beloved Celtic for more money. He would have had no real desire to go – for it involved leaving the village he loved and the football team that he loved. But if he felt that he was being 'taken the loan of' by employers, no matter who they were, the struggle of the miners in the 1920s may well have been a significant factor in the Delaney subconscious – something that is hard to fully comprehend in the relatively prosperous early years of the 21st century. Sadly, the middle-class, affluent and out-of-touch Celtic directors in 1946 also found this hard to understand – to the detriment of all concerned.

There was also another struggle that must have affected Jimmy's early life. Across the Irish Sea a nation was being born, but the process was long and grievous. By 1923 there was some sort of a resolution, with a 26-county Irish free state in existence. This was virtually autonomous but technically still swore allegiance to the British crown and very definitely missed out the six counties of the industrial North. But the struggle, the ongoing struggle, would have an effect on the Irish throughout the world.

One could of course say, 'but this is Scotland!' So it was, but one would be very naïve to think that the Irish did not view with concern and alarm the things that had gone on in Ireland. The brutality of the British Army and their criminal henchmen the Black and Tans was nothing more than a continuation of the work of Oliver Cromwell, William of Orange and the Redcoats, and the Irish in Scotland had no reason to believe that they were entirely safe there. Indeed, when Celtic won the Scottish League at Morton in April 1922, scenes of sectarian violence marred the game.

It did not help, for example, when the General Assembly of the Church of Scotland in 1923 urged the Government to 'appoint a Commission to inquire into the whole [Irish Catholic] situation, with a view to the preservation and protection of Scottish nationality and civilization'. They went on to say, 'If therefore the Scottish people wish to safeguard their heritage, they cannot afford to lose time in taking whatever steps may be necessary to secure this just and patriotic end.'

'Whatever steps may be necessary.' Does this include violence? One hopes not, but there seems little doubt that some fanatics (and there were many in the 1920s – disturbed people who had seen too much violence and bloodshed in the khaki of the British Army) could take that statement as some justification from the Church of Scotland itself for their violent actions.

It is of course incomprehensible for the Church of Scotland in modern times to take such a view. The Kirk now has a reputation for being boring, benign, tolerant and sadly utterly useless, and most members would be appalled and embarrassed by anything like that. But the 1920s were not normal times. The Irish rebellion of 1916 was still seen as a stab in the back to the British Army fighting in France and elsewhere. The struggle of the early 1920s, which had created its own martyrs like Kevin Barry and Terence McSweeney (who would soon be fêted in song throughout the Irish Diaspora) was not supported in Protestant Scotland, even though the Glasgow working class surely had a great deal more in common with the Irish working class than it did with the English upper class.

There was thus another factor in Jimmy's background. Job discrimination was not so widespread or as institutionalised as it was in Ulster, but one would have to be blind not to notice the 'No Catholic need apply' notice appended to some job adverts. Often it was much more subtle than that, but it certainly did exist in a way and to an extent which, 80 years down the line, seems indefensible and even ludicrous. The chances of Jimmy getting himself a well-paid, middle-class, professional job in the 1920s would not have been good.

Jimmy had left school when he was 14 in 1928, and did apparently work for a short time in the pits before, for one reason or another, losing his job. For a while things had looked slightly more optimistic with the advent of the Labour Government of Ramsay MacDonald in 1929. But he was a disappointingly weak character with no real grasp of the situation and unemployment not only failed to stabilise, it actually rocketed in the wake of the Wall Street Crash in the US.

Delaney would say in later years that he had been idle 'for some considerable time' before he became a professional footballer. Football was the recreation, the palliative care and even the cure to economic woes. Jimmy played for a local team called Cleland St Mary's in the early 1930s. They were a juvenile team and the next logical step in Scottish football was the juniors. He played a trial with Wishaw Juniors, but when season 1933–34 started in late July, Jimmy Delaney, at the age of 18, was playing for Stoneyburn Juniors.

Stoneyburn is considerably to the east of Cleland: sufficiently far east for them to play in the Midlothian Junior League, rather than one of the many junior leagues in Lanarkshire and the west. Stoneyburn was a mining village some four miles to the south of Bathgate. It had much in common with Cleland. It was one of the many villages in Scotland in the 1930s which had little to offer other than football for the young men of the area, most of whom were victims of the general industrial depression of the times. An indication of the poverty of the area can be gleaned from the winding up of the senior team Bo'ness United in spring 1933 because of bankruptcy and inadequate finances.

Even more dire news was forthcoming from Germany in early 1933. Adolf Hitler had been appointed Chancellor at the end of January and had immediately banned any further elections. As if to prove this point, at the end of February, the Reichstag or German Parliament was burned to the ground, and the Jews were used as the scapegoats. The British Government under

Ramsay MacDonald ('the boneless wonder' as Churchill called him) bumbled along without a clue about how to stop Hitler or do anything to arrest the dire economic situation.

Stoneyburn Juniors had had a dreadful season in 1932–33, finishing third from the bottom of the Midlothian Junior League. It is not known how they heard of the young Delaney but Jimmy, at the age of almost 19, was with them at the start of season 1933–34. This was still amateur football, although often a 'signing-on' fee of around £5 (an enormous amount in 1933) would be paid, which would be a retainer for all season, with the guarantee that the club would get something if a senior Scottish or English team came along.

The games would be well supported with crowds occasionally reaching 1,000. Scottish junior football being what it was, there are many reports of players being sent off, crowds invading the park, referees being attacked, referees abandoning games, officials of clubs receiving short suspensions for 'failing to provide adequate protection against riotous spectators' or life suspensions for 'attempting to bribe a referee', and so on. It was definitely not a game for softies or innocents, although paradoxically the teams all had lovely names like Primrose, Thistle or Bluebell. But how would the slightly-built youngster from Cleland cope with all this?

Saturday 28 July 1933 seems to have been Delaney's debut for Stoneyburn against Ormiston Primrose. Amazingly for July, the game had to be abandoned because of rain shortly after half-time. Stoneyburn were losing 1–3 at the time. The only mention of Delaney was that he 'sent in a rocket drive' according to the *West Lothian Courier*. The team was Collins; Hunter and Sherrat; John McKay, Tennant and Hutton; Delaney, James McKay, Murray, Fry and Muirhead.

The following Friday evening, Stoneyburn were at Fauldhouse United watched by a crowd of 'at least 1,000' enjoying the pleasant summer evening and a good game which Fauldhouse just edged 2–1. 'Jim [sic] Delaney showed promise' on the right wing and the following Saturday he was 'conspicuous' against Blackburn Athletic. Then, in a game against Edina, Stoneyburn's forward line 'knitted well together' as the team registered a 5–1 victory.

Although the team lost its next game to Linlithgow Rose by 0–3, Delaney 'had a number of sparkling runs'. However, the game that made everyone sit up and take notice was on 26 August when the team won 4–1 against Dalkeith Thistle and Delaney scored three goals, two of which were 'well taken and crafted'. It was probably this game which alerted the attention and interest of Willie Maley, the manager of Glasgow Celtic.

The next game, on 2 September, was less happy. It was against a team with the strange name of Bo'ness Cadora and the score was 1–7. Admittedly, Bo'ness were a fine side, and Stoneyburn were without some of their regulars, but the writer of the *West Lothian Courier* does go out of his way to praise Delaney, who had a 'fine try' for the club. Delaney was at this stage offered a trial with Hibernian. He accepted the offer of a trial, but then Celtic came in with a similar offer. Crucially, the Celtic trial was before the Hibernian one. On Friday 8 September 1933, Delaney went to Celtic Park (where presumably he had attended as a spectator in the past, although some sources claim that he had never been there before) and impressed Maley so much in a bounce game that he was signed the following day, a few days after his 19th birthday. According to one source he was given a signing-on fee of £20 plus £2 per week, rising to £4 if he made it to the first team.

This does seem to be a trifle high for a 19-year-old in 1933, but if it were as high as this, one can imagine what a godsend it was for the Delaney family. It would be looked upon as a sort of retainer, whereby young Delaney was now a Celtic player and could not be poached by anyone else in the sometimes-dirty world of 1930s Scottish football. It is also an indication of how highly he was rated.

He was also of course now a professional footballer. He had made a meteoric rise to stardom with barely any junior career at all, and he knew now that he would have to work hard for the club that his father and everyone else in Cleland loved. It would be some time, however, before he could contemplate a first-team breakthrough, but he was allowed to play one final game for Stoneyburn. Sadly it was yet another thrashing, this time 1–6 to Waverley Bluebell of Edinburgh. But Delaney was now a Celt.

Chapter 2

Celtic
1933–1936

THE CELTIC that Jimmy Delaney joined on 9 September 1933 was in a bad way. True, the Scottish Cup had been won the previous April thanks to a solitary McGrory goal in a dull final against Motherwell. But of real concern to the team's vast following was the chronic inability to win the Scottish League, or even to come close. Since the league had last been won in 1926, Celtic had only really pushed Rangers in 1931 – when, with a little more determination and luck in the last few games, they might just have made it. The other years had been grim disappointments, although the particular Saturday of Delaney's signing saw a creditable 2–2 draw against Rangers with McGrory scoring twice and missing a penalty.

Had it not been for Motherwell winning the title in 1932, Rangers would have equalled that year and beaten in 1933 the record set by the great Celtic side that won the League six years in succession from 1905 to 1910. Celtic had won the Scottish Cup in 1927, 1931 and 1933 – something that brought a great deal of pleasure to the fans – and occasionally the Glasgow Cup or Glasgow Charity Cup, but even these tournaments were bringing no great or consistent success to Celtic. The most recent victory in these tournaments had been the Glasgow Cup in October 1930.

There were several factors to explain the inability to keep pace with Rangers. One was the death of John Thomson in September 1931, so lovingly chronicled in story and ballad, and not least in a well researched and brilliantly written recent book by Tom Greig called *My Search for Celtic's John*. The tragedy had cast a huge pall over Parkhead and in particular Willie Maley, the ageing manager, who had seemed occasionally almost catatonic in his inability to shake himself out of his lethargy and depression about the death of his great young goalkeeper.

Maley had been with the club from the beginning and had been manager since 1897. He had an aura, a presence about him. The atmosphere changed when he came into a room. He was a famous Glasgow and Scottish institution, justly proud of the team which he had virtually created. The trouble was that no one else was allowed anywhere near the team. Any suggestion, however well intended, would be seen as criticism or even as an insult, and the result was that when something was wrong with the club, as it clearly was in the early 1930s, little was done to arrest or rectify the damage.

There was also a financial problem. The club had virtually bankrupted itself in 1929 to pay for a new stand, although Maley despicably had tried to sell Jimmy McGrory to Arsenal to pay for it. McGrory would not go, so Tommy McInally and Adam McLean had to be offloaded to Sunderland instead. Even with the money that these two brought, Celtic now clearly lacked the financial clout of Rangers on the other side of the city – where grim determination, cynical manipulation of religious and national prejudice and a certain business acumen were paying great dividends. In contrast, Celtic seemed to lack even the desire to succeed.

This was of course the early 1930s, the depth of the Depression which had started in Wall Street in 1929 and would have such dire consequences throughout the world, not least in the rise of Hitler in Germany. In Scotland, unemployment hit everyone hard, and Celtic supporters most of all, as they were victims of a certain amount of anti-Catholic and anti-Irish prejudice, which was even encouraged by the Church of Scotland. The Irish and their descendants would be the first to lose their jobs. Celtic fans simply did not have the money to pay to get in to watch their favourites every week. Gates slumped, particularly at home where crowds of less than 10,000 were commonplace, even though the club laudably tried to introduce an Unemployed Gate offering admission at a specially reduced rate.

The figures for attendances at Celtic's home gates are quite depressing. According to David Ross in *The Roar of the Crowd*, Celtic averaged 12,053 in 1931–32 and 11,553 in 1932–33, before sinking to a scarcely credible 9,579 in 1933–34. Rangers were top of the attendance table, but Celtic were also beaten by Hearts, Hibernian and Aberdeen, and were only marginally ahead of Dundee and Motherwell. Maley's reaction was often to berate his players and his supporters for not trying harder – hardly a constructive approach to the problem.

In 1933, Celtic's team were getting old together. Peter Scarff was ill with tuberculosis, that scourge of the 1930s, and died in December 1933. Bertie Thomson had fallen out with Maley and was now with Blackpool. Various others had seen better days – Jimmy McStay, Peter Wilson and Alec Thomson, for example. Youth was not yet coming forward in sufficient numbers to replace them, a result of the crazy decision some 10 years earlier (now mercifully but belatedly rescinded) to do away with a reserve team.

However, Celtic still retained two great assets in 1933. One was the mighty Jimmy McGrory, the darling of Scotland following his great goal in the Hampden international against England in April, and the other was the support. The low crowds must not in any way be mistaken for a lack of interest or passion for the club. The potential was enormous. The club still retained the undivided affection of the Irish population of west central Scotland, even though they were now second or even third generation immigrants. It was also becoming increasingly obvious that Celtic did not lack support in the Protestant community, particularly in the east and north of the country. Great players like Jimmy Quinn, Patsy Gallacher and Tommy McInally had won them over in the past and their love for the club remained.

The economic depression may have deprived Celtic supporters of the wherewithal to support the team as frequently as they would have liked to, but the enthusiasm remained undiminished. Every Celtic game would see a huge crowd outside the gate, standing patiently, listening to the roar of the crowd and waiting to be allowed in to see the last 10 minutes of the match when the exit gates were opened to allow the crowd to leave. Celtic's support in 1933 was as massive and as committed as it had ever been, and the potential was undiminished.

This was the state of the club as Jimmy Delaney appeared in September 1933. He could not of course have expected to join the first team immediately, although the longer that season 1933–34 went on, the more strident came the calls for change. The team finished in third place in the Scottish League, some 19 points behind Rangers. Both Old Firm games were draws, but it was the miserable form against teams like Ayr United, Aberdeen, Dundee, Queen of the South and Falkirk which caused the damage. In addition, there was a dismal tendency to draw games that should have been won and a tendency to miss penalties – always an indication that things are not quite right.

The Scottish Cup, traditionally Celtic's favourite tournament, was given up at Love Street, Paisley, in the quarter-final. Celtic went down 0–2 with Peter McGonagle and Peter Wilson both missing penalties. McGrory had a great goal disallowed for offside and then missed several other chances. All in all, it was an extremely painful experience for the Celtic fans. Rangers also beat Celtic in each of the Glasgow tournaments, so Celtic finished the season with nothing. Excuses were forthcoming to justify the poor performance. There had been injuries, particularly to McGrory in the latter part of the season, but the general feeling was that Celtic were going nowhere.

This state of affairs clearly presented an opportunity to the young Delaney. He was learning his trade in the reserves, who played in the Alliance League, and sometimes he was 'farmed out' to a junior team for a game or two. Indeed, by the end of the season he had established himself as heir apparent on the right-wing position. That he had not got there already was due to another talented youngster called John Crum. When Bertie Thomson had fallen foul of Maley and departed in August 1933, the right-wing spot was given to Crum. Crum had not disgraced himself, but like many a youngster in subsequent years for Celtic, found that it was difficult to break in and establish himself when the side itself was not doing well. Nor would he have the courage to tell Maley that there were other positions he could play apart from right-wing.

Meanwhile, Delaney was doing well for the reserves in the Alliance League, starring in particular in the game on Tuesday 24 April 1934 when the Celtic reserves beat their Rangers equivalents 4–1. He was rewarded by being given an outing for a Celtic side which played a benefit match against the Scottish Juniors on 1 May at a place called Newlandsfield Park. It was a harbinger of great things to come: Crum played in the centre and scored a hat-trick. The slender looking Delaney, already showing signs of losing hair, took his place on the right-wing and impressed everyone. He scored a goal and fed Crum constantly as Celtic beat the Scottish Juniors 6–1. Another youngster called Malky MacDonald, who had been in and out of the Celtic team, also caught the eye.

Delaney might have expected a game in one or other of the Glasgow Charity Cup games but was disappointed. So too were the fans, as they lost in the final to Rangers on 12 May 1934. The Glasgow Charity Cup was traditionally contested in May, after the official end of the season in April. The profits were indeed for charity and players were expected to play for nothing, or only the most minimum of wages. Whether this actually happened or not, no one seems to know, but it is hard to imagine professional footballers agreeing to play for nothing!

However, immediately after the Charity Cup disappointment, it was off for a two-day tour of the Highlands. Delaney did not play in the game at Inverness, but on Tuesday 15 May 1934 he played for Celtic against Wick Academy. The opposition were weak, but the team once again shone and won 5–2 with Delaney on the right wing and Crum in the centre. Once again, Crum scored a hat-trick.

Delaney might now have thought that his season was over, but Celtic had received an invitation to play in France against a select team called Entente Nordiste in Roubaix. For propaganda reasons (even after bad seasons), Maley was always keen to go abroad with his players in the summer, and especially to a town like Roubaix which had been in German hands during World War One. The pitch was dry and bumpy and Delaney on the right wing made little impact against a left-back called Payne, as Celtic conceded two late goals to go down 2–4.

As the team crossed the Channel in late May 1934 and travelled by train back to Glasgow, Jimmy was well aware that the next season would be the one in which he really had to break through. He had had his one season in the reserves, he had impressed sufficiently to be in the squad for tours and foreign travel by the end of the season and now was the time in which he had to keep himself fit all through the summer and be prepared for the season restarting in August. He knew too that the team was at a low ebb. Seldom had there been as bad a season as 1934. The supporters would be demanding change and success.

Nevertheless, there were a few grounds for optimism. Crum clearly had a future, as indeed did Malky MacDonald and Willie Buchan. McGrory was still going strong, although he was more and more injury prone, but some of the older players were now departing. Jimmy McStay, Peter Wilson and Alec Thomson would not be back. Change was necessary. Would Maley be able to create another great team, or even a team good enough to wrest the League Championship from Rangers? He was now into his late sixties. Could he adapt?

The outside world in 1934 still presented a grim scenario. Unemployment and short-time working, although diminishing from a peak of a few years ago, were still far too high. Too many of those who had fought in World War One were still not being given the opportunity to work to feed and clothe their families, and there was the worry of what was happening in Germany. Although the world still laughed at that funny little man called Adolf Hitler with his funny walk and his moustache, it was now painfully obvious that the German people did not share the mirth. Indeed, they looked upon him as some kind of a hero. This was a dangerous attitude.

Delaney might have hoped for a game in the first team at the start of the 1934–35 season, but the team's right-winger that day was Charlie Napier. Charlie Napier was a superb player and much loved by the fans. He was called 'Happy Feet' and had songs sung about him like *Clap, Clap Hands, Here Comes Charlie* and the Jacobite anthem *Charlie is My Darling*. Napier had been the left-winger in the great 1931 team, but was versatile enough to play on the right-wing as well. Sadly for young Delaney, 'Happy Feet' was versatile enough to keep him out of the opening game of the season against Kilmarnock on 11 August.

Delaney was disappointed, as he felt he had done well in the pre-season trial in which he played for the Greens against the Green and Whites. He also knew that Johnny Crum's broken foot, which he sustained in a five-a-side tournament, would give him an opportunity. He had been told by many that his time would come, not necessarily by the aloof and autocratic Maley but by some of the players – not least the great Jimmy McGrory who, being an utter gentleman, always went out of his way to cheer up youngsters.

But Jimmy's moment came the following week. Napier had injured himself in the Kilmarnock game and Celtic's teamsheet for the trip to Tynecastle to play

Hearts on 18 August 1934 contained the name Delaney in the right-wing spot, where it would remain, barring injury, for the next 10 years and more.

There was a crowd of 39,270 at Tynecastle that day. Delaney was visibly shaking with nerves and tension on the train to Haymarket station as he tried to enjoy the chit-chat with the players and supporters. The supporters who had travelled through from Glasgow with the team 'escorted' the players as they walked the short distance up the road to the ground. For their efforts, the fans saw a game which was exciting and contained everything except goals. Delaney was considered good enough to be given another go. The press ran a few comments about Delaney 'doing some good work'.

Delaney's next few games were unfortunate in that Celtic seemed to hit a goal famine, with even the great Jimmy McGrory unable to find the net with anything like the frequency that was expected of him. The goalless draw against Hearts was followed by a 0–1 defeat at Motherwell, a goalless draw against St Johnstone and then, perhaps most embarrassingly of all, a 0–4 defeat by Rangers in, of all games, Jimmy McGrory's benefit.

The press were quiet about Delaney's role in those early games, but clearly Maley thought that he was good enough to be persevered with. The team eventually scored a goal on 4 September in a Glasgow Cup game against Queen's Park after five games without doing so. Delaney then had his first really big game when Rangers came to Celtic Park in the Scottish League on 8 September. Press reports mention him giving 'good service' in this 1–1 draw. Celtic should have won the game, but the team's bad luck from the penalty spot continued as Chick Geatons hit the bar.

Celtic were certainly going through a very inconsistent spell. Optimists pointed to the enthusiasm of the side, praising youngsters like Delaney and another youngster on the left-wing called Frank Murphy. Both fledgling wingers had splendid games when Celtic beat Hibernian 4–0 at Parkhead on Tuesday 11 September, a game in which Delaney scored his first Celtic goal. The following Saturday, although Delaney scored again, the team went down to Hamilton Academicals. The rollercoaster continued with a fine win against Aberdeen and a narrow, unlucky loss to Rangers in the Glasgow Cup before the month of September finished with a defeat at Albion Rovers.

Form like this tended to suggest that the League Championship was not a realistic proposition in season 1934–35. The youngsters were good, but needed time to develop, and what really seemed to be lacking was a driving force. It was now being said quite openly that Maley was far too old for the job, but he still retained the aura, the mystique, the gravitas which made it difficult for anyone to challenge him.

Fortunately, Maley was aware of all the undercurrents and mutterings among the support. In mid-October he made the momentous decision that would turn Delaney and Celtic into the team of the moment in the years immediately before World War Two. He appointed as trainer Jimmy 'Napoleon' McMenemy, one of Celtic's greatest-ever players and presumably named after the great French emperor because both men were geniuses.

McMenemy had played at inside-right in the great side of 1905 to 1910 that won six titles in a row. He then moved to inside-left to accommodate Patsy Gallacher and create another great forward line in 1914. McMenemy played during World War One, and when Maley mistakenly thought he was finished, he finally moved to Partick Thistle where he won a Scottish Cup medal to add to the six that he had already won with Celtic.

McMenemy had been coach with Partick Thistle, albeit without any great success, but made no secret of his lasting love for Celtic. Like Tommy McInally of the previous decade, McMenemy pined for home. He would, however, have more success than the wayward Tommy did. McMenemy's return to Celtic Park in October 1934 was Maley's last great brainwave.

The job of 'trainer' nominally consisted of making sure that the players kept fit. He would be seen on matchdays with a bag and sponge, and would run on to the pitch to attend to an injured player in the days when no one had heard of a physio. In theory, he did not have much to do with things like team selection or tactics. In practice, things with an astute character like McMenemy could be radically different – particularly in a situation where the manager was clearly burned out and tired.

Napoleon immediately saw talent in Jimmy Delaney, as did everyone else. 'Delaney is a heartening discovery' it was said about a 3–0 win over Clyde and the goal he scored. McMenemy had seen other great wingers in Alec Bennett, his old friend whom he had played alongside, and subsequently Andy McAtee, and knew what he wanted in a right-winger. He approached Bennett for advice on how to develop the talent of the young Delaney. Bennett's statement was that the key thing in a winger is variety. 'Never let them know what you are going to do next. Go for the corner flag, cut inside, move about, but above all else, enjoy your football, play it cleanly and *want* that ball.'

The great forward lines that McMenemy had played in – Bennett, McMenemy, Quinn, Somers and Hamilton of the 1900s and McAtee, Gallacher, McColl, McMenemy and Browning of a decade later – had one thing in common and that was an ability to interchange with each other. Somers would occasionally appear on the right-wing during the course of a game, while Bennett took the left-wing and Hamilton appeared in the centre. Until now, forward lines had tended to be rigid, but McMenemy clearly wanted the Celtic team of the late 1930s to imitate and emulate the teams in which he had played, with fit young men interchanging at will.

McMenemy worked tirelessly with his two wingers, Delaney and Murphy, convinced that they were what Celtic required. They were both shy young lads, possibly still a little in awe of folk like McGrory and Geatons, not to mention the intimidating Maley, but with McMenemy they were completely at ease. McMenemy had sons of his own who played professional football (John played for Celtic in the late 1920s but was always compared unfavourably with his great father) and he knew what young men needed at this stage in their career in professional football: reassurance, encouragement, stability and the knowledge that they were trusted. As Jock Stein would be for youngsters at Celtic Park in the 1950s, so McMenemy was the pillar on which Delaney and Murphy could lean.

This meant that if young players were occasionally relegated to the reserve team they did not feel any shame or disgrace about it. This in fact happened to both Murphy and Delaney, but in the early winter of 1934–35 the team embarked on an unbeaten run as the new management team seemed at last to be able to get the best out of the underperforming O'Donnell brothers. Although Delaney was outstanding in a 7–0 defeat of Ayr United in early November, he was soon given a rest while his place on the right-wing was taken by Jimmy McGrory of all people. This allowed Frank O'Donnell to play in the centre and his brother Hugh to play on the left-wing.

The team was playing splendidly, winning all their games apart from an unlucky reverse at Easter Road where old Celt Peter Wilson engineered their downfall. Had it not been for the bad start, they might even have been in contention for the 1935 League Championship. Delaney returned on Christmas Day and, with Johnny Crum as his inside-right partner, played brilliantly in a 4–2 victory over Queen's Park. He scored twice and clearly the rest had done him a great deal of good. He could not really be dropped again.

There were clear signs that the fans were coming back, as was always likely to happen when a good team was being assembled. A crowd of 35,000 were at Celtic Park for the last game of 1934 to see Celtic beat Hearts 4–2. McGrory scored a hat-trick as Delaney tore past the Hearts full-back 'as if he was not there'.

The dreadful Celtic year of 1934 was now over. There were signs that the team were on the way back and it was felt they might even come back this season and win something. But a stern test awaited them at Ibrox on New Year's Day and for the young Delaney it was a grim example of how brutal Old Firm games could be – and how disappointing. A crowd of 80,000 fans were there: yet more proof of the tailing off of the Depression and the return to work giving more money for fans to attend football matches.

The Celtic forward line of Delaney, Crum, McGrory, Napier and Hugh O'Donnell looked good on paper. But the right-wing pair of Delaney and Crum was inexperienced and possibly shocked by the rough treatment that they received from the Rangers defenders and the religious intolerance that they received from the Rangers fans. McGrory was well policed by Jimmy Simpson, Napier was injured and spent the second half of the game in hospital, and Hugh O'Donnell had an off day. In addition, left-back McGonagle was sent off for throwing the ball at a Rangers player who had charged Joe Kennaway, the Celtic goalkeeper, very violently. Celtic in fact did well to keep the score down to 1–2, but it was an awful experience for young Delaney, who also picked up enough bruises that day to rule him out of the next game against St Johnstone. His fault lay in that he had not expected it to be like this. Previous Old Firm games that he had played in were tough but sporting – this was an example of the ugly side of the game, and the unpleasant side of supporters.

This defeat effectively ended what little chance Celtic had of the League Championship. They would lose another three games that season – away at Aberdeen and Ayr and at home to Clyde – and that, allied to their bad start, was simply not good enough to land the Championship. Yet there were many good days as well, and there was the general belief that with a little strengthening in a few areas, the team might soon be back at the top.

There was a general need of a centre-half, now that Jimmy McStay had gone. Malky MacDonald and Chick Geatons were deployed there, but both were out of position. The forward line was chopped and changed rather too often. But of one thing there was little doubt and that was that in young Delaney, Celtic had a winner. Spring 1935 saw Delaney learn his trade, observe the best, keep himself very fit and develop a little street wisdom so that he knew how to avoid the meaty challenges of coarse defenders. In Willie Buchan he had a superb inside partner. Willie, like Jimmy, was learning his trade, having been in and out of the team, but the two of them, serious-minded and hard workers at training, developed a fine understanding.

Delaney had clearly taken to heart McMenemy and Maley's instructions about varying his approach. He had a tremendous amount of speed, was very nimble and quick on his feet, could turn and now had a great deal of ball control, something that had not perhaps been his forte at the start. His crosses were usually deadly accurate, but he could also get a goal himself, scoring for example a fine hat-trick in a snowstorm in February against Albion Rovers.

The Scottish Cup, in which Celtic with 14 wins topped Queen's Park's 10 and Rangers' 8, represented their best chance of a trophy in 1935. Indeed, it has often been the case throughout Celtic's history that inconsistency has deprived them of the League but a few fine and dramatic performances have landed them the Scottish Cup. It seemed cut out for just such an occasion in 1935.

A knock to an ankle prevented Delaney from playing in the 4–1 win over Montrose at Parkhead, a victory that was not as easy as it seemed, for most of the goals came late after the Angus part-timers tired. Then came Partick Thistle, who shocked Parkhead's 54,180 by going ahead inside the last quarter of an hour. Fortunately, Hugh O'Donnell equalised soon after to set up a midweek replay.

Amazingly, this midweek replay with a 3pm kick-off attracted 39,644 to Firhill, where they saw 'Delaney dashing about like the fire brigade' in the words of one member of the press. Such imagery may seem quaint, but it indicated the speed that he had. He possibly also set off alarm bells in the Thistle defence. Once again it was an incredibly tight game, with goalkeeper Joe Kennaway saving a penalty kick before Hugh O'Donnell opened the scoring early in the second half. Another three goals came within the last 10 minutes: fortunately two were for Celtic, who won 3–1. Delaney set up McGrory for the final goal of the game.

Celtic were drawn away to play Hibernian or Aberdeen in the quarter-final. That tie was only decided in Aberdeen's favour five days before the quarter-final and Celtic thus had to go to Pittodrie. A couple of months previously, Celtic had lost 0–2 in the League and the forebodings of the support were justified. The team travelled up to Aberdeen on the Friday night accompanied by lots of supporters and fellow travellers. With a large local support, a massive 40,108 appeared at Pittodrie on the Saturday. Hundreds and possibly thousands more were locked outside as the crowd swayed dangerously on the terracing.

This was the heyday of Aberdeen's two great forwards, Willie Mills and Matt Armstrong, and hopes were high in the Granite City that the black and golds might this year win the Scottish Cup. They were a fine side and difficult to beat at home, but tended to suffer from travel sickness and a general sense of being overwhelmed by the occasion when they played in Glasgow. This day, however, saw Aberdeen at their best and Celtic's display was a major blow to the huge Glasgow support. Armstrong scored two penalties (neither of them being 'definites' in the opinion of the press) and Mills scored another before Delaney eventually engineered a consolation goal for McGrory.

Little was now left of the 1934–35 season other than to play out time in meaningless League games, friendlies in places like Forfar, Inverness, Brora and Wick and a rather curiously lacklustre display in the Glasgow Charity Cup where the team went down 1–4 to Queen's Park. McMenemy put this down to immaturity and inexperience and said it would be learned from.

And so ended Delaney's first season in the full Celtic team. It had been a steep learning curve, but Delaney was a quick and enthusiastic learner. Already he had developed a rapport with the fans, for they appreciated his studied earnestness and his enthusiasm for the cause. Perhaps next season would bring better, but before that could happen there would be one or two changes in the close season.

Maley bit the bullet with the two O'Donnell brothers. Frank was a passable centre-forward, Hugh a speedy left-winger but the sad fact is that they underperformed grossly at Celtic Park, even though both came from a Celtic-daft family in Buckhaven, Fife. Hugh had the same name as a medieval Irish rebel and the song *O'Donnell Abu* was sung on the terraces in his honour:

> *Many a heart shall quail*
> *Under each coat of mail*
> *Deeply the merciless foeman shall rue,*
> *When on his ears shall ring*
> *Born on the breeze's wing*
> *O'Donnell's dread war cry*
> *O'Donnell Abu!*

Sadly, Hugh failed to bring the consistent performances that were needed in order to win the League Championship. Frank suffered from being a centre-forward when McGrory was around, so was only played when McGrory was injured, or occasionally he was played out of position.

The brothers were inseparable, so when Preston North End came in with a bid for the two of them in May 1935, Maley accepted the money. To a certain extent, Maley was sad at this, for they were honest triers and genuine Celts, who were just a little short of what was required. Perhaps, however, it was Maley himself that was the problem, for Frank subsequently gained six international caps for Scotland and Hugh won the English Cup with Preston North End in 1938 in their legendary team that was dominated by Scotsmen, notably Andy Beattie and Bill Shankly.

Charlie Napier was a more ticklish problem for Celtic. 'Happy Feet' was undeniably a class player and an established international. In fact, in the Scotland versus England game in 1935 it had been Napier who had taken the two corners from which Dally Duncan had scored the goals to give Scotland victory. He had also played well for Celtic at various positions, even right-half for a while the previous season, but Maley did not like him. He was a flashy dresser, wearing bowler hats and spats on occasion, and did not always fit in well with the rest of the players. Maley wondered whether he really needed Napier, for he felt that Napier, good though he was, had to carry a certain amount of the blame for the club's repeated inability to win the League Championship. Like two subsequent Charlies, Tully and Nicholas, he was often guilty of showing off and playing to the gallery – to the detriment of the team.

The *casus belli* came at the same time as the O'Donnell transfer. Napier refused to sign for the following season unless he was guaranteed a benefit. Maley would not be dictated to like that and reckoned that he now had enough young forwards in any case. Napier was put on the transfer list. Derby County expressed an interest and with a suddenness that baffled everyone, Napier joined the Baseball Ground team for an undisclosed fee but one that was reckoned to be about £8,000. The Celtic fans were amazed and dumbfounded at this and so too, one feels, was Charlie Napier himself, whose bluff had been called when he really did not want to leave Celtic. It meant that he would not be part of the success that was to come.

Delaney must have wondered what was going on, but he realised that Maley was not a man to be trifled with and he also figured that the departure of these three forwards would cement his position in the Celtic team, if indeed it needed any cementing. But he noticed with pleasure that Celtic signed a little-known Englishman called Willie Lyon from Queen's Park. This tall and authoritative man, from anything but a traditional Celtic background, was a great centre-half, a great communicator and a natural leader. Lyon would soon be appointed captain and thus there was a great triad of Celtic leaders for the next few years – Maley himself in the stand, McMenemy on the touchline and Lyon on the field.

Delaney felt immediately comfortable in this set-up, and season 1935–36 would be one of the best in the club's history. It would be pay-off time for Celtic's fans, who had suffered dreadfully over the last decade. Delaney now had the added ingredient of confidence to complement his debonair looks, his speed, his crossing ability and his ability to score goals. A particular speciality of his was when he ran in himself to score. While everyone was expecting a cross to McGrory, the defence would fall back and grant Delaney the space he needed.

The forward line of Delaney, Buchan, McGrory, Crum and Murphy came together, and it was good enough to exclude Malky MacDonald. It was also lucky in that no one suffered long-term injuries, although Delaney himself missed a few games in mid-winter. The football was a sight to behold and it was the year that McGrory scored 50 League goals, a remarkable amount of them with his head from crosses created by the sparkling wing play of Jimmy Delaney and, to a lesser extent, Frank Murphy.

The team lost four League games: on the opening day of the season at Aberdeen; one at Tynecastle; another in the New Year's Day game at Parkhead, which ended 4–3 to Rangers; and an inexplicable loss at Dunfermline in December when the team simply underperformed. Perhaps they underperformed because it was in the middle of the spell when Delaney was laid off with an injury.

Celtic also drew with Kilmarnock on 5 October. Delaney was not playing in this game either, but this time it was for a far better reason – he was winning his first international cap for Scotland. He had actually played for Scotland on 21 August against England at Hampden in what was known pompously as the

King George V Silver Jubilee International. It was, however, a one-off and has not been deemed an official international. In truth, it was little more than a pre-season friendly in which several potential internationalists were given an opportunity to shine. Jimmy was picked and grabbed this opportunity, scoring the first goal in the 4–2 victory for Scotland.

Such was Delaney's subsequent form that he could hardly be denied his opportunity for the official Scotland team and he was duly picked for the trip to Ninian Park, Cardiff, on 5 October 1935. It was a time when world peace was being threatened in a very concrete and obvious way, as Mussolini's Italians invaded Abyssinia for no apparent reason other than Il Duce thought that his tanks would do rather well against the spears of the Abyssinians. The Abyssinian leader Haile Selassie appealed to the feckless and ineffective League of Nations for help. He got none and Mussolini's friend Hitler realised that there would be little resistance to his seizing any bits of Europe that attracted him.

The game in Wales was a close one and ended in a 1–1 draw, with Dally Duncan of Derby County scoring Scotland's goal. It was of course a tremendous experience for the still young Delaney, who had only recently celebrated his 21st birthday, and it was an indication of how far he had come in one year. To be picked to play for Scotland was a far greater honour then than it is in the early years of the 21st century. It was a particular honour for a Celtic player, whose supporters often felt that there was more than a little religious discrimination in the awarding of Scotland caps.

Certainly there seems to be little doubt that Jimmy McGrory was ludicrously under-capped, and there is the appalling fact that McGrory never played for Scotland at Wembley. However, this may be explained more by the ineptitude of Scotland's selectors rather than by any deliberate anti-Celtic policy. The selectors were directors of clubs normally and were themselves selected at an AGM by fellow representatives of other clubs. They did not necessarily have any great knowledge of football. The process was not in any way professional or even logical and the wonder is that Scotland consistently did so well against the other home nations. It would be some time before a professional manager would be appointed.

Delaney, however, had been considered good enough and justified their faith to such an extent that he was also picked for the Ireland game at Tynecastle on Wednesday 13 November. Thus the city of Edinburgh saw Jimmy Delaney at his sparkling best twice in five days. On the previous Saturday, Celtic had ripped a poor Hibernian side (Peter Wilson and all) apart in a 5–0 thrashing with 'dazzling Delaney' leading the way. He was no less impressive in the international before 30,000 on the Wednesday afternoon as Scotland triumphed 2–1.

The right-wing pairing of Jimmy and Hearts' Tommy Walker delighted the Scottish fans. Walker scored the equalising goal in which Delaney had been well involved in the build-up and then, after intense Scottish pressure, Dally Duncan eventually scored the winner more or less on the final whistle as darkness was beginning to descend on Tynecastle.

The following day, Thursday 14 November 1935, saw the British General Election in which the national (but Conservative-dominated) Government of Stanley Baldwin was returned, albeit with a reduced majority. Labour's defeat may well have disappointed Delaney, as it would most people of his background, but the fact that the British people were content with the status quo was perhaps an indication that the 'doctor's mandate' of the national Government was now working and unemployment was on the wane. Certainly attendances at football matches were greatly increasing with Celtic's average now over 16,000, only slightly below the returns of Hearts and Rangers.

There was perhaps a sinister reason as well for the decline of unemployment and the regeneration of the British economy. Although the Colonel Blimps of the Conservative Party gave the impression that they did not appreciate the realities of the situation in Europe, wiser elements within the Government and the Civil Service realised that it might be an idea to be prepared for the eventuality of another war. Thus more ships were to be built on the Clyde, parts for aeroplanes were needed from various sources and more jute would be required from the factories of Dundee for sandbags in the event of air attack.

Celtic's form had been very impressive. The opening day at Pittodrie was disappointing, but the recovery was instantaneous, with McGrory and Delaney a sparkling combination. Wins were recorded at difficult grounds, like St Johnstone's Muirton Park (on 24 August, the day that Tom Maley, brother of manager Willie and a founder member of Celtic, died), Queen of the South's Palmerston Park and notably at Ibrox on 21 September. The win against Rangers was an even more remarkable victory for it was achieved without the injured McGrory. It was the first Celtic win at Ibrox since New Year's Day 1921 and was a clear indication that this Celtic team was going places. Delaney's contribution was massive. He took the corner kick which landed directly at Frank Murphy's feet for one of the goals and ran through the Rangers defence so often that even rough tackling was not enough to stop him. 'He ran so fast that they couldn't even foul him', chortled the *Glasgow Observer*. The Celtic fans in the 72,000 crowd at the end invaded the field to congratulate their heroes.

It was small wonder that two things dominated conversation around Celtic Park in the autumn and early winter of 1935–36. One was the goalscoring exploits of McGrory, who on 19 October overtook Steve Bloomer's British record of 352 goals before it was discovered that Bloomer was not in fact the record holder. Hugh Ferguson of Cardiff City and Dundee (before his tragic suicide at Dens Park in 1930) had in fact scored 364. It would of course only be a matter of time before McGrory would beat that one as well.

The other topic of conversation was the fine play of the team, whose forward line of Delaney, Buchan, McGrory, Crum and Murphy was so similar to Bennett, McMenemy, Quinn, Somers and Hamilton. The common factor of course was Jimmy McMenemy, whose tactics and team talks were stimulating and positive. It was a task that the ageing Maley now happily left to Napoleon. It was almost like the apostolic succession as the hero of one generation passed on the Celtic torch to the next.

There was one setback and that was the loss of the Glasgow Cup Final on 12 October 1935 to Rangers. Celtic had been expected to win this game but had suffered when Joe Kennaway, the inspirational Canadian goalkeeper, was injured and replaced by Chic Geatons in an eerie replay of the John Thomson tragedy of four years previously.

But there was little wrong with the League form and, by the time that the team visited Ayr's Somerset Park on 23 November 1935, Celtic were only one point behind Aberdeen with a game in hand. A crowd of 15,000 were at Ayr that day to see Celtic win 2–0 with an early goal from McGrory and a clever one just before half-time from Jimmy Delaney. The game was won, but tragedy hit Celtic when Delaney had to be carried off with a leg injury. The details of how it happened are sparse, but it was a serious one, enough to rule Delaney out for the rest of 1935. It may be a coincidence, but with Delaney on the sidelines, the team began to struggle. They only drew with Partick Thistle and then appalled their fans by losing 0–1 at Dunfermline Athletic on 14 December. Fortunately, the team were able to redeem themselves on midwinter's day with a fine 5–3 win over Aberdeen at Parkhead, on a frozen pitch which had had to be covered with sand.

This was the day that McGrory scored his favourite goal, but it was also the day that established beyond any doubt that he was the greatest scorer of them all, for by the end of the game he had 366 goals, clearly more than Hugh Ferguson or anyone else. It must have been a matter of tremendous regret for the young Delaney that he was not on the field on the day that the old maestro became immortal. In fact, of course, McGrory had already been immortal for some time.

Celtic then won at Hamilton unconvincingly, when McGrory was out as well, but better news came when it was announced that Delaney would be fit for the New Year's Day game against Rangers at Parkhead. Not only was he fit, he even scored the first goal of the game after Jimmy Simpson was short with a pass back to Jerry Dawson. At one point, Celtic were 3–1 up, but Rangers came back to win 4–3. It was a tough, unpleasant kind of a game in the 'glaur' (mud of a Scottish winter's day) and Celtic felt that they were worth a draw at least. It was a view shared by the commentator of the BBC Scottish Home Service on the radio when he gave his 10-minute report that evening.

In spite of this, however, Celtic were still in a better position than Rangers and there were clear signs that Aberdeen, the other challengers, were finding it difficult to sustain the pace at the top. Celtic won their next game against St Johnstone at Parkhead, but Delaney aggravated his leg injury and was taken off with 25 minutes to go. He missed the next two games, which Celtic won rather easily against Queen of the South and Albion Rovers. The next game should have been a Scottish Cup game against Berwick Rangers at Parkhead. However, it was postponed on the Saturday because of flooding and, as the Berwick team simply could not afford to come to Glasgow in midweek, they had little option but to withdraw from the competition.

The postponed game would have been played on 25 January, Burns' Day, but it was as well that it was not, for Celtic might well have been embarrassed. On Monday 20 January 1936, King George V died at Sandringham Palace. There would have had to be two minutes silence for the late monarch as Willie Maley, an ardent royalist, would have insisted on it, but the Celtic fans might not have respected the silence. King George was replaced by 'David', who would become King Edward VIII – but not for long.

King George was thus well buried by the time that Celtic played again and Delaney was fit for the trip to Tynecastle to play Hearts. It was always likely to be a difficult match and Hearts scored first through Tommy Walker, who would in later years become their manager. The second half saw a great deal of Celtic pressure but Delaney, still not quite match fit, was up against a solid defender in Herd. Celtic simply could not score – Delaney himself had three opportunities early on – and the feeling that this might just be Hearts' day gained ground when their famous goalkeeper Jack Harkness (immortalised as a Wembley wizard in 1928 and soon to become a great journalist for the *Sunday Post*) saved a Willie Lyon penalty. Delaney 'will want to forget this one' said the *Dundee Courier*.

Things became a lot more serious for the young Celtic side when St Johnstone came to Celtic Park on Scottish Cup business the following week. The pitch was very hard and players struggled to find their footwork, but the 1–2 result for the Perth men is still inexplicable in terms of form. Delaney certainly struggled on the hard pitch. He was 'completely bottled', particularly when he was playing in the shadow of the main stand in the second half, which had not had any sunshine, and the 26,647 crowd were plunged once again into the sort of depression that they had suffered so often in recent years.

At moments like this, one needs good management. Here, Maley read the situation well. He fulminated and thundered at the players on Monday before handing them over to the gentler Jimmy McMenemy on the Tuesday. McMenemy knew that there was great potential there and that what a team of youngsters do not need is abuse and vituperation. Tactics were discussed and in particular more stress was to be laid on the play of wingers Delaney and Murphy. It would be their job to get round the defence and lay on the passes and the crosses for McGrory. They were to stay wide, unless they actually had the ball, and the excellent midfield of Geatons, Lyon and Paterson was to spread the ball wide. This would not of course preclude the swapping of positions now and again to fool the opposition. Meanwhile, the inside trio of Buchan, McGrory and Crum was to press forward – McGrory for the high ones and the two inside men just a little behind for the ground passes.

To say that this worked is stating the obvious – Celtic had 12 League games to play and won them all. With the single-mindedness that their untimely exit from the Scottish Cup provided for them, they began to play a brand of football that delighted their fans and impressed the rest of Scotland. McGrory scored at least once in every game he played in, as the team had a settled look about it and victories were gained at difficult grounds like Airdrie and Dundee where wins had not been all that forthcoming on previous occasions.

The young Delaney revelled in all this. He was now quite clearly a hero with the Celtic support and could do things which veterans, for all their street wisdom, could not. In the first game after the St Johnstone defeat, for example, in front of a sparse crowd of 6,000, Celtic were awarded a free-kick. The Kilmarnock defence lined up. In a move which was unusual in the 1930s (although more common now), Delaney joined the Kilmarnock wall. Willie Lyon took the free kick, Delaney ducked and the ball flew into the Killie net.

On 29 February (for it was a leap year), against Clyde at Shawfield, Willie Lyon was injured and had to play on the right wing, allowing Delaney a roving commission in the centre of the field. He sprayed passes like Peter Wilson used to do, feeding Crum, Buchan and McGrory to do what was needed. Celtic were given a standing ovation at the end of their 4–0 victory and, as they came off, McGrory clearly gestured to the crowd that the bulk of the adulation should be directed at the youngster from Cleland. Delaney looked shyly at McGrory then the crowd and smiled.

On 7 March 1936 came possibly a pivotal day for Celtic's season – as well as a day which had vital bearing on the future of Europe. While Rangers and Aberdeen were engaged in their Scottish Cup clash at Pittodrie, Celtic, no longer interested in the Cup, were playing a League game at Airdrie. Broomfield had been a notorious Celtic graveyard in the past (and would continue to be until its demolition in the early 1990s) and things looked grim when Celtic were two goals down at half-time. Once again it was Delaney who took charge in the second half. McGrory scored twice and Crum once, but 'the influence of twinkle-toes in the wing was significant'.

On this day, however, the gauntlet was thrown down to France and Britain. Hitler issued his first challenge to the Treaty of Versailles by invading and seizing the demilitarised Rhineland. All this territory was of course within Germany, and nobody was hurt, but the world waited to see how France would react to the presence of German soldiers now looking over its eastern border. Hitler would later admit that had there been any armed response from the West, he would have retired 'like a dog with its tail between its legs', but all the French did was protest. A large body of opinion in Britain was of the view that Germany should do whatever it wished with its own territory, irrespective of what the Treaty of Versailles said. The memory of World War One, only 18 years ago, with all its horrendous casualties, was still too recent for anyone to provoke a repetition. Hitler now detected a weakness among the French and the British – a weakness that he would exploit fully in the next few years.

The *Sunday Post* of 8 March 1936 was worth its money. Obviously the international situation is well dealt with, but there is also a vivid account of Jimmy Delaney's great day at Airdrie, Rangers' narrow win over Aberdeen at Pittodrie and the eight-goal thriller at Cappielow in which Third Lanark beat Morton 5–3. There was also a new cartoon series launched about a working-class Scottish family called 'The Broons'.

On 14 March, when the legend of 'goal-a-minute' James McGrory was created (he scored in the 65th, 66th and 67th minute), Delaney had a part in all three goals:

> *And on the wing Delaney's speed*
> *Created goals for Jimmy's heid;*
> *The Cleland boy, so fast and true*
> *A loyal Celt, straight through and through.*
>
> *And wait a bit, don't be so fast*
> *We've left the star turn till the last*
> *There in the midst o' his glory,*
> *Goal-a-minute James McGrory!*

A week later at Dens Park, Dundee, it was Delaney himself who scored from within seconds of the kick-off from a rebound off the post. A crowd of 20,000, including a vast travelling support now sensing that something might be happening for Celtic this season, thrilled to the demolition of Dundee by the spectacular wing play of Jimmy Delaney and Frank Murphy. Celtic won 2–0 and it really ought to have been a great deal more. The *Dundee Courier* seemed to be suffering from sour grapes when it damned with faint praise: 'not a great win but a great result for the Celts'. Celtic gave a slightly different impression, as they marched through the streets singing about *The Dear Little Shamrock*, *Erin's Green Valleys* and the praises of their great team.

It was all the more amazing that year, therefore, when the Scotland team was announced to play at Wembley on 4 April 1936. It had been confidently predicted, and even expected, that the right-wing berth would go to none other than Jimmy Delaney and the centre-forward berth to the mighty Jimmy McGrory. In fact, it was stated with great confidence in the press that 'that combination would shake Wembley to the core'.

It was not only Celtic fans, therefore, that gasped with sheer amazement when neither of the two Jimmies were included. The centre-forward spot went to David McCulloch of Brentford – presumably on the grounds that having played for Hearts he would read inside-right Tommy Walker well. The outside-right spot went to a Celtic man, but not the talented young winger who had done so much to set the world alight that year. Johnny Crum was certainly a talented and versatile forward and a man who had in the past played on the right wing, but he was now a brilliant inside-left!

The selection was outrageous and it was possibly this one decision more than any other that led to the belief and accusation that Celtic supporters were not also Scotland supporters. It would be difficult for a Celtic fan to wish that Scotland team well. Delaney and McGrory laudably held their tongues and Johnny Crum was presumably very embarrassed, for it looked as if he were being chosen as the token Celt and not for any tactical reason. Don John in *The Courier* said, 'It is difficult to understand. Few thought that the young Celt (Delaney) would not be included.'

It was indeed crazy. The Scotland team drew 1–1 and that was satisfactory, but with Delaney and McGrory in full cry, as they undeniably were in 1936, it would have been hard to imagine Scotland not thumping England by a considerable margin. Those who had seen that combination for Celtic in recent weeks, and the dynamic football that they were creating, simply shook their heads at the folly of it all.

Meanwhile, Celtic still had the League to win. It was neck and neck between them and Rangers with Aberdeen not entirely out of it. Four games remained for Celtic, while Rangers, who were still involved in the Scottish Cup, had more. If Rangers could win their games in hand it would be all square, although Celtic appeared to have the better goal average. The atmosphere was tense, akin perhaps to that in more recent years in 1998 when Celtic at last won the Scottish League after a decade of supine underachievement.

No slip up could be permitted. The week after the international, on 11 April, Celtic were at Arbroath. A crowd of 10,000 were there to see the game at

Gayfield, Arbroath's trim little ground only yards away from the North Sea, and they saw a titanic struggle as the local side, who still needed to save themselves from relegation, threw everything at the Celtic defence, which had an unaccustomed frailty about it. Delaney had cut in from the wing to score in the 12th minute, but it was not until the very last minute that McGrory scored the second to make Celtic safe. Arbroath claimed a foul, but it was the claim of the desperate.

Just as the crowd were leaving, rumours began to circulate that Hamilton had beaten Rangers. Such rumours spread readily nowadays and even as far back as the 1950s, when radio began to provide such information, but in 1936 one could only know such things from the newspaper men in the press box who would phone their office. In fact, one of the writers for the *Dundee Courier* was a crypto-Celtic fan and, forgetful of his professional gravitas, had shouted the information 'Hamilton 1 Rangers 0' to all concerned. Willie Maley, apparently unhappy about his team's performance up to that point, relaxed and smiled.

This now meant that Celtic would probably win the League if they won two games out of their remaining three. One of the games was against Clyde at Parkhead on the Holiday Monday immediately after the Arbroath game. Once again it was tense, with the players visibly nervous and fraught. It was almost a carbon copy of the Arbroath game, with Delaney scoring early from a Murphy corner, and McGrory hitting the target in the second half. But in the meantime Clyde had missed a penalty and then made it 1–1 before McGrory's second-half goal. The last few minutes, with the score at 2–1 to Celtic, saw Jimmy Delaney joining the panicky defence to keep out Clyde who, like Arbroath, were desperate to avoid relegation. The final whistle was a great relief to the 15,000 fans inside Parkhead.

It so happened that both the Scottish League and the Scottish Cup were decided within half a mile of each other on Saturday 18 April 1936. While Rangers beat Third Lanark 1–0 in the Scottish Cup Final at Hampden, Celtic were thrashing Ayr United at Parkhead. Delaney did not score, but was outstanding throughout. McGrory scored three to record his 50th goal and his seventh hat-trick of the season, but then ill-advisedly took a penalty kick after having picked up an injury. He missed the penalty and aggravated his injury so that he missed the last game of the season. Late goals from Willie Lyon and Willie Buchan saw Celtic to a 6–0 victory.

This result meant that Celtic would have to lose their last game by an improbable margin and Rangers win their remaining three by an equally improbable margin to deprive Celtic of the title. Thus both members of the Old Firm celebrated that night – Celtic for winning the League and Rangers for the Cup. The League was definitely confirmed the following Wednesday night when Rangers could only draw 1–1 at Tynecastle.

It was akin to feelings expressed at the relief of Mafeking in the Boer War in 1900. Those supporters who remember the tremendous relief that was felt in 1998 when Celtic prevented Rangers from winning 10 League titles in a row will appreciate the feelings that their fathers and grandfathers experienced in 1936. A biscuit or a sandwich is much valued when one is hungry, but this was much more than that. It was a full-scale meal, for a new team had been born. And how!

Thus, as Delaney ran out at Firhill for the last League game of the season, Celtic had won the championship for the first time in 10 years. Their success was due in no small measure to the emergence of this slightly built, already balding young man from Cleland, who had brought a form of wing play which Celtic fans had not seen since the days of Alec Bennett 30 years previously. The mood was upbeat and happy, and Delaney revelled in it all. The press were trying to get Delaney to sign for Newcastle United, but Delaney laughed it off, although he did say that if he were to sign for any English team it would be the Geordies because of their geographical proximity. This remark was taken out of context and grossly distorted to fool the gullible – but only the gullible, for at this time he had no desire to leave the team he loved.

The importance of this season for Celtic in a historical context cannot be underestimated. It is always easy to assume that a strong Celtic team would automatically arise simply because the circumstances of Scotland demanded it. This is not so. By 1935, Celtic were certainly in decline, with their gates a long way below those of their rivals. Without the Delaney inspiration of season 1935–36, there would have been a real possibility of a permanent decline in the affairs of Celtic FC. The Celtic fans had suffered terribly during the Depression. Football attendance had ceased to be a habit and there is no reason to believe that the disaffected fans would, as a matter of course, return to see their team. Fortunately, the team turned the corner with Jimmy Delaney and the improvement in the attendance figures over the next few years became quite phenomenal.

There were two postscripts to this successful season. One was a light-hearted tour of Ireland the following week and the other was the Glasgow Charity Cup Final on 9 May. This tournament, often the 'Cinderella' of the Scottish season, was this year contested with more enthusiasm than normal for the final was an Old Firm occasion at Hampden and each side, having won a major national trophy, was keen to prove the point that they were the best in Glasgow.

It was one of Delaney's finest hours. He took on a roving commission, playing almost deliberately out of position to disorientate the Rangers defenders. Delaney scored first and, after Rangers had scored twice, he headed (unusually for him at this stage of his career) an equaliser in the middle of the second half. With five minutes remaining, the score was 2–2 but, in the event of a draw, Rangers would win on corners – they had won seven corners to Celtic's six. This was the crude and crazy way of settling the issue in the tournament at this time. Delaney sensed this. He immediately scored a great goal from the wing and then crossed for the inevitable Jimmy McGrory to do the needful and win the game 4–2.

The Celtic fans, who outnumbered their opponents in the 43,162 crowd, were delighted with this brilliance. The man of the moment accepted the congratulations of his teammates and his chivalrous opponents, then the warm-hearted Jimmy McMenemy. But then, as he went into the tunnel, he met the towering bulk of his manager, Willie Maley. Maley 'made as if to pass me', as Delaney said, then as the youngster bravely said something like 'How did you enjoy that, boss?' the gruff reply was, 'Don't let that go to your head, son!'

But that was just Maley's manner. Maley knew, as indeed did all of Scotland, that Celtic had unearthed something special in Jimmy Delaney. Certainly *The Glasgow Observer*, the outrageously pro-Celtic newspaper which catered for the Catholic population of west central Scotland, was in no doubt. A contributor called OLO had a piece entitled, 'He Gets It', which gently took Jimmy to task for being out of position.

'Jim [sic] Delaney, match winner. Twice out of position, two goals – his first and second. He won the Glasgow Charity Cup by being where he oughtn't to. Naughty lad. And, not being content, he had to have a third.

A fault most reprehensible
Was that, you will agree,
When Nelson stuck the telescope
To the eye that couldn't see;
He realised the act was wrong
But knew that he was right
And we know that disobedience
Won the Copenhagen fight.
I know one other little lad
Who risked a fall from grace
When he coolly blinked at orders
By wandering from his place;
'Where's Jim Delaney roving to?'
His mates cried in a fret,
And up pops Jim from nowhere to
Plant one snugly in the net.
The flabbergasted partisans
Had scarce recovered, when
This naughty lad, with calm affront

Does the self-same thing again.
We've got to give him something for
His breach of discipline –
So we'll hand the bouquet out to –
Jim Delaney.

The young Delaney was also out of place that night. He knew that there would be a reception committee waiting for him at Cleland Station, for he was undeniably the hero of the Celtic community that night. But he did not really like a fuss being made of him, so he got off the train at Carfin, the next station up the line, and walked home across the fields to his mother's house. The reception committee waited and waited as several Glasgow trains came in, then assumed that he must have got a lift home from someone in a car. So they eventually went to his mother's house to find him having a cup of tea and talking away to his mother and a neighbour. 'Where were you, Jimmy? We were waiting for you!' 'Ach, I didnae want any fuss, so I just got off at Carfin. The walk would dae me guid, as well!' he said. 'I might hae stiffened up!'

Chapter 3

Celtic
1936–1939

IF 1936 was good (and indeed it was) for Celtic, there was better to come. The support enjoyed their holidays 'doon the watter' at Rothesay and Dunoon as champions for the first time in a decade. It was a sweet feeling, made all the better by the obvious improvement in the general economic situation as the country slowly recovered from the depression of the early 1930s. A British tennis player, Fred Perry, won the men's singles at Wimbledon and, in an equally unlikely scenario, Derbyshire were winning the County Cricket Championship in England. The gossip columnists talked animatedly about the new King Edward VIII, his Coronation next year and whom he would marry. They were not, however, allowed to mention, even obliquely, his relationship with Wallis Simpson, which was already the talk of the American and French newspapers.

Nevertheless, realists were aware that a great deal of the economic recovery was driven by preparations for war. And in July that year an event occurred which indicated all too clearly that world war was not far away. This was the outbreak of the Spanish Civil War, when General Franco rebelled against the legitimately-elected Spanish republic. This war lasted until 1939 and was basically a military coup which was resisted with a courage and determination that would cost millions of lives. The event split the Celtic-supporting community down the middle, for a cruel choice would have to be made whether to back the Spanish government, which was a broadly Socialist coalition, or to side with the Catholic Church, who were all for Franco. Possibly the best solution to all this was to do what the British Government did; stick one's head in the sand and hope it all went away.

It did not, of course, and Britain, France and the US doing nothing was a very dangerous policy as it gave the impression that the West was weak and would do anything to avoid another war. 'Non-intervention' was the operative phrase. Other powers were not so coy. The Soviet Union gave limited and not always helpful support to the beleaguered republic, whereas Mussolini and Hitler unreservedly backed Franco. However, Hitler was not quite asserting world domination on the sports field. The first two weeks of August 1936, just as the Scottish football season was starting, saw the Olympics held in Berlin. It was meant to show everyone that Germans were superior in everything, but sadly for the Führer, the high-profile events were won by a distinctly non-Aryan character. This was Jesse Owens, the American black athlete who won four gold medals and was openly befriended by his German rival, Lutz Long, who was no Nazi. The Führer was not best pleased.

On 14 October, Germany's football team came to Scotland to Ibrox to play against Scotland. They made history by being the first football team to fly to Scotland for a game. That Wednesday afternoon was arguably one of the saddest days in the history of Rangers, for they were compelled, much against their judgement and conscience, to fly the swastika, which was after all the flag of Germany.

Not only was the already hated flag on show, but the German team stood in the centre of the field and gave the Hitler salute to the flag, as the Govan Burgh Band played *Deutschland Uber Alles*. Fortunately, with the game being played in the British Isles, there was nothing as offensive as what happened to the England team in Berlin on 14 May 1938, when ashen-faced and tight-lipped, acting on the orders of the craven British Foreign Office, men like Eddie Hapgood, Stanley Matthews and Cliff Bastin gave the Nazi salute. Although nothing like this happened at Ibrox that day, there were nevertheless many ex-servicemen from World War One and many who knew at first hand what was happening to the Jewish population of Germany, who found this exhibition of vulgar nationalism to be deeply nauseating.

But it was Jimmy Delaney who had the last laugh. Recalled to the Scotland team from which many argued that he should never have been dropped, Jimmy was part of a superb forward line which contained Tommy Walker of Hearts, Matt Armstrong of Aberdeen, Bob McPhail of Rangers and Dally Duncan of Derby County. It was Delaney who scored the two second-half goals which gave Scotland a superb victory. Jimmy was outstanding and was helped by the presence of the other great forwards.

In the same way that he was part of an outstanding combination at Celtic, so too he had fine players along with him for Scotland on this day. The defeat of the Germans was much celebrated in the land, for the Germans were still much disliked after World War One, and eyed with justified suspicion and distrust for Hitler's aggressive statements and bellicose foreign policy. Hitler had apparently refused to shake hands with the 'racially inferior' Jesse Owens. How would he have reacted to Jimmy Delaney, one wonders? It had certainly been a bad few weeks for the 'master race'.

A Scottish poet penned the following:

Wha' put Hitler off his tea?
And made'im swear at Mussolinee!
'Twas Cleland's bhoy baith true and free
The one and only Jimmy D!

Why did Goering shout at the maid
And cause the floo'ers tae wither and fade?
Why did he spew below the bed?
'Twas Scotland's Jimmy D!

Celtic's start to the 1936–37 season was not all that it could have been. Notably there was a defeat in the Glasgow Cup semi-final to Rangers – a matter of nine days after a creditable 1–1 draw against them in the League – and there had been disappointing results against Kilmarnock and bogey team St Johnstone. To an extent this poor start had been due to an injury to Jimmy McGrory and it was certainly true that form picked up when the centre-forward returned, even though it was becoming more and more apparent that, at the age of 32, he was beginning to struggle with injuries.

But there was no such problem with the other Jimmy. Words like 'delightful nippiness and cleverness' were used about him. He had a chance to impress on a broader stage as well. Celtic, in a harbinger perhaps of the European Cup competition which would arrive 20 years later, organised a double-header friendly against Sunderland, the English champions, in a game which they called the 'Champions Match'. After a 1–1 game at Roker Park, the teams came to Celtic Park on 30 September 1936 and it was there that Celtic became the unofficial champions of Great Britain. Jimmy McGrory scored twice and, although the lead was cancelled out by Sunderland, Jimmy Delaney scored the winner. It was all pleasant, friendly stuff and both teams were given a great ovation from the Celtic crowd.

It had long been one of Celtic's ambitions to play in a British cup, or even a British league, and there is little doubt that a trophy like this would have meant a great deal to them and to manager Willie Maley in particular, who never really laid aside his 'missionary' vision for Celtic: they were expected to show the world, not just Scotland, how the game should be played. Delaney would have another trip to England that autumn, this time to Goodison Park to play for the Scottish League against the English League and to win 2–0.

Another clear sign that Celtic were beginning to mean business once again was when they appointed an assistant-trainer in the shape of the old full-back, the much-loved Joe Dodds of Shaw, McNair and Dodds fame. Once again,

Delaney had expert help. As left-back, Joe would have been Delaney's direct opponent if their paths had ever crossed on the field. No doubt he could have told Delaney the tricks of the trade of the left-back and how Delaney could best get past the most doughty of left-backs. Certainly very few right-wingers ever got past Joe Dodds.

Delaney had in the meantime lost his Scotland place. The trip to Ireland on Hallowe'en had Alex Munro of Hearts, a competent player although hardly of Delaney's class, on the right-wing and the same player would play at Dens Park against Wales on 2 December. Considering that Delaney had scored the two goals against Germany and was playing well for Celtic, this is odd. Scottish selectors, of course, were quixotic and peculiar, and wiser counsel would prevail for the important England game in April, but in the meantime Delaney's omission did little to dispel the widespread feeling among Celtic fans that their players were not always welcome playing for Scotland.

Delaney might have missed the Wales game anyway, for he picked up an injury in the 3–1 win over Dunfermline Athletic on 28 November and missed the next Celtic game. By the time that he returned on 12 December 1936 to play Motherwell, Britain had a new king, her third in the calendar year of 1936. In a move unprecedented in Britain's long history, King Edward VIII had been compelled to abdicate in order to marry Wallis Simpson. He was replaced by his shy, nervous, stammering brother Bertie, who became King George VI. He would have to rely to a very great extent on his Scottish wife, Lady Elizabeth Bowes-Lyon of Glamis Castle, whom he had married in 1923.

The first Celtic game of the new king's reign was a remarkable one for Delaney. He was taken off in the first half with what looked like a broken arm, but it turned out to be nothing more than a slight muscle tear. He was able to resume in the second half and scored the two goals which won the game. The team then played an appalling game at Dumfries to lose 0–1 to Queen of the South before Delaney finished the calendar year of 1936 by scoring twice in a routine 4–0 demolition of Albion Rovers at Parkhead on Boxing Day. The defeat at Palmerston Park had cost Celtic the lead in the League race, but they were still there among the other contenders – Aberdeen, Rangers and Hearts.

Celtic continued their melancholy tradition of losing at Ibrox on New Year's Day. They had not had a Happy New Year at Ibrox since Joe Cassidy had done the deed in 1921. Indeed, it would not be until Charlie Nicholas did the needful in 1983 that this particular bogey would be laid to rest. In 1937, they went down 0–1 on a heavy ground and from then on in the Scottish League Celtic struggled with inconsistent form. Two draws in January were not championship-winning form in this tight race and then, with Delaney out injured and McGrory chosen eccentrically for the left-wing, the team lost to Aberdeen at Pittodrie. From then on Celtic were outsiders in the League race and eventually ended up in third place, some nine points behind Rangers. Delaney was affected by injuries and the general malaise which hit the team in League matches, although he still got a good press report more often than not. 'Delaney dazzles and delights', 'Delaney was simply Delaney' and 'Delaney on song' are among the reports, but sadly he was not able to lift the team to a second successive League Championship.

Crucially his goals seemed to have dried up. He was suffering from what in other sports is called 'second season' syndrome, whereby the season after a brilliant one is not quite so good. Perhaps this was because defences had sussed out his tactic of cutting inside and detailed an extra man to deal with him – none too gently, for he was injured four times before the end of the season. Perhaps he was being supplied less well by his defence and midfield, or maybe he found that the heavy grounds of that exceptionally wet winter were too much for his comparatively slight frame. In any case, the Scottish League campaign of 1937 was a disappointment, both for Celtic and Delaney.

But ample compensation was forthcoming in the Scottish Cup. After a stuttering, unimpressive start against minor teams on heavy pitches, Celtic really turned it on in the spring with some epic games. Yet it nearly did not happen. Delaney, having missed the League defeat at Aberdeen on 23 January, was still out for the Cup game at Stenhousemuir at Ochilview. The Warriors of Stenhousemuir did not seem to be any huge problem for Celtic, but it so happened that Stenhousemuir played the best game of their somewhat impoverished history and were distinctly unlucky not to cause Scottish football's greatest-ever sensation. In fact there would have been two sensations on the same day for, as it happened, Rangers went down to Queen of the South at Dumfries.

Delaney was forced to sit in the stand and watch Celtic play a feckless first half against a spirited Stenny side in foul weather. Then McGrory scored and the 3,000 crowd expected a shower of goals. But Howie scored for Stenhousemuir from the left-wing and gradually Celtic were penned back more and more until, in the last minute, it looked to the press and all the Stenhousemuir supporters that Celtic left-back Jock Morrison handled inside the penalty box. Referee Peter Craigmyle from Aberdeen said 'No' and Celtic were given a reprieve.

The Celts were none too brilliant in the midweek Cup replay at Parkhead either, but this time Delaney was fit and he probably made a difference to the forward line which had let itself down so badly at Stenhousemuir on the Saturday. McGrory's two goals, one in each half, were enough to send Celtic through to the next round. Meanwhile, in the war in Spain, heroic defending by volunteers from all over the world (the International Brigades) was saving Madrid, for the time being at least, from Fascism.

The Celts were next drawn against Albion Rovers at Cliftonhill on 13 February

1937. Another upset was feared when the Rovers went ahead in the first minute and then took the lead again after McGrory had equalised, so that the half-time scoreboards throughout the country told everyone that Celtic were down 1–2. This time, though, there would be no mistake, as Delaney, now fitter than he had been since his injury, took charge. He fed Willie Buchan for a couple of goals, McGrory for another and finally scored himself near the end.

A couple of weeks later, Celtic reached the quarter-finals with a regulation victory at Methil against East Fife in front of a packed crowd of 12,069 and thousands more thronging the main street outside and listening to the shouts of the crowd. The local crowd cheered on Celtic as well as their own favourites, according to the *Dundee Courier*, for Methil and Buckhaven 'having yielded up so many players to Celtic in the recent past' was a pro-Celtic area. In this game the difference lay in the wing play, with both Jimmy Delaney and Frank Murphy outstanding as Celtic beat the Fifers 3–0. Delaney was particularly impressive in the second half when playing against the wind.

A huge crowd was expected at Parkhead for the game against Motherwell in the quarter-final. These teams had the reputation of being the best pure football teams in the country, as Motherwell had excellent players like Ellis, Blair, Wales and Stevenson. In addition, the memory of those epic Scottish Cup Finals of 1931 and 1933 were deeply ingrained in the psyche of Celtic supporters. There was too a certain needle in the atmosphere, for Motherwell were perceived as being a pro-Rangers team, a perception that has not entirely died among Celtic fans to this day. Sadly, a late fall of snow delayed the game until the following Wednesday afternoon when the crowd, although respectable at 36,259, was about 20,000 or 30,000 down on what might have been expected.

Those who took that Wednesday afternoon off on 17 March 1937 may well have had uncomfortable interviews with their employers or headmasters the following day, but they saw a remarkable game of football about which the press quite rightly went into ecstasies. The first 15 minutes contained a flurry of goals, during which Delaney laid on one for Johnny Crum, but the balance of goalscoring was 3–2 in Motherwell's favour. Then, just inside the second half, George Stevenson scored for the 'Well again and Celtic were 2–4 down and looking as if they were heading for the exit door of the Scottish Cup.

But the tradition of a Celtic fightback against Motherwell had started with the 1931 Scottish Cup Final and was maintained that day. First, Delaney was brought down in the penalty box and captain Willie Lyon, a lion indeed, who was absolutely inspirational, took the penalty kick and scored.

> *For there's surely no denyin'*
> *Wi' our captain Willie Lyon*
> *We will win the Scottish Cup once again!*

However, Motherwell's goalkeeper McArthur was in inspired form and the minutes began to tick past with no addition to the Celtic score. McGrory was well policed and now lacked the speed that he once had, and wingers Delaney and Murphy worked hard but could not quite break through. It was left to Willie Buchan, the inside-right, to pick up a Delaney pass and dribble his way through the Motherwell defence to score the crucial late goal which gave Celtic the replay. Indeed, such were the cries of encouragement in the remaining minutes that Celtic might well have gone on to win the game.

Delaney had picked up an injury and McMenemy and Maley considered that he was such a vital part of the machine for the replay the following Wednesday that he was given a rest for Saturday's League match in order to have him fit for the trip to Motherwell. It was also a tacit admission that the League had been lost this season, although Celtic did beat St Mirren that day.

The team bus going to Fir Park on Wednesday 24 March would have been aware of passing many fans on the way. They were actually walking to Motherwell from Glasgow! Losing a day's pay, and needing what money they had to get into the ground, meant they could not pay for transport, so they were compelled to use nature's resources. Frankly, such was the interest in this game that it should have been played at Hampden or Ibrox, as Fir Park was grossly inadequate for the purpose.

Wednesday afternoon or not, the gates were closed before kick-off with 36,500 inside – plus many more who climbed over the wall. The crowd massed outside in its thousands, while inside dangerous swaying took place at the north-west corner to such an extent that spectators were allowed onto the running track and were lined five deep round the pitch, with boys at the front sitting on the ground. Mercifully there were no fatalities or even serious injuries, although it was a close run thing. Such was the enthusiasm of the Celtic support for this team.

Motherwell again took the lead and were still one up at half-time, but in this frenetic atmosphere, Celtic thrived and the forward line of Delaney, Buchan, McGrory, Crum and Murphy played delightful football, combining to allow McGrory to equalise in the 50th minute. At this point, they lost goalkeeper Joe Kennaway, who was engulfed in the throng which invaded the park from behind his goal.

Order was patiently restored and the game continued. Once again Jimmy Delaney was outstanding, giving left-back Ellis a terrible roasting, and it was from a break down the right that Willie Buchan scored what turned out to be the winner in the 65th minute. Full-time arrived and serious fears were entertained for the safety of the players. Delaney was seized by the fans, as indeed were Kennaway and Crum, but only so that they could carry them off the field. Jimmy would later describe this as a scary moment, but at no point was he in any real danger, for there was nothing malicious in these fans, merely hero worship for their idol.

The massive crowds and the enthusiasm for the game were due to several factors. One was quite simply the love of the game which the Scottish nation possessed – and still does. The country was coming out of a dreadful depression and money was now more plentiful. In particular, the Celtic-supporting community of Scotland had suffered dreadfully in the depression for they had had to endure racial and religious discrimination, in addition to other problems. Small wonder that they had huddled together in their enclaves, awaiting the resurrection of their football team to restore their morale and fortunes. Now the depression was over, they had emerged in all their glory to support their team, the one thing that gave them a collective self-respect and feeling of their own importance.

The imminence and inevitability of war is often adduced as a factor to explain the size and enthusiasm of Scottish football crowds at this time. People were determined to enjoy themselves while they still could. This is at least half true. Certainly only a fool could deny the menace of Hitler. Even in 1937, Europe was at war in Spain and any trip to a football match, or indeed the centre of a city, would see many posters urging everyone to join the International Brigades in order to defeat the Fascist menace. The Roman Catholic Church, ever a supporter of Franco, maintained an embarrassed silence about the involvement of Hitler and Mussolini in the Spanish conflict, and the outrages that they were committing on the Catholic Basque population of northern Spain.

But it was not just a matter of enjoying themselves while they still could. Rather, it was a matter of sharing the euphoria. It is a sad fact that people enjoy life when there is a crisis. They feel part of everything and they feel needed. In 1937, people would be listening to the news on the radio, reading more newspapers, talking more about current affairs, going to the cinema more often – and of course going in even greater numbers to football matches. Excitement was in the air and it was an excitement that even the huge amount of crippled and disabled war veterans from 20 years earlier could not dispel.

There was also the undeniable fact that Celtic were playing some superb football. 'To play the game in the good old Celtic way' is a line from one of the present day supporters' songs. This mighty team of the late 1930s played football the way that it was meant to be played. The forward line in particular was very impressive. The spearhead was McGrory, now ageing and threatening to give up before injuries permanently crippled him, and the inside men of Willie Buchan and John Crum had few equals, but the real icing on the cake was the dazzling wing play of Jimmy Delaney and Frank Murphy.

To say that Murphy was not as good as Delaney is no slight on Murphy. Yet it may be that Frank's miserable total of one full international cap and one Scottish League cap came about as a result of his being compared unfavourably to 'Jay Dee', as Jimmy Delaney was now commonly called by the crowd. Murphy was a fine player – fast, direct and a great crosser of the ball – all the things that a good winger must be.

But Delaney was this – and more. There was an added zest to get the ball, a great deal more panache and style, and a greater variety in his play. His normal tactic would be to get the ball, beat the left-back, go to the dead-ball line and cross, but he could also cut inside and score himself or go across the field and pass back to the waiting Geatons or Paterson who had joined the attack. Delaney had now filled out a little but remained a superb athlete who was much loved by his adoring Celtic crowd and much respected by his opponents for his chivalrous and sporting behaviour.

Those who saw Jimmy Johnstone in his prime in the late 1960s and early 1970s will have been impressed. Jimmy Johnstone was frequently compared to Jimmy Delaney. Both had lots of talent, skill, speed, determination and a mutual love affair with the Celtic public. The difference was that Johnstone was trickier, whereas Delaney was more direct. Johnstone could never resist beating a man again, thereby giving a full-back another chance. Once Delaney was past the defender, he stayed past the defender, either delivering a cross or heading for goal.

An endearing quality of Delaney was his modesty. He was never rude or discourteous to his fans, but he hated being made a fuss of. Other members of the team would love being in the limelight and would even go out of their way to court publicity and attention, but not Jimmy. He would come out of Parkhead after a game and pull his cap over his eyes, hoping not to be recognised as he made his way to his tram to the centre of town and then to get his train home. He was quite happy standing in the queue as if he had been a spectator at the game rather than the man they all came to see.

With Motherwell out of the way, the next game in the 1937 Scottish Cup campaign was the semi-final to be played at Ibrox against Clyde on 3 April. A crowd of 76,000 were there – yet another astonishing attendance – and they saw a good game. Delaney found himself directly opposed to Willie Hughes and this time Delaney was quieter than usual as Hughes, with a point to prove to the Celtic management about why he had not been kept at Parkhead, played a fine game. But keeping Delaney quiet did not in itself win the day for Clyde. In the first half the other winger, Frank Murphy, drove across a low ball for a stooping McGrory to dive on and score a brilliant goal. In the second half, Clyde's centre-half Robb, under pressure from McGrory, had the misfortune to score an own goal. On the same day, Aberdeen beat Morton to earn their first ever place in the Scottish Cup Final.

Any fears that a somewhat indifferent display in the Scottish Cup semi-final might prejudice Delaney's chance of a cap against England were dispelled when the team was announced. Delaney was the only Celtic player in the team – when a case might have been made out for all 11, some thought. The centre-forward place went to Frank O'Donnell, ex-Celtic but now of Preston North End. Frank had taken on a new lease of life at Preston and had become a better player than he ever had been with Celtic.

Following severe overcrowding at the Scotland v England game in 1935, this game was made all-ticket (the first time ever at Hampden) and the attendance was given as 149,407, but other sources give a greater amount. In fact there were many more than that who had climbed the walls, rushed gates and forged tickets. Such was the enthusiasm to see this game on 17 April 1937 that it would remain a world record attendance until the World Cup Final of 1950 in South America. As well as issuing tickets for the first time ever, the Scottish Football Association also gave a few simple instructions to the crowd along the lines of 'obey the stewards', 'arrive early', 'move down the terracing' and, to those of less humble origins, 'leave at home your bowler hat and wear a "bunnet" instead' – to allow the man behind you a better view presumably. Curiously, there does not seem to have been any patronising advice about abstaining from alcohol.

Celtic had been due to play Arbroath that day at Parkhead, but the wise decision was taken to play this inconsequential League game on the Friday evening. Thus Delaney and his Scotland teammates were given the opportunity to sit in the Parkhead Stand and watch Celtic, a privilege shared by the English team and many of the visiting English supporters. Celtic, with a few reserves playing, won 5–1.

Meanwhile, Glasgow was building up to the big occasion. Tartan scarves and tammies were much in evidence as trains and buses arrived from very early in the morning. Railway stations and even department stores resounded to the strains of bagpipes. One heard a great deal of Robbie Burns and Harry Lauder as fans sang the praises of *Bonnie Doon*, *Sweet Afton*, *Loch Lomond* and *Mary, My Scotch Bluebell*. Little hatred was expressed for the English, but there was an uncomfortable reminder of the world situation as the way from Mount Florida railway station to Hampden was festooned with posters encouraging everyone to fight Fascism by joining the International Brigades in Spain.

Delaney's direct opponent that day was Sam Barkas of Manchester City, but he would inevitably be compared with England's right-winger, a youngster called Stanley Matthews from Stoke City. They would be compared again in the future but this day both played well. There had been a great deal of rain, and England played better in the first half, deservedly leading 1–0. But in the second half, with wave after wave of thunderous roar coming from the Hampden terraces, Frank O'Donnell equalised following a fine move involving Delaney and Tommy Walker of Hearts, and then twice within the last 10 minutes Bob McPhail of Rangers (Greetin Boab as he was called) scored to give Scotland a 3–1 victory, although most fair-minded observers would admit that there were not two goals of a difference between the two sides.

But in Scotland there was no such thing as a fair-minded observer and the nation went crazy to celebrate the victory over the Auld Enemy. Every one of the 11 was feted as a hero and Delaney was hailed as joyfully as anyone for his part in this triumph. Don John in *The Courier* said, 'Delaney may not be a dazzle player, but I rank the Celt as one of the most dangerous members of the party'. And Delaney had another, almost identical, experience to come the following Saturday.

This was the Scottish Cup Final between Celtic and Aberdeen on 24 April, a date that would become very significant in Delaney's career and family life. Astonishingly, another crowd of equal proportions turned up. This one is sometimes given as 146,433, sometimes more than that. Those who were at both games argue that the Scottish Cup Final actually had more than the international. It matters little: crowds of astonishing proportions watched both games and Jimmy Delaney was the only player to have played in both. Counting the 76,000 that were at the semi-final against Clyde at Ibrox and various League games, Delaney's 'tally' for the month of April 1937 is not far short of half a million!

Unlike the international, the Scottish Cup Final was not all-ticket. The Scottish Football Association, however, clearly misjudged the sheer size of the Aberdeen support that day, which would not have come far short of the Celtic crowd. It was the first time that the Black and Golds had been in the Scottish Cup Final and their huge, dormant support had not previously been measured. As early as Thursday afternoon, buses and trains were leaving Aberdeen full of supporters, who were clearly out to enjoy a long weekend in Glasgow. The mother and the children would go shopping or visit some relatives in the west of Scotland while the father would watch the game.

Celtic's 'far-summoned allies' were also there in large numbers, for on special occasions like this, the Celtic support becomes more of a national or even an international institution. The hard-core, first or second generation Irish from the immediate area around Glasgow, are of course there in strength, but so too are supporters from Ireland itself, from various parts of England and a substantial multi-denominational support from the east of Scotland. Indeed, it had been one of the triumphs of Willie Maley that he had been able to attract a large following of supporters of religions other than Catholicism.

About half an hour before kick-off, it was obvious that Hampden was dangerously overcrowded and the decision was taken to close the turnstiles.

This in itself caused more than a little mayhem, for the turnstiles were not all closed at once and supporters rushed round the ground trying to find a turnstile that was still open. It was truly a massive crowd, with thousands locked out. These poor unfortunates, many from Aberdeen, could, in this age before transistor radios, do little other than listen to the shouts of the crowd and try to judge the progress of the game from that.

Willie Buchan and Jimmy Delaney would both testify to the sheer wall of noise that they passed through that day as the teams came out. Buchan indeed said that he almost fainted, such was the tangible tension among so many people. It was billed as McGrory's last Cup Final. He had scored in 1925, 1931 and 1933, been injured in 1927 and had played on the losing side in 1926 and 1928. This man, who now had 'more records than Harry Lauder', would have been a very popular goalscorer, but it was Crum and Buchan who scored the goals in a 2–1 Celtic victory. The match was rated as one of the best Scottish Cup Finals of them all for the sheer standard of the play.

Delaney's contribution to the Celtic cause was not unlike that of the previous week for Scotland. He was not outstanding, but he was always there, always a threat and always needed to be well marked by the Aberdeen defence. The full-time whistle saw him congratulate his Aberdeen opponents rather than indulge in any triumphal victory celebration – the sort of thing that Delaney despised. Indeed, the Scottish Cup itself was presented in a dignified way to the Celtic directors in the board room of Hampden and photographs were only allowed after the players had dressed and the crowd had gone home. It was Celtic's 15th capture of the Scottish Cup and Jimmy Delaney's one and only Scottish Cup medal.

Thus, for two weeks in a row, Delaney enjoyed the limelight. But if there were any doubt that the moment should be seized it was dispelled when the news came a few days later of how German bombers had obliterated the Basque town of Guernica in the Spanish Civil War, for no reason apparently other than to show the world that they could do it and they could therefore browbeat Britain and France into giving away more of Europe. Once again the Roman Catholic Church maintained an embarrassed silence.

The League season ended on a discordant note on Friday 30 April when Celtic played their last League game. They were to be taken to Wembley the following day to see the English Cup Final between Preston North End and Celtic's old friends Sunderland, who had apparently offered a king's ransom of £20,000 in an unsuccessful bid for Jimmy Delaney. Delaney refused to go, for he was happy playing for Celtic in those heady and tumultuous days.

The Celtic players would travel down on the overnight sleeper from Glasgow on the Friday night but first they had to go to Motherwell to play their last League game. They managed to lose 0–8! Excuses were possible in injuries to

Morrison and Kennaway, but Alec Stewart of Motherwell could hardly believe his luck in scoring six goals against the mighty Celtic.

It was certainly an odd way to finish a League season and the high scoreline did little to dispel rumours about liaisons with bookmakers and so on. But Delaney and company enjoyed the trip to Wembley, where many believed he should have played the year before in the England v Scotland international. Sunderland won 3–1 in the 1937 English Cup Final, which was the first ever to have a portion of it televised live to the few homes who had a television set. Ex-Celt Frank O'Donnell, playing with brother Hugh in the Preston side, scored Preston's consolation goal.

Celtic would go on to win the Glasgow Charity Cup, but they did so without Jimmy Delaney. This was for the excellent reason that he was away in central Europe with Scotland, playing against two countries that were living under perpetual fear of the German jackboot: Austria and Czechoslovakia. Delaney played well in both games, with the team drawing 1–1 in Vienna and winning comprehensively 3–1 in Prague.

The summer of 1937 was thus spent happily by Jimmy Delaney as he had now won a Scottish Cup and Scottish League championship medal after only four years at the club. He was an established Scottish internationalist and was playing for the club that he loved. He knew that old Maley, for all his crusty misanthropic exterior, appreciated his play and he was confident that his career would continue to develop. He did, however, worry about the possibility of war. The Coronation of King George VI on 12 May 1937 (celebrated when the Scottish team was abroad) was a great occasion, full of pageantry and pomp, but the feeling was growing that this might be the last such occasion. Stories had now reached Britain in detail of the saturation bombing of Guernica. What could those bombers do to London and Glasgow? There had been some aerial bombing in World War One but this was different; far more comprehensive and efficient, and a great deal more terrifying. Meanwhile, Prime Minister Stanley Baldwin resigned and the poisoned chalice passed to Neville Chamberlain.

Apparently oblivious to the sufferings and anxieties of the world, or perhaps all the more determined to give people something to help them forget, the Scottish football season for 1937–38 started again on 14 August, with Celtic determined to mend their inconsistent ways and to make a determined challenge for the Scottish League once again. The massive crowds continued to come to the games, revealing a truly insatiable appetite for the game in Scotland, and the area around Glasgow in particular. Yet there often seemed to be a curious problem about Celtic fans: they did not attend Celtic Park in as large numbers as they clearly did away from home and particularly in big games like Cup Finals at Hampden.

This may have been behind Maley's strange decision to transfer Willie

Buchan to Blackpool for £10,000. This astonishing piece of asset stripping may well have upset Delaney in the short term, but the odd thing was that it was the right decision for Malky MacDonald. 'Callum', as he was called, came in almost immediately to replace Buchan and very soon Delaney was able to strike up the same rapport that had previously existed between himself and Willie Buchan. Indeed, the consensus of opinion was that MacDonald was a better player than Buchan. Delaney himself would in later years deny that he was the best player in the team. 'How could I be when Malky MacDonald was in the side?' MacDonald on the other hand would always claim that, 'You didn't play with Delaney – you played to him, and he did the rest!'

Another departure that autumn was Jimmy McGrory. This had been coming for a long time, for he had been threatening to give up the playing side of the game for some time, as he was now 33 and struggling to recover from his repeated injuries. He played his last game in mid-October against Queen's Park and by 18 December had been appointed manager of struggling Kilmarnock. On Christmas Day, McGrory was back at Celtic Park with Kilmarnock, sadly for him on the receiving end of an 8–0 drubbing, with Maley giving strict instructions to his players not to let up, irrespective of who Kilmarnock's manager was.

Not surprisingly, in view of these massive changes in personnel, the Celtic team did not do all that well in the early part of the season. Two defeats to Rangers, one in the Scottish League and the other in the Glasgow Cup, did little to help morale, but this must be balanced against some fine high-scoring performances as St Johnstone, Partick Thistle and Hibernian were all put to the sword. McGrory was of course irreplaceable, but the team was reasonably served by Joe Carruth before Johnny Crum was moved into the centre and John Divers II (so called to distinguish him from an earlier John Divers who played in the 1890s and another in the 1960s – John Divers III – the son of John Divers II) brought in to the inside-right position.

Delaney personally continued to play excellent football on the right-wing and twice starred for the Scottish League, against the Irish League in early September at the Belfast Oval and at Ibrox later that month when his goal was enough to defeat the English League and for the press writers to ask, 'Where would Celtic and Scotland be without the Delaney dazzler?' He also impressed them yet again at Sunderland when the two teams continued their friendship and played a game called the Cup-Winners' Match in another harbinger of things to come.

But he had bad luck at Arbroath on 9 October. Willie Lyon had already been carried off when Delaney clashed with Arbroath's Atilio Becci. Delaney was carried off on a stretcher and taken to Arbroath infirmary for X-rays on a suspected broken leg. Fortunately, there was nothing broken, but it was enough to lose Celtic this match and to knock Delaney out of a few games, notably the Wales v Scotland clash at Ninian Park, Cardiff, at the end of the month. Scotland would lose that game, but fortunately Delaney was fit again for the game against Ireland at Pittodrie on 10 November. Scotland fared slightly better in that one, drawing 1–1. However, Becci, a committed Celtic fan, would have the misfortune to inflict a far more serious injury on his hero 18 months later.

On 4 December at Fir Park, Motherwell, Delaney was again in the wars. He limped off at half-time and did not reappear after suffering a torn muscle. He was thus unavailable for Scotland's midweek game against Czechoslovakia at Hampden and a few games after that. Rather foolishly, he was played in the 8–0 beating of Kilmarnock on Christmas Day in circumstances where clearly a longer rest should have been in order. He scored the first goal, but thereafter was quiet, a virtual spectator as goals rained in from other parts of the pitch. He had aggravated his torn muscle and would be out for some considerable time.

In fact he did not return until 26 February 1938. In his absence the team prospered. They lacked the flair of Delaney, but his deputies Joe Carruth and Matt Lynch were adequate and the inside trio of MacDonald, Crum and Divers were very impressive and thoroughly deserving of the huge crowds that they attracted. They broke records at Cathkin Park, Tynecastle and at Celtic Park itself on New Year's Day when 83,500 (some record books say 92,000) saw as comprehensive a beating of Rangers as they were ever likely to get.

Delaney's return brought a 5–1 win over St Mirren, a result that saw Celtic clear at the top of the League, three points ahead of nearest challengers Hearts and 11 clear of Rangers, whose form had collapsed after their New Year's Day defeat. The Scottish League seemed secure, but disaster hit Celtic in the Scottish Cup. It is this defeat which means that the 1938 side, although good, cannot be considered as great as the 1908 and 1967 teams who won every trophy that they entered. The sides of 1916 and 1917 also won every trophy entered for, but that was in the unreal circumstances of World War One and when there was no Scottish Cup.

The Scottish Cup demise was a strange one, and it was at the hands of Jimmy McGrory's Kilmarnock on 5 March 1938. It will be recalled that Celtic thrashed them 8–0 on Christmas Day, giving poor McGrory a managerial baptism of fire. But Jimmy had clearly worked on his team since then and there had been a tremendous improvement. Still, it was confidently expected that Celtic would win comfortably.

The only possible excuse that Celtic could have was the absence through injury of Chick Geatons. That had been a management decision. Geatons was actually fit and indeed playing in a reserve game that day, but it was felt that he should not be hurried back after an injury and that he be given a run in the reserves instead. Thus, Matt Lynch played at right-half. Celtic were wearing their 'Hibernian' strip of green and white sleeves. Following this game, it was considered unlucky and seldom worn again. The 'Hibernian reverse' of white with green sleeves was a more common alternative to the hoops (or the stripes as they were called).

Quite simply, Celtic underestimated Kilmarnock and the 39,538 crowd were distressed to see Killie score in the first 10 minutes and then again before half-time. Celtic did not really get back into the game until Malky MacDonald scored a penalty in the last 15 minutes. The story goes that they had an extra supporter that day in the second half, for Chick Geatons, hearing that they were 0–2 down, had feigned injury in the reserve match at Clyde and rushed to Parkhead to cheer on the team. Sadly his heroics were to no avail, for Celtic failed to equalise.

Delaney had a frustrating afternoon. As happens to all great players, there are times when things will not go well. He tried to move around the forward line hoping for the crucial ball that might just turn things around, but it did not happen. Full-time came not to a chorus of booing, but something that is perhaps worse: a cemetery silence apart from the delight of the few Kilmarnock supporters.

Maley was furious with his team. Had Celtic reached the Scottish Cup Final, there is no reason to doubt that the previous year's record crowd would have been equalled. Money had therefore been lost – always an important consideration with Maley. But that hardly excuses his boorish behaviour towards Jimmy McGrory. He gave him the most cursory of handshakes and then ignored the man who had scored so many goals for his club. McGrory went to Maley's office for a chat, thinking that he would be welcome. He was told to come in but left standing while Maley continued his paperwork.

Delaney met McGrory, however. The two Jimmies, once comrades in arms but now in separate camps, found this meeting an embarrassing one. Delaney was as chivalrous and sporting as always and McGrory clearly felt bad about what he had done to the team that he still loved. 'I wish it had been Rangers', he confided to Delaney. Delaney smiled and wished McGrory all the best for the rest of the campaign. Killie in fact would reach the Final, only to lose to Second Division East Fife.

There was still the League, which Celtic duly won with one or two stutters. Delaney's unlucky season continued with another injury. This time he was carried off towards the end of a game against Ayr United with a repeat of the leg injury that he had had earlier in the season. He missed two games and, gallingly for him, the chance to play for Scotland at Wembley in the international. He had not been picked for the 1936 Wembley international either and missing an opportunity to play at the Empire Stadium (as it was known) must have upset him, particularly after his visit there to be a spectator at the previous year's English Cup Final.

In his absence the team had gone down appallingly to Falkirk, raising the possibility that the League title might not be the foregone conclusion that everyone seemed to think that it was. But Delaney was back by the Easter weekend, when Celtic had a double header against Dundee, and two other games after that. Five points were required from four games (with two points for a win in 1938) and it was certainly the presence of Delaney in full power that made all the difference at Dens Park in the thriller which Celtic edged 3–2. Delaney it was who laid on the two goals for Divers and the one for Carruth.

It was the same two teams at Parkhead on the Holiday Monday, but this time it was a great deal easier as Celtic won 3–0. Then, at St Mirren on Saturday 23 April, the League was clinched. Crum scored in 20 seconds, Delaney scored one of his great goals before the half-hour mark and Celtic coasted home to the delight of their fans in the 16,000 crowd. Thus Celtic won their 19th League championship and Delaney had his second League championship medal in three years.

But 1938 was not finished yet. There were two trophies to be played for and won. Delaney, not having been picked for the Wembley international because of his injury problems, could not reasonably have expected to be picked for Scotland's tour of Europe either, even though he had participated so brilliantly in last year's tour. He was naturally unhappy about this, but the good news was that he was available for the Glasgow Charity Cup games in early May. Queen's Park put up a brave fight in the first round, as did Partick Thistle in the semi-final, but Celtic's pace was just a little too much for them and Celtic won 3–2 in both cases. Delaney's mazy dribble in the Queen's Park game, which allowed Frank Murphy to score the second goal, attracted a certain amount of praise in the press. 'Delaney's dribble douses doubters', says the alliterative writer in the *Glasgow Observer*.

Ironically, the easiest opponents were a dispirited Rangers team who had had a poor season. On 14 May, Celtic easily lifted the Charity Cup with two first-half goals, one from Delaney and the other from John Divers II. Rangers in fact missed two penalties, but even if they had scored, Celtic could easily have upped a gear or two and won the game. A feature of the forward play on this occasion was the interchanging of position at full speed, as Delaney, Crum and Murphy would suddenly appear all over the forward line and baffle the defence. This was the old trick of Jimmy McMenemy, who himself used to interchange with Peter Somers and Patsy Gallacher to devastating effect. The difference was that it was now done in a far more sophisticated and planned fashion. The game finished with Celtic well on top and Rangers were glad to hear the final whistle.

There was yet more to come. In 1938, there was an all-Britain tournament called the Empire Exhibition Trophy. Bellahouston Park hosted the Empire Exhibition, a successful piece of propaganda and morale-boosting exercise in view of the now inevitable and perhaps imminent struggle against Nazi Germany. This exhibition was opened on 3 May by King George VI and Queen Elizabeth at Ibrox Park, which would be the venue for a football tournament to which were invited the best teams of Great Britain: Celtic, Rangers, Hearts, Aberdeen, Everton, Sunderland, Chelsea and Brentford. The games were played in the long summer evenings and certainly attracted great crowds.

A total of 53,791 saw the tournament open with a goalless draw between Celtic and their old friends Sunderland on 25 May. The problem for Celtic was an injury to Jimmy Delaney early in the first half. He was able to play on, but with a pronounced limp, and he had to play on the left-wing to allow the right-sided Carruth to be the right-winger while Frank Murphy was given a chance to show his prowess at inside-right. This ploy did not work and the game went to a replay.

Delaney missed the replay but Matt Lynch was adequate in his place and Celtic, despite conceding the first goal, went on to win 3–1. The semi-final saw the team against Hearts. Once again, Delaney missed the game but the team won 1–0 with a goal from Johnny Crum. Everton beat Aberdeen in the other semi-final, so it would be a Scotland v England clash. In the 1930s, Everton were one of the leading lights of English football. They had won the League championship in 1928 and 1932 and the English Cup in 1933. They had a huge support and many fine players, like Torry Gillick, Tommy Lawton and Joe Mercer. Beating them would surely entitle Celtic to call themselves the champions of Great Britain, and perhaps the world. Curiously, in 1933, on the very day that Delaney had signed for Celtic, Maley had turned down the chance of a game against Everton, believing (correctly) that his 1933 team would be no match for the Toffees. In 1938, however, it was a different matter.

The great thing about this tournament for Delaney was the time between his injury on 25 May and the final on the evening of Friday 10 June. Delaney's leg, which had given him more than a few problems during the 1938 season, had a chance to recover for its final fling. It was with great pleasure that Celtic announced the recovery of Jimmy Delaney to take his place on the right wing. They would certainly need his tricks and his wiles, but the match programme was clearly printed too early to allow for Delaney's recovery – his name is missing from the team.

It was most unusual to see a football game played in such brilliant evening sunshine. The newspapers (even the Scottish ones) of the following morning, although giving a detailed account of the game, are far more interested in the Test Match at Trent Bridge in which England had scored 422 for 4 against the Australians with centuries from Charles Barnett and Len Hutton.

A crowd of 82,000 saw Mr Thomson of Northumberland start the game. The teams were as follows. Celtic: Kennaway; Hogg and Morrison; Geatons, Lyon and Paterson; Delaney, MacDonald, Crum, Divers and Murphy. Everton: Sagar; Cook and Greenhalgh; Mercer, Jones and Thomson; Geldard, Cunliffe, Lawton, Stevenson and Boyes.

The game was tough and determined, but clean, and full-time came for the 82,000 fans at the ground and those listening on BBC Radio with the score at 0–0. Rex Kingsley had provided the radio commentary for the second half. It would be Celtic who won this titanic struggle after extra-time with a goal from Johnny Crum, followed by his immortalised dance of delight in front of his adoring crowd. It would thus be Willie Lyon who picked up what was eccentrically called the Empire Exhibition Tourney Tower, a replica of Tate's Tower in Bellahouston Park. Delaney 'chased every ball' and played his part in this great triumph, having had hard luck in the first half with an acrobatic turn and shot which skimmed the bar. This victory made sure that everyone in the world knew all about Glasgow Celtic.

It could not have come at a better time either, for Celtic's Golden Jubilee dinner came less than a week later, celebrating 50 years of the club. Although they were founded in November 1887, as they did not play a game until 1888 it is perhaps appropriate to say that 1888 is the year of their birth. Old players like Gallacher, Quinn, McInally and Loney attended the occasion. Delaney, still shy, was in awe of such men, but it was a grand experience for him. The aged Maley spoke eloquently and it was expected that he would announce his retirement, though as it turned out he did not. Tears were shed, everyone was happy and Celtic were at the apex of their history. Jimmy Delaney was one of the heroes.

From then on, Celtic began to slide badly. Indeed, it would be the mid-1960s under Jock Stein before they really got back to where they were in 1938. Yet 1938 was a time when football was increasingly being used by millions of people as a shield from the grim reality of the European situation. Autumn 1938 was the time in which Hitler laid claim to Czechoslovakia and Europe looked down the barrel of a gun.

There was perhaps a certain justification for some of Hitler's claim, as the Sudetenland had a preponderance of German speakers. The Treaty of Versailles of 1919 had taken those German speakers from Germany to form the artificial land called Czechoslovakia, and now even the liberal press was agreeing that Versailles had been too severe. The problem was that the Czechoslovakians were not taking very kindly to the threats of dismemberment of their country.

During the whole of September 1938, the world held its breath as British Prime Minister Neville Chamberlain flew back and forward three times to talk to Herr Hitler. Everyone knew that failure in these talks would lead to war, but eventually, on 30 September, Chamberlain came back with his paper which guaranteed 'peace in our time'. All that really meant was that there would be no war – this year. The Sudetenland was given to Germany in spite of the unavailing protests of the Czechoslovakians.

History has not been kind to Mr Chamberlain. It is important to remember, though, that criticism of Chamberlain was far from widespread in 1938. Indeed, he was treated as a hero by newspapers like *The Times* and by the adoring public in London as he drove from the airfield to Downing Street. This feeling was paralleled throughout the British Empire. For example, the crowd that assembled at Cliftonhill on the stormy day of 1 October to see Celtic at Albion Rovers were happy, cheerful and saying nicer things about a Conservative Prime Minister of Great Britain than Celtic supporters normally do! Peace was the important thing. It was only 20 years since the last war and there was ample evidence in the comparatively young men of only 40 years of age of the damage that could be done in such a war. Men like Churchill were not happy, but when had he ever been right on any decision?

Delaney and Celtic had started the season as brightly as they had finished the last one, although not without a few fallibilities. Jimmy McGrory's Kilmarnock, the previous year's Scottish Cup finalists, were thrashed 9–1 on the opening day, but the Ayrshire men held Celtic to a draw at Rugby Park 11 days later. Then Celtic lost to Aberdeen, but delighted their fans by beating Hearts 5–1 in Edinburgh on 3 September (Delaney's 24th birthday) and Rangers 6–2 on 10 September, in a fantastic display of football in which Delaney scored with a brilliant bullet header.

October began with an 8–1 win at Albion Rovers. On that day, when peace was apparently secured, Delaney scored twice. The following week, while playing for Scotland against Ireland, he scored another goal. Yet another good Saturday came his way the next week as Celtic won the Glasgow Cup by beating Clyde 3–0, Delaney scoring the first goal in front of 43,976 fans.

But that was as good as it got for Celtic. Delaney personally had a good game for Scotland as they beat Wales 3–2 at Tynecastle on 8 November 1938 to compensate for a relatively poor showing for the Scottish League against the English League. However, on the heavy grounds of November, the nimble Celtic forwards all began to struggle, as the team stuttered with a few draws and then lost to Motherwell.

Sunderland made one of their periodic attempts to sign Delaney, offering, yet again, an astronomical sum (believed to be in the region of £22,000) for him and Crum, but Maley laudably turned this down – and Delaney himself apparently made no protest. Perhaps it might have been better for Jimmy if he had gone to Roker Park, because from then on, albeit through no fault of his own, Delaney's Celtic career went fast downhill.

Only an injury to Malky MacDonald can really explain the total lack of form that Celtic suffered in November, December and January of that last season before war broke out. Delaney was sufficiently out of touch to lose his place in the Scotland team that played Hungary on 7 December, but that was the least of his troubles as Celtic drew games that they should have won and lost to Aberdeen at Pittodrie on Christmas Eve, before a truly awful spell at the beginning of 1939.

A crowd of 118,567 – a Scottish League record which will probably never be broken – were at Ibrox on 2 January to see Rangers get the better of Celtic by 2–1, in spite of the brilliant part played by Delaney in Carruth's goal, which threatened a Celtic fightback. Delaney was injured in the feckless display on 3 January which Queen's Park won 1–0, their first victory at Celtic Park since 1927. Delaney thus missed a sensational 0–4 collapse at Kirkcaldy to an incredulous Raith Rovers, who had been promoted the previous year and were battling against relegation.

There was a limited improvement after that, but Celtic were effectively out of contention for the Scottish League. Delaney missed a few games with injury in any case, but the impression was that, not for the first time, Maley had sunk into one of his depressed moods. It is not certain whether this was due to Celtic's collapse, the imminence of war or simply old age (he was now nearly 71).

Maley should have resigned when things were good the previous summer, but refused to give up on the thing which made his existence valid. McMenemy, who was himself approaching his 60th birthday, was now beginning to struggle too. Yet the Celtic crowds stayed loyal and large, and for a spell it looked as if the Scottish Cup might yet provide some solace.

The campaign opened at Kirkton Park, Burntisland, Fife, against Burntisland Shipyard. A crowd of 1,427 were there at the public park, where wooden fences and screens had been hastily erected to satisfy the Scottish Football Association requirement of an 'enclosed ground'. Burntisland had had difficulties assembling a team due to the amount of overtime available in early 1939 in the shipyard, which made ships for the Royal Navy. For a while though they matched Celtic, and indeed soon after half-time it was all square at 3–3, until Celtic took charge and ran out 8–3 winners.

Next it was a trip to another east-coast venue, this time Montrose. Delaney scored before the 6,389 had all got themselves into the tight Links Park ground and Celtic had little bother, winning the game 7–1. There then followed two phenomenal games against Hearts with huge crowds. At least 50,709 crammed into Tynecastle on 18 February to see Delaney again give Celtic an early lead and feed MacDonald a couple of minutes later to put Celtic two up in the first five minutes. Hearts pulled one back before half-time and then, with only two minutes left, grabbed a late equaliser, which was not undeserved on the run of play but galling for the Celtic men nevertheless.

Celtic's management were less upset when they saw 80,840 appear at Parkhead for the replay. This was on a Wednesday afternoon and is probably still the record for a midweek Scottish game (other than a final or an international), although the 1966 game between the same two teams would probably run it close. It was yet another tribute to the love of the game that the average Scotsman had. Hitler or no Hitler, football was still on the agenda!

The game was worthy of the huge crowd. Both teams scored in the first half, the second half was goalless and the game went to extra-time. For a long time it seemed that the game would still be level until, with only three minutes left, John Divers II seemed to scramble the ball over the line, although Hearts goalkeeper Waugh insisted that he had pushed it out. Referee Peter Craigmyle of Aberdeen, the most famous referee of the day, agreed with Divers and gave the goal to Celtic. As Hearts went berserk and chased and pleaded with Craigmyle, 11 Celts and a single Hearts player (Tommy Walker, who would one day become their manager) accepted the decision and waited patiently until the other 10 players calmed down and restarted the game to play out the remaining three minutes.

It was back to old Cup-tie foes Motherwell in the quarter-final at Fir Park. This time the game was all-ticket. This did not prevent another 10,000 or so supporters standing outside the ground to hear the cheers of the crowd, but this time it was a disappointing game for Celtic. Celtic were two down at half-time and clearly some fight was required. Delaney provided a source of hope when he scored with 15 minutes to go, but then Celtic lost a third and vital goal to go out of the Scottish Cup.

This brought to an end to what can be described as a silver age for Celtic. If the Edwardian team of the six League championships produced a golden age, and if Jock Stein's team of the European Cup did likewise, then the Celtic team of 1935 to 1939 is worthy of the epithet 'silver'. Martin O'Neill's team of the early 21st century awaits history's judgement, but 'silver' looks more appropriate than 'golden'.

Just 11 days after the defeat at Motherwell, on 15 March 1939, Hitler seized Czechoslovakia. This time there was no attempt at justification or diplomacy: it was sheer naked greed and nothing more or less than that. Mr Chamberlain's policy of appeasement had now clearly failed. Delaney won his last peacetime international honour on Friday 17 March when the Scottish League were invited to celebrate St Patrick's Day at Dalymount Park, Dublin, against the League of Ireland. The Irishmen shocked Scotland by winning 2–1.

Dublin was a curious place to be at that time. With Europe on the very cusp of war, people in Britain wondered which way DeValera would jump. Recent history would hardly allow him to support the British, yet what would happen to Ireland if Britain fell under the Nazi jackboot? Some of the country would support the Germans, even though the German support for the 1916 Easter Rising had been half-hearted, to put it mildly. On the other hand, Britain, whatever it had done in the past, was hardly a threat to the Irish free state now. Indeed, Britain was probably the lesser of the two evils.

Delaney's poor show in the League international in Dublin probably ruled him out of contention for the Scotland v England international on 15 April. As it turned out, he would not have made it anyway. It was as if Fate or some malignant Destiny had decided that, one way or another, the glory days of Jimmy Delaney with Celtic were about to be curtailed. Meanwhile, the bells of hell were also ringing very loudly for Spain, for the weekend which would have such dire consequences for Jimmy Delaney would also be the one that would see the final surrender of republican Spain to General Franco and his Fascist allies.

Only 7,000 appeared at Celtic Park to see the visit of Arbroath on 1 April. The League, indeed the whole season, was over as far as Celtic were concerned, and little was at stake. The Arbroath side were struggling against relegation and contained one or two ex-Celtic men like John McInally and Willie Hughes. Delaney's direct opponent was Atilio Becci, with whom he had had dealings in the past. Becci, of Italian descent, had more reason than most to worry about the future, for the spectre of internment or worse appeared on the horizon however much his family tried to distance themselves from Hitler's friend, Benito Mussolini.

There were thus two ironies about Becci. In fact, he would be conscripted to the British Army and fight honourably in Italy. In war-torn Italy, he would meet an RAF man of the Celtic persuasion and confess that the worst moment of his life was the Delaney incident, for Becci was a great fan of Jimmy and indeed of the green and white brigade.

Celtic were two up early in the second half and playing far better than they had done for months, when they won a corner on the left. Frank Murphy took it, and as Delaney and Becci both rose together, they were nudged by another player and fell clumsily on the hard ground. Delaney hit the ground with a thump and Becci, trying to regain his balance, stood on Delaney's arm. Delaney's arm may have been broken when he hit the ground, but the break was certainly aggravated by the accidental contact with Becci's boot.

Delaney did not rise. A few Celtic players milled round Becci and a certain amount of pushing and shoving occurred. It is even possible that in the mêlée Becci stood on Delaney's arm yet again. Once the referee restored order, wisely taking no action against Becci, trainer McMenemy was summoned for Delaney. Delaney stirred, made to get up but then collapsed: he had fainted with the pain. A stretcher was summoned. He took no further part in the game and was taken to hospital as the game fizzled out into a 2–0 win for Celtic.

Delaney's arm was not so much broken as shattered. The surgeon said that if Delaney had not been a professional footballer, amputation might have been the preferred option. He also graphically said that fitting together the bones was like a jigsaw puzzle. It would be more than two years before Delaney was fit again. There is a picture of Delaney listening in his hospital bed to the Scotland v England game of 15 April 1939. In fact, Delaney would have to listen to a great deal more than that on radio: the outbreak of war, the departure of Willie Maley, Dunkirk, the fall of France and the Battle of Britain. With his arm in plaster or sling, Delaney would suffer a real form of depression which comes from a long layoff and the feeling of being useless, as well as acute and prolonged pain.

He was due to be married in June 1939 and this went ahead in Waterfoot, Ireland. Thus, the great changes to his personal life which marriage entailed all happened when he was out of football. By the time of his return in August 1941, 'large parts of Europe had fallen ... into the hands of the Gestapo and all the odious apparatus of Nazi rule', as Mr Churchill so eloquently put it. Great Britain had been saved by the RAF, but only just, and was now fighting a monstrous tyranny on its own apart from the new and uncertain ally of the Soviet Union. The Prime Minister had changed, the Celtic manager had changed and the world was an altogether different place.

The statement by the surgeon that had Delaney not been a professional footballer, amputation might have been the preferred option is a curious one. In the first place, a one-armed man playing football is rare, but not unheard of. It might have happened. Indeed, Hector Castro of Uruguay, the man who scored the vital goal in extra-time in the 1930 World Cup Final, had lost a considerable part of one arm in a childhood accident.

Also, what sort of job could a one-armed man do that would have been suitable for the war effort? The one positive spin-off was that the fractured arm made sure that he would not be required for the Army. He was allowed back to play football on a part-time basis in 1941, but only on the condition that he had another job as well. In Cleland, this meant coal mining.

Chapter 4

The War Years 1939–1945

SUMMER 1939 was far from pleasant for the world. Everyone wondered not if, but when hostilities would start. The British Government had one slight hope of preserving peace. Even Chamberlain now reluctantly agreed that appeasement of Hitler was not an option, but he might yet have averted war by concluding an alliance with the Soviet Union in summer 1939. This might just have deterred Hitler from seizing Poland and certainly would have put Britain and France in a stronger position when the inevitable happened. A half-hearted attempt was made when an embassy was sent to Moscow (by boat because there was no aeroplane available) under a junior officer with the unlikely name of Reginald Ranfurly Plunckett-Ernle-Erle-Drax, but no agreement was possible. Neither side tried particularly hard and in any case the Poles refused to play ball, for any Anglo-Soviet agreement might have involved allowing Soviet troops inside Poland in order to defend them.

The truth was that both Chamberlain and Poland considered the Soviet Union to be more dangerous even than Hitler himself. Yet there are times when one must take unpopular or unwholesome choices, if a war is to be avoided. The British Government could not bring itself to do so. The folly of all this became apparent when the Soviet Union and Germany astonished the world by signing a pact in August. Poland thus found itself with two enemies, one on either side, rather than just one.

While all this was going on and Glasgow was girding itself for the inevitable bombing of the docks and other important strategic sites on the Clyde, Delaney was in and out of hospital undergoing operations and treatment for his shattered arm. Amputation, which was considered at one point by surgeon Mr Beattie of the Victoria Hospital, no longer seemed necessary. For a spell it looked as if the setting was working and, although it was obvious that no football was possible for Delaney for some time, he was allowed home.

Delaney had in any case another very important event in his calendar. He had fallen in love with an Irish girl called Annie McCormack and at Waterfoot in County Antrim, in June 1939, the pair were married. Delaney had been on holiday the previous summer with the Celtic players in the wake of their Empire Exhibition Trophy success. He was introduced to Annie. Letters were exchanged, love developed and as the popular song said, 'Love and marriage, love and marriage. They go together like a horse and carriage.'

A cursory glance at the wedding photograph will show nothing unusual, but a closer look will show that Jimmy has a plaster on his left arm. It would turn out to be a long and happy marriage, with Jimmy absolutely devoted to Annie and vice versa. They would celebrate their golden wedding anniversary in 1989, although, by that time, Jimmy was a very sick man. They would have five children: Pat or Patsy was born on 24 April 1940; the tragic Michael on 26 September 1942 (he died of leukaemia in 1944); Kathleen on 26 March 1944; John on 27 September 1951 and Anne-Marie, the mother of John Kennedy (who would go on to play for Celtic), on 4 April 1956.

The world was still at peace when the football season started in August as usual. Everyone went around trying to look unconcerned. 'Cheer up – it might never happen' became a cliché. The press asked questions about 'Who will replace Delaney?' on Celtic's right wing and occasionally made vague statements that Delaney should be back by the 'turn of the year' – a grossly over-optimistic assessment of Jimmy's chances.

Celtic had played four games – losing twice to Aberdeen and beating Hearts and Cowdenbeath – with Matt Lynch, Oliver Anderson or Johnny Kelly on the right wing, when the world awoke on Friday 1 September 1939 to hear the news that Hitler had invaded Poland. There was now no avoiding war, although the British Government did try one last-ditch attempt through diplomacy on 2 September. Celtic played Clyde at Parkhead that day as Parliament met in emergency session – they beat them 1–0 through a Johnny Divers goal, but football was not the main topic of conversation. Even the playing of *God Save The King* – not a sound that one heard very often round Celtic Park – was greeted with polite respect.

War was declared on the Sunday and the Government, fearing air raids, immediately issued its famous knee-jerk reaction edict of closing down all football, cinemas, places of entertainment and schools. This was of course too ridiculous for words and the authorities had to backtrack to a certain extent, but there was the long-term effect that official football was cancelled 'for the duration'.

This meant that international matches, the Scottish League and the Scottish Cup were suspended. The Glasgow Cup, the Charity Cup and regional leagues would be allowed, the idea being that they would not involve a lot of travel. Crowds would be restricted to 8,000 or half the capacity of the ground, whichever was the greater, lest the *Luftwaffe* spotted easy targets. There would of course be exceptions and exemptions. Illogically, wartime internationals between Scotland and England were permitted on the grounds that they were good for morale.

Full-time football was not allowed. Teams were permitted to pay their players a maximum of £2 per week, and in exceptional circumstances a bonus of £1, as long as they had another job as well. This was to ensure that football players were seen to be doing something for the war effort. 'Guest' players were allowed and there were no long-term contracts.

For Delaney, who was able to go for walks with his arm in a sling but not yet able to train, this had little immediate impact, although it was clear that once his arm recovered he would have to do some work in addition to professional football. Before the war, he had earned £4 per week as a fully-signed player but this had gone up by increments, so that in 1938 and 1939 he had been reasonably affluent on £7 10 shillings per week. It hardly compares with the superstar bracket of what is earned in the 21st century, but it was nevertheless considered to be a more than adequate wage for the late 1930s. Jimmy was 'on the sick' with Celtic supplementing what his insurance gave him, but when he had fully recovered, his wages would be much reduced – a point that he would be very aware of in 1945 when the war ended.

Life had changed radically and seemingly permanently from those heady days of 1938, but Jimmy remained cheerful and optimistic that things might again improve. Indeed, during that autumn of 1939 and even the first few months of 1940, people wondered what all the fuss was about in this 'phoney war' when nothing seemed to be happening. British troops were in France on the Maginot Line and elsewhere, and there had been a few naval actions, particularly in the South Atlantic, involving the capture of the Admiral Graf Spee. There were restrictions with the blackout and on travelling, but cities had not yet been bombed, casualty lists were not yet being published in newspapers and people wondered why there was no 'real' football.

Football historians have largely neglected the chaotic arrangements of football in wartime – Celtic historians in particular because of their team's abysmal showing. But it would be a mistake to think, as many have implied, that football was not taken seriously. If anything, the opposite was the case. In the same way that the cinema became even more popular than it had been already, providing a release from the grim reality and drudgery of wartime, football too offered another world in which Tommy Lawton, Wilf Mannion and Stanley Matthews became superheroes.

In spite of the 'phoney war' idea, people did have a fear of imminent death. Many people still remembered the horrors of World War One, and indeed there was still enough evidence in the shape of limbless ex-servicemen to remind them. The threat of attack from the air was a particularly potent one and everyone was expected to carry round with them their 'wee gas mask' that Glasgow singers and comedians like Dave Willis and Will Fyfe talked and sang about.

> *In my wee gas mask, I'm working out a plan*
> *Tho' all the little bairnies think that I'm a bogey man*
> *The girls all smile and bring their friends to see*
> *The nicest lookin' warden in the ARP.*
>
> *Whenever there's a raid on, listen to my cry*
> *An airy-plane, an airy-plane away-way up-a-kye*
> *Then I run helter-skelter but don't run after me*
> *You'll no get in my shelter for it's far too wee!*

Football matches were as well attended as could be realistically expected in the circumstances – and every spectator should have had his gas mask with him. Sadly this was not the case, and the gas mask soon became a joke.

There was a certain amount of 'football must stop' from those who felt that 22 fit men should be in the services, but there was nothing like the amount of emotional blackmail that had been apparent during World War One, with white feathers being presented to men who were not in khaki. The main reason for this was that conscription was in force and every man was either in the forces or had a good reason (according to the Government) for not being so employed. This meant of course because they were needed on the Home Front.

One major change did happen to Celtic, however, and this was the sacking early in 1940 of manager Willie Maley, who had been in that post since 1897. It was euphemistically described as a 'retiral'. Maley was now over 70 and had clearly struggled to cope in the new circumstances of the war without star players like Jimmy Delaney. In addition, he had seen fit to pick a quarrel with the board over an honorarium awarded to him in 1938 on which he now found that he had to pay tax. He was replaced by Jimmy McStay, Celtic's fine centre-half and captain of the years immediately before Delaney. As players, the paths of McStay and Delaney had barely crossed, for McStay was departing as Delaney was arriving. Delaney must have wondered how he would get on with McStay.

The team's form continued to shock and horrify the fans, as the death wish continued to hang over Celtic Park. The team was clearly struggling without Maley in the background and Delaney on the field. Maley had led the team for good or bad for so long that there was little possibility of any improvement unless someone with a little more dynamism than the current board of directors was in place. They gave every impression of knowing nothing about football. In particular, opportunities presented themselves with the possibility of signing guest players for a few games. Matt Busby, for example, wished to play for them when stationed near Glasgow and dropped quite a few hints to this effect – on one occasion even turning up at Parkhead and offering his services – but the board did not see what this could offer.

There was seemingly good news about Jimmy's arm. He was certainly keen enough to return, and by March 1940 he was able to come to Celtic Park for some light 'track work'. But almost a year after the accident, his arm was still in plaster and his return would be some time away. He was, however, happy enough to give an interview to the *Glasgow Observer*. Talking happily about his prospects of returning the following season, Jimmy continued to be unrealistically optimistic when he said that 'Celtic could always stage a comeback and I don't see why not very soon'.

This may have cheered up the fans in France and the munitions industries, but an early return was far from likely, though Jimmy's arm seemed to be making an improvement. According to one press report in early May 1940, a few days before Chamberlain resigned and Churchill became Prime Minister, Delaney was now fully fit but 'dare not risk another fall on his arm as yet'. This might have been good news for the faithful, had Hitler not knocked any mention of football out of the headlines. He invaded Belgium, Holland and France soon afterwards, obliterating places like Rotterdam from the air. This offensive compelled the British Army to scurry to a small place called Dunkirk at the end of May, shortly after Delaney had been seen with his arm in a sling (not a plaster) at the Glasgow Charity Cup semi-final at Hampden on 22 May 1940. His arm and general state of mind would hardly have improved with what he saw – a 1–5 defeat in a disgraceful game in which Johnny Divers was sent off.

The anxious summer of 1940 was spent with at least the consolation for Delaney that he might be back playing soon. The British Army was brought back from Dunkirk, defeated but not broken and with a comparative lack of casualties. But by the middle of June, France surrendered and Britain was on her own as Mr Churchill encouraged everyone to 'brace themselves for their duty'. The football season would start again in August, but an invasion was imminently expected. Yet there was a grim, steely determination among everyone, with hardly a trace of defeatism or disloyalty.

For the mining community in Cleland, there had been no reason historically to love either Winston Churchill or the British Empire. It had, after all, been Churchill who had wished to 'starve the bastards out' in the General Strike of 1926, but he was seen as the man of the hour and reluctant respect was given to him. He was of course infinitely preferable to the man on the other side of the Channel, now only 22 miles from the British Isles. Churchill himself was aware of this. On one occasion when accused by some of his staff of being a dictator he said, 'Very well, but there is another dictator in Europe. Which one do you prefer?'

The first game of the 1940–41 football season saw no Jimmy Delaney as Celtic drew 2–2 with Hamilton Academicals in the Southern League. Newspapers said vaguely and briefly that Delaney was 'still out'. One could hardly blame the newspapers for not going into more detail, for there was a shortage of printers' ink and paper was rationed. In any case the Battle of Britain was raging over the skies of Kent, as the RAF stood between the western world and barbarism. But on 28 August it was announced that Delaney's arm had 'new complications' and, on 31 August, Celtic fans heard that a 'bone graft operation' was required.

It is not known what had happened to cause a deterioration from the heady, optimistic days of May. Perhaps the reports had been too sanguine in the first place. More likely, the ever-determined Delaney had jarred it on one of his training runs, or perhaps he had fallen. In any case, further serious treatment was required and it was at this point that amputation was once again considered. Indeed a surgeon said, not for the first time, that if he had not been the great Jimmy Delaney, the famous footballer, he might indeed have recommended that course of action.

Fortunately, an alternative was available. It involved the in-grafting of a pig's bone into the arm with the idea that it might solidify all the other shattered bits. This bizarre sounding treatment was difficult, and carried a great deal of danger with it, for the body would initially reject a foreign body and there was a tremendous danger of infection. But Jimmy and Annie decided that this should be done. There was no guarantee of success, but they felt that it should be tried.

This brave decision meant another prolonged stay in hospital. The next reports about Delaney came on 8 December 1940 when the news was that 'the bandages will come off following the successful bone graft'. By this time the RAF had averted, at least temporarily, the threat of invasion, and former Prime Minister Neville Chamberlain had died of cancer and perhaps a broken heart after his policy of appeasement had so spectacularly failed. On the football front, Celtic had notched a rare wartime success by winning the Glasgow Cup when George Gillan scored the only goal of the game to beat Rangers on 28 September.

After the New Year of 1941, Delaney's arm was definitely on the mend, although in February he was given a medical for the Army (conscription having been in force since the beginning of the war) and classified as Grade 4. This meant that it was highly unlikely that he would ever have to serve and was far from bad news for Jimmy and Annie. The peace-loving, gentle Jimmy was no soldier. It meant that once his arm healed, he could play football for the rest of the war, provided of course that he had another job as well.

Yet the recovery was still slow. Months of physiotherapy were required as he had to learn how to grasp things once again. There was also the psychological problem of worrying about damaging his arm again. He had to be careful not to swing his arm and hit it against a wall, for example, and he would have to try not to fall in case he automatically stuck out his arm to save himself. But the treatment was successful, for Jimmy was fit again by the start of the 1941–42 season and did not appear to have any further problems with his left arm in later life. He was also able to do a daytime job down the pit at the Kingshill Colliery, near Cleland.

The war news continued to be depressing. The casualty figures, although nothing like as bad as those of World War One, were by no means negligible. Very close to home, in the middle of March 1941, Clydebank had suffered terribly in air raids aimed at the Singer's munitions factory. Even closer on 10 May 1941 was the bizarre arrival of Rudolf Hess, Hitler's deputy, who parachuted down on Eaglesham Moor near Hamilton, apparently to negotiate peace, but more likely because he had gone mad.

Generally, though, little progress was being made. It was similar to World War One in that Britain and Germany were at a stalemate with neither side able to deal a knock-out blow to the other. There was a feeling of going nowhere, although there was the occasional success to cheer – the sinking of the *Bismarck*, for example, which had been creating havoc in the Atlantic and the North Sea. Churchill knew that the only real chance of success was the entry of the United States, but President Roosevelt, although sympathetic, was still hamstrung by the isolationist (and the profiteering) lobby. In the event, Hitler would give Britain a great boost in June 1941 when he invaded the Soviet Union. At least Britain now had an ally, however sinister and prickly.

For Celtic, 1941 had been bad. Malky MacDonald and Johnnie Crum provided the occasional good moments, but the team lacked direction. It is difficult to be too critical in the unreal circumstances of wartime, but the fact was that their still massive support deserved better than what they were being given. The Glasgow Cup in September 1940 had given them a certain amount of cheer and the press kept saying things like 'Celtic's revival is about to begin' or 'Celtic will soon be out of the doldrums', although there was little cause for permanent happiness. But Jimmy Delaney would be back from August 1941; great things would be expected.

A huge crowd assembled at Parkhead to see the Celtic trial match on 2 August, for it was the much-heralded return of Jimmy Delaney, who played on the right wing for the Green and Whites against the Greens. He was cheered to the echo every time he touched the ball and supporters were delighted to see that there was no deterioration in his speed, crossing or general desire to play the game. Crucially, his arm seemed to be strong and there was no shirking of the tackle, something which indicated that confidence had returned as well as fitness.

It had been almost two and a half years since Jimmy had been seen at Celtic Park in a playing capacity, and how the world had changed! Celtic's manager and Britain's Prime Minister had changed, men like Willie Lyon, the centre-half and captain in 1939, were in khaki and the map of Europe had been altered drastically and, it seemed, permanently. Britain had not been invaded (apart from the Channel Islands), although it had been a close run thing. Clydebank had been badly bombed though Glasgow itself, surprisingly, was comparatively unscathed. Many of the Celtic supporters were watching the game in the uniform of the British Army, enjoying what leave they had left before they departed to an uncertain future.

For these reasons, the return of Delaney assumed a tremendous importance, for everyone needed something to cheer them up in those grim circumstances. Yet it would be naïve to assume that the return of one man could change everything at a stroke, particularly in those uncertain and unpredictable days. Negative-thinking directors had done too much harm to Celtic and manager Jimmy McStay, a great player in his career, was very unfortunate in the times in which he lived and operated.

Chaos is the word that springs to mind to describe the running of Celtic. Wartime circumstances were difficult, but undeniably other teams, notably Rangers, were better organised. In World War One, when Maley was vigorous, energetic and at the height of his powers, it was Celtic who won the trophies. Maley had now gone and Celtic lacked direction. Delaney was only half-joking in later years when he said that he turned up at Parkhead for a game 'and had to be introduced to my right-wing partner'. Celtic paid dearly for such lack of guidance.

The first game, for example, in the Southern League of 1941–42, saw Celtic lose 0–3 to Hearts at Tynecastle. This must have been a grave disappointment for Delaney and he would be forgiven for having a feeling of *déjà vu* about this, for Tynecastle was where he had made his competitive debut seven years previously in 1934 and now the resurrection of his career was in Edinburgh as well. It would have been a poignant moment for him.

Be that as it may, and in spite of the Celtic forward line being the very familiar Delaney, MacDonald, Crum, Divers and Murphy, Celtic disappointed their fans by going down 0–3. If ever there was a brilliant example of the proverb 'You can't jump into the same river twice', this was it. The forward line simply could not get going for the defence and midfield contained men, with the laudable exception of Bobby Hogg, who frankly would not have been invited to don the green and white in normal times.

While this was going on at Tynecastle, it was on this very day (9 August 1941) across the Atlantic Ocean that significant events were taking place. Having travelled in conditions of the greatest secrecy, Winston Churchill met Franklin D. Roosevelt on board a ship in Placentia Bay, Newfoundland. Together they drafted the Atlantic Charter, which allied the US to the British cause in a far more tangible way than ever before. Although Churchill was not quite able to persuade the President to declare war, it was a tremendous boost for Churchill and for British morale.

Back in Scotland, Delaney's second game back was far better than his first. Delaney laid on the first two goals for Johnny Crum and Joe McLaughlin as Celtic beat Albion Rovers 4–2. By the end of August, Celtic had beaten Dumbarton and Queen's Park, with Delaney scoring in both games, and Celtic fans went around Glasgow with smiles on their faces. The crowds at these games were about 10,000, which was remarkably good in the summer of 1941 considering, for example, that travel from any distance to support Celtic would have been almost impossible in wartime circumstances, when posters would ask the famous question, 'Is your journey really necessary?'

The early season euphoria, however, quickly evaporated on 6 September when Celtic went to Ibrox. One might have hoped that the fact that the western world was heavily involved in a struggle for survival might have encouraged supporters at a football match to behave a little better and see themselves as being on the same side. Not a bit of it! The game was little short of a shambles, with both sets of players and fans disgracing themselves as Celtic went down 0–3. Rangers' first goal was offside, so Celtic were nursing a grievance. It was further inflamed by the repeated fouling of Jimmy Delaney by Rangers defenders who were not even spoken to by referee Willie Webb. Delaney was playing at centre-forward that day, which meant that his direct opponent was Willie Woodburn, who 13 years later would become one of the very few players in Scottish football to be suspended 'sine die' – indefinitely.

Halfway through the first half, Rangers scored again. Celtic were given a chance to get back in the game when Delaney was brutally fouled and injured in the penalty box in front of the Celtic fans. As Delaney was being treated behind the goal, the referee was being badgered and manhandled by Rangers players on the field who claimed that Delaney had taken a dive.

Mr Webb would not change his decision and Frank Murphy took the penalty. Jerry Dawson in the Rangers goal saved brilliantly, but as Murphy ran in for the rebound, he was brutally fouled again by a Rangers defender, although the penalty was not retaken. This was too much for the Celtic fans and a hail of bottles and stones came from their end of the ground as they indicated their severe displeasure.

Hooliganism like this can never be justified, but it must be stressed that there was a feeling of injustice, particularly as there seemed to be a concerted and deliberate attempt to injure Celtic's star man, Jimmy Delaney. The fact that Delaney had just come back from two years of injury seemed to make him a weak link in the eyes of the Rangers defenders, who were encouraged in their foul play by weak refereeing and the incitement of their support. The *Glasgow Observer* states categorically, 'So many fouls were committed against Delaney in the opening minutes that one could be pardoned for thinking that Jimmy had been labelled "Dangerous – must be stopped at all costs".'

The second half continued to be a travesty. Delaney resumed, but both he and Crum were carried off as further ferocious tackles continued. Rangers scored again and the game finished to the sounds of triumphalism, reminiscent of what was happening all over Europe at this point as violence, intimidation and thuggery won the day. After the game, Celtic were punished for their fans' misbehaviour by having Celtic Park closed for a month, even though the game had been played at Ibrox. Rangers got off scot-free for the behaviour of their players.

Celtic's season never recovered after this, but Delaney recovered from his bruising and continued to play in the centre-forward position. He was less than happy about it and the war word 'utility' was used to describe it. This meant that it was not ideal, but one must make do in the meantime. Celtic lacked a centre-forward and McStay obviously felt that Delaney was the best he had available. It was only after Celtic lost at home to Motherwell on 4 October that Delaney was restored to his best position. That game was actually played at Shawfield because of the ban on the use of Celtic Park.

By this time, Celtic had lost again to Rangers in the Glasgow Cup semi-final on the Holiday Monday at Hampden Park. This time the crowd and the Rangers players behaved a little better and Celtic were clearly under orders to keep calm. The referee was a little eccentric, however, awarding penalties all over the place. Rangers took theirs better than Celtic did and won the game.

Delaney disappointed his fans in this game. He had scored a few goals from the centre-forward position, but he needed more room. He was not a Quinn or McGrory type of centre-forward who could barge through using his muscular frame. The right wing was a far better place for his sophisticated style of play. It was where he had played before with tremendous success and, in any case, it did not entirely prevent him from having the occasional charge down the centre, for a feature of Jimmy's play had always been his ability to interchange with other attackers. In the centre of the field, he often felt enclosed and restricted.

In addition, he must have been very upset to discover that he would be unlikely to win any more international caps – even the unofficial wartime ones. The Scottish Football Association (SFA) claimed that his arm would be too expensive to insure. This was a bizarre claim. It is uncertain how or even if his arm was insured when he played for Celtic, but certainly there seemed to be no problem there. Why was it that the SFA were being so intransigent and self-destructive in denying themselves the services of their best available player? As a reader's letter to the *Weekly News* stated, 'Delaney may have a pig's bone in his arm, but it is the SFA who are showing the most signs of being pig-headed!' They were certainly penalised in full for their folly, as England repeatedly beat Scotland in the early years of the war, something that caused immense distress to the Scottish soldiers listening to the game on the BBC World Service. In North Africa or on the High Seas, such games took on undue importance in the minds of the war weary.

Late autumn 1941 did show an improvement in Celtic's performances and results, although a tendency to draw rather than win games precluded any serious attempt on the Southern League. In addition, the impression gained by reading reports of games is that Delaney was a one-man forward line, as previous stars like Crum and Divers began to struggle. Single-handedly, he saved Celtic against Airdrie on 8 November by scoring a hat-trick, and that was against a team with only nine fit men available that was forced to employ a couple of juniors.

'Where would Celtic have been without him?' asks the *Glasgow Observer*. Two weeks later, when Delaney scored two late goals to give Celtic a scarcely deserved 4–4 draw against Hearts, the journalist praises his wing play but adds that he was 'a deadly menace in the middle'.

The result the following week was a similar scoreline when Albion Rovers drew with Celtic at Cliftonhill. There is the enigmatic quip that 'as a winger, Delaney was a great centre' – an acid comment on the fact that Delaney was having to do several jobs at once. Something unusual happened in that game as well; Delaney was booked. Details are sparse other than that Dunsmore of Albion Rovers received a similar punishment. Mitigation seems possible in that the referee was the notorious M.C. Dale, who was frequently suspected of having drink on his breath (famously at the Victory Cup semi-final of 1946) and who would surely not have been allowed to officiate in more normal times. Dale also sent off Frank Murphy in this game and Frank, like Jimmy, was a gentle, inoffensive player.

In December 1941, Celtic won three and drew the other game and Delaney got good reports in every game. 'That man Delaney again' it was said for example of the game against Dumbarton on 6 December, although some Dumbarton players seemed to think that he had used a hand in the build-up to his goal in the 4–2 triumph. This game, however, was not the main topic of conversation in Glasgow or anywhere else on the Monday morning, for on the Sunday evening the Japanese had attacked Pearl Harbour and destroyed the American Pacific fleet.

This at least meant that the US joined the Pacific War. Then, a few days later, Hitler continued his self-destruction programme by declaring war on the US as well. Earlier that year he had invaded the Soviet Union and thus, in the space of six months, Britain had gained the two largest powers on earth as her allies. Christmas and New Year were miserable experiences during wartime, but there was a new feeling of optimism that all would be well in the long run. Churchill may have shed tears at the loss of the American fleet but he, like everyone else, was delighted at this turn of events. It meant that Britain was saved and that the war would eventually be won. The road would be long and hard, but victory would be achieved.

But for Celtic, victory remained an alien concept. This was proved on New Year's Day, when Rangers came to Parkhead to play in front of 30,000 – the maximum allowed under war regulations. Tickets for this game had been much sought after and, as with other things in wartime Glasgow, a black market had sprung up as 'spivs' sold tickets for outrageous prices. People were able to pay such money for, as always happens on the home front in wartime, the standard of living had actually improved in a new era of full employment and plenty of overtime.

On New Year's Day 1942, although Delaney teamed up well with Willie Fagan (ex-Celtic and now back on loan from Liverpool) on the right wing, there was little else to boast about and Rangers won comfortably 2–0. In spite of fears, there was no crowd trouble and the game passed peacefully but depressingly. Delaney picked up a leg injury in the second half, robbing Celtic of what little chance they had of pulling back two goals and forcing him to miss the next game against Clyde.

Celtic's Southern League season fizzled out. Delaney could cross for others to score or he could score them himself, and often he was called upon to do both. He scored twice against Airdrie, for example, on 14 February 1942 in a game where the crowd were distressed by the bad news from Singapore. The beleaguered garrison could not hold out against repeated air attacks and would be compelled to surrender to the Japanese the following day. This had happened thanks to dreadful military incompetence. Fingers were pointed with justification at General Percival, who had also played an inglorious and brutal part in the repression of Ireland 20 years earlier, until he fell foul of Tom Barry's Flying Column. The loss of Singapore was a low point of the war, for the guesses about what would happen to the British and Australian prisoners would turn out to be all too correct.

For Celtic, and their vast army of disgruntled fans, there was still a chance of something for the fans to shout about in the Southern League Cup. This was a new trophy and had been introduced the previous season to replace the Scottish Cup. It was played on a sectional basis and was such a success that it was continued in peacetime when it became known as the Scottish League Cup. It was played for in the late winter and early spring.

Celtic were in the same section as Queen's Park, Hibernian and Hamilton, and at long last Celtic seemed to be giving their fans something to be proud about. They beat all the teams in the first round of matches and then Queen's Park again. But when they lost to Hibernian at Easter Road, there was a chance that Hamilton could catch them if they beat Celtic in the one remaining fixture. This was at Douglas Park on 4 April 1942. Hamilton went ahead in the 50th minute, and for a while it looked as if they could eliminate Celtic, but 'Delaney was here, there and everywhere' and 'lifted Celtic to victory'. He scored in the 71st minute then, after a brilliant run down the wing, crossed for John Riley to earn one of his few moments of glory in a sadly underperforming Celtic career.

Celtic were thus in the semi-final of this Cup, but had to play Rangers at Hampden in front of its 50,000 limit on 2 May. They lost 0–2 but there was an extraordinary prelude to the game. At St Enoch's Hotel, Celtic players discovered that because of the strict limit, there would be no free tickets for family and friends. Their dependents would be admitted, but would have to pay. The Celtic players sat on the bus in sullen silence until they reached Hampden and threatened to strike.

Wartime or not, this was strange behaviour, and it is hard to believe that the ultra-professional, dedicated Jimmy Delaney was involved in this, although he did seem to go along with the demands of some of his more militant colleagues. They were talked out of refusing to play, but not for the first or last time in Celtic's history (compare Arthurlie in 1897, Airdrie in 1998 and Inverness Caledonian Thistle in 2000), player unrest led to disastrous consequences on the field as Rangers won 2–0 with a great deal of ease. Delaney failed to get the better of Rangers' left-back, Jock Shaw.

It was Rangers too who beat Celtic in the Glasgow Charity Cup on Wednesday 13 May, but this time Celtic played far better. Delaney was in the centre again to allow Matt Lynch to play on the right wing. Jimmy equalised for Celtic and, for a long time, Celtic were the more likely winners until Rangers reasserted themselves and Jimmy Duncanson scored a late sickener.

All season, Delaney had been playing with a bandage on his left arm. By the end of May when Celtic were playing (badly) in the wartime Summer Cup, discerning spectators noticed that he had been able to remove it. It was another clear sign of recovery, but the way that he was playing had indicated that anyway. He would never have said this publicly, but he must have felt in summer 1942 that he really did deserve to be playing with better players and for a better set-up than the shambles that was wartime Celtic.

He was also working in the pit, as war regulations compelled him to do. Every ounce of coal was needed for the war effort. The war was still going badly for Britain. By the summer, the Germans were only 65 miles from Alexandria in Egypt and if they captured the Suez Canal, they could strangle the British Empire and eliminate entirely the Jewish population of the Middle East. On the Atlantic, the convoy system had not yet managed to get the better of the U-boat menace and Britain thus faced a constant threat to its supplies.

Delaney suffered a slight accident at his work in the pit, injuring his head and leg in a minor cave in, and was thus unavailable for the trial match on 1 August. But he was playing in the first three games of the season against Dumbarton, Queen's Park and Hamilton. All three games were 2–2 draws. Delaney played in the centre and scored five goals. The press had this to say about the Hamilton game: 'All Celtic's problems are forward, only Delaney is in the least dangerous.'

This was a typical and hardly surprising comment. Celtic had offloaded Johnny Crum and Johnny Divers (to Morton) and Frank Murphy (to Albion Rovers), experienced players all, albeit possibly past their best. But no effort was made to replace them with quality. The result was that Delaney was indeed by himself. After a profoundly depressing 4–0 defeat on 12 September to a Morton side which contained Crum, Divers and the great Billy Steel, it was stated: 'Delaney had to fetch and carry for himself. He is surrounded by immaturity.' Indeed he was, and by the end of September Celtic were out of the Glasgow Cup and had won one Southern League game out of seven.

In normal circumstances, this would not have been allowed to go on. McStay would have been sacked, the board perhaps replaced, supporters would have organised boycotts and protests and newspapers would have carried in-depth features on 'What is wrong with Celtic?' Delaney himself would have gone elsewhere, disgusted by the lack of support.

But these were not normal times. All one could do was soldier on, and hope that things would get better with what little resources that were available. As Vera Lynn would sing:

> *Keep smiling through*
> *Just like we used to do.*

It was particularly galling to see the Celtic-daft Matt Busby playing for Hibernian and beating Celtic 3–0 on 26 September. This was the day that Delaney's son Michael was born. For Delaney's future career, this would be a very significant game, for Matt Busby would remember him and how well he played. Indeed they already were good friends.

In October, things improved slightly with three wins out of five games, but the pattern remained depressingly familiar of one man trying to carry a team of youngsters, of whom only one, Pat McAuley, seemed fit to wear the colours. In a game against Partick Thistle, which was won 3–2, the *Evening Times* praises McAuley and says, 'Delaney's second goal only a master of angles could have scored'. In the 2–4 defeat by Third Lanark the press said, 'Stop Delaney, you stop Celts … Delaney carried the Celtic attack on his shoulders'.

By the end of October, things on the world scene improved significantly with news of the victory in the tank battle of El Alamein. 'A bright gleam has lit up the helmets of our soldiers', said the Prime Minister, and the rest of the year was taken up with the rapid British advance over North Africa, capturing key places like Mersa Matruh, Sidi Barrani, Tobruk and Benghazi. 'It is not the end, it is not even the beginning of the end, although it is perhaps the end of the beginning', said Mr Churchill. The British recaptured Mersa Matruh on Sunday 8 November, with the vital aerodrome being secured by the RAF regiment with a Celtic supporter (the author's father) in the vanguard.

On 7 November, Celtic showed signs of returning to winning ways with a 3–0 win over Hearts in which Delaney had sent over 'banana bend' crosses. The following week Celtic were at Cliftonhill to play Albion Rovers. It was a splendid game of football which delighted the 8,000 crowd and ended up 4–4, but it was more significant for two other reasons. One was the debut of a 'raw, lanky, junior trialist' for Albion Rovers called Jock Stein and the other was an injury to Jimmy Delaney which would keep him out of action for a month.

On his return on 19 December, he scored twice from the centre-forward position in a good game against Motherwell, but then on Boxing Day, in the 2–0 defeat against Morton, he looked lethargic and out of touch, as if the leg injury sustained at Albion Rovers was returning to haunt him. It was probably unwise to play on New Year's Day at Ibrox and one feels that if he had been anyone other than Jimmy Delaney, he would have been rested.

He certainly would have wished he had, as the game was a shambles. Celtic were two down in the first five minutes before Davie Duncan pulled one back, but then another was lost before half-time and goalkeeper Willie Miller was badly injured following a coarse challenge. After half-time, Rangers scored again with a blatantly offside goal, and MacDonald and Lynch were both sent off, MacDonald for arguing with referee W. Davidson of Glasgow and Lynch for fouling out of sheer frustration while calmer elements like Delaney tried in vain to take the heat out of the situation. The farce continued and Rangers ended up winning 8–1 – one of the reasons why Celtic fans are keen to keep wartime football unofficial.

Meanwhile the German general, von Paulus, trapped in Stalingrad, was able to wish everyone in Germany a Happy New Year – but the voice was a fake. The war was now swinging decisively towards the Allies. By January, Churchill was telling the Eighth Army that 'it will be sufficient to say – I marched and fought with the British Eighth Army' as Rommel reeled.

Celtic's melancholy season continued, however, and only three more League games were won. Delaney finished up scoring 19 League goals, far more than any other Celtic player. A little self-respect was regained for the team on 10 April 1943 when Celtic achieved an honourable draw against Rangers at Parkhead, thanks to two Delaney goals. His second came after he picked up a ball on the right wing near the halfway line, cut inside past several defenders, ran about 40 yards and hammered home a goal which even earned a few reluctant rounds of applause from the Rangers fans.

The Southern League Cup was a disaster involving two beatings from Rangers, and similar things happened in the Summer Cup, but in May there was some cheer for the Celtic fans in the triumphant Desert Army which had now reached Tunis and was mopping up the Afrika Korps. Celtic won a trophy. It was the Glasgow Charity Cup – not exactly the most prestigious of trophies, even in wartime, but the win was much celebrated by fans both home and abroad, who had clearly not lost their love for the club. Celtic beat Queen's Park 3–0 when 'frequently Delaney seemed to take on the whole opposition by himself'. This was followed by wins over Clyde 3–1, with two great Delaney goals, and Third Lanark in the final on 22 May before 25,000 at Hampden.

This success shone like a beacon in that dreadful season of 1942–43 in the same way that Delaney shone round the rest of the team. He was almost all that they had. McAuley showed promise, Miller was a good goalkeeper and Hogg was a reliable defender, but there was little else for anyone to enthuse about in the many letters that were written to troops abroad. But there was always Jimmy Delaney. It was often said that in during World War One, the most talked about man in the trenches was Patsy Gallacher. Delaney seemed to take over this role in World War Two.

With the focus of the war now moving to the soft underbelly of Sicily and Italy, the 1943–44 season opened on 14 August with a 2–1 win over Clyde, but there was a familiar refrain in the press: 'If you take Delaney out of the match, Celtic were impossible winners'. Celtic won their next game against Morton, but then exited the Glasgow Cup at the first time of asking to Partick Thistle before going down 1–4 to Dumbarton. After this the fans' patience cracked and they held a demonstration against how the club was being run, in particular highlighting the need to acquire the services of an accredited centre-forward.

All this was against a backdrop of how the club had been forced to appeal to supporters for clothes coupons to help obtain new strips, for the green was becoming mighty faded by now, as the same strip had been used since 1939. This was not anyone's fault, of course, nor was it a problem peculiar to Celtic, but it gave the press the opportunity to make comments about the fading glory of Celtic.

Celtic diverted some of the pressure by beating Rangers 1–0 at Ibrox on 11

September 1943, three days after Italy had surrendered and disclaimed Mussolini. The Old Firm game was in truth a dreadful game played on a dry, bumpy pitch, won by an own goal, but it was a victory and for a spell things looked promising for Celtic and Delaney was playing in a winning team for a change.

There was a very unlucky 4–5 defeat to Partick Thistle in October, but apart from that Celtic did not lose again in 1943. Delaney was playing well and the clichés about 'Delaney was the one and only Celtic forward' became less frequent, as Jackie Gallacher (son of the great Hughie) and Gerald Padua McAloon emerged to give Delaney some support and goals began to be scored. November was a particularly prolific month with five goals against St Mirren, and four each against Third Lanark and Clyde. 'With Celtic, goals are no longer on the ration', the press stated, and the hearts of the faithful, now in Italy rather than North Africa, were stirred and cheered by the news that Delaney's ex-captain Willie Lyon, now a Major in the Royal Artillery, had been awarded the Military Cross in Tunisia for gallantry.

For Delaney this comparatively bright period came to an end at Boghead on 18 December 1943 when he broke a rib in an accidental collision with Watson of Dumbarton. This was to rule him out of football until the end of January 1944, by which time Celtic had lost twice to Rangers and to Hearts, and any chance of landing the Southern League Championship had gone.

However, as often happens after a lay-off, the injured player came back to play even better than previously, and by now an irresistible groundswell was building up to have Delaney chosen for the Scotland v England international at Hampden on 22 April 1944. This grew in intensity after Scotland sustained a 6–2 thrashing at Wembley on 19 February, the same day that Delaney had scored twice for Celtic to beat Motherwell at Fir Park.

The problem was still, ostensibly at least, about the insurance of Jimmy's arm against further injury. A Glasgow insurance firm offered to cover Delaney's arm for up to £4,000 in an international appearance and on 12 April a crowd of 500 demonstrated in favour of Delaney outside 6 Carlton Place, the headquarters of the Scottish Football Association. Rex Kingsley, the *Sunday Mail* journalist, wished to be associated with such popular manifestations of support, stating that 'If the selectors don't pick Delaney for Hampden Park, the next job will be to be to pick new selectors!' Faced with such pressure, the selectors yielded, having arranged adequate insurance, a problem which many people thought need not have existed in the first place. Delaney was in the side.

Celtic's glorious form continued in the spring of 1944 as the Allies continued their slow advance up Italy and speculation increased about where and when the Second Front was to be opened in Europe. It had to come soon, for the country was thronged with Americans 'over paid, over sexed and over here' and other Allied forces. The Southern League Cup section was won at a canter with

Gallacher, McAloon and Delaney all in sparkling form as Hamilton Academicals, Falkirk and Partick Thistle were put to the sword. The game against Partick Thistle at Firhill saw a huge crowd reminiscent of the great pre-war days with turnstiles closed and one or two daredevils on the roof of the stand.

A feature of Delaney's life had always been tragedy and misfortune. This was seen in injuries, great and small, but now there was to occur the saddest tragedy that anyone could imagine having to bear – the death of a small child. There had been good news on the family front when Annie had presented Jimmy with his first daughter, Kathleen, on 26 March. But on 15 April, the day that Celtic beat Queen's Park at Hampden in the Glasgow Charity Cup, it was reported that 18-month-old Michael Delaney was in Motherwell County Hospital, seriously ill with a form of leukaemia.

This clearly presented the family with a dilemma. Should Jimmy play in the international against England on 22 April? The decision became an acute one when the young boy was returned home, clearly because the hospital felt that there was little that they could do for him. A large part of Delaney must have felt that football should take a back seat, but the counter-argument was that life should go on and that, in any case, Michael might rally and even recover. Being a religious couple, no doubt the Delaneys discussed the matter prayerfully and in consultation with their parish priest, and the decision was the brave one that Delaney would play.

It was also the correct one. Many people in 1944 faced the reality or imminence of death, either of themselves or loved ones, with a great deal of fortitude and the Scottish nation looked to Delaney as a hero to give them something to cheer about, particularly after the campaign that had been waged about insurance. A Scottish soldier, for example, visited his badly wounded brother-in-law in an Italian military hospital. It was an emotional reunion and after the family questions about letters from home came the inevitable one: 'How's Delaney playing these days?'

It was a fine day and 132,000 were at Hampden to see the game, breaching all sorts of regulations but showing the love of their country's football team that prevailed in spite of, or perhaps because of, all that was going on in Italy, the Far East and on the High Seas. Unannounced in advance (for security reasons), Field Marshall Montgomery, the hero of El Alamein, walked out to be presented to the two teams. He was greeted rapturously, as befitted a man who was spearheading the Allied effort, and everyone knew that the invasion of Europe was not imminent for a few days at least because he would not have been here, if it were. Or perhaps it was a double bluff? 'Monty' did have a *doppelgänger* who managed on many occasions to fool crowds, newsreel camera crews and journalists.

Scotland certainly played better than they normally did in wartime internationals, but they still lost 2–3. Jimmy Caskie scored for Scotland and there was an own goal, but Raich Carter and Tommy Lawton (twice) scored for England. Delaney played well, but as often on the really big occasions, did not star. There were of course extenuating circumstances and soon after he got home that night to his house at 72a Main Street, Cleland, young Michael died. Jimmy and Annie were devastated, but one of the great things about a village like Cleland is that there is plenty of support when required in such desperate circumstances. In this case, the whole nation mourned as well. His son's death certificate describes Jimmy Delaney as a 'general labourer'. This is correct, for in wartime his job as a general labourer was the main one, yet it is curious to see this phrase used of a man whom everyone knew as one of the best and most famous footballers in the British Isles.

After the funeral rites were observed, Delaney turned out for Celtic in the Southern League Cup semi-final against Rangers. A crowd of 87,121 were at Hampden (restrictions on attendances had now been relaxed), but they saw a 4–2 win for Rangers. Delaney set up McAloon for the first Celtic goal and then scored the second with a 'screaming shot' from the edge of the penalty area to beat Jerry Dawson in the Rangers goal. For a while, the score was only 3–2 and Celtic were deserving of extra-time, but it was Rangers who got the crucial and fatal fourth goal. The Rangers players made a point of shaking hands with Delaney, who had played so well in such desperate circumstances.

Celtic's season ended on 13 May 1944 when the team unaccountably folded and went down 1–4 to Clyde in the Charity Cup semi-final. Delaney scored a penalty, but only after Celtic were 0–4 down and their supporters were streaming from the ground, unable to understand how a team who had done so well earlier in the season could now collapse so comprehensively. Perhaps it was because their star man was still suffering from grief. Perhaps it was for other reasons; but it was a very unfortunate way to finish a season which had promised so much.

By the time that football resumed in August 1944, the world had changed. The D-Day landings had been a success, but there was no immediate surrender as might have been hoped. The Germans were still fighting in Italy as well, although Rome was now in Allied hands, and every day seemed to bring liberation to another part of France. Paris itself was liberated on 25 August. Hitler had survived an assassination attempt on 20 July as some generals hoped to dispose of him and then negotiate peace with the Western Allies while they were not yet on German soil. In the Far East the war continued to be waged with merciless savagery on both sides.

On 5 August 1944, Jimmy Delaney played for an Edinburgh Select XI against Aston Villa at Tynecastle. It is strange that he managed to get himself picked for Edinburgh, for his connections with that city were tenuous to say the least, but Bill Shankly, Jimmy Caskie and Billy Steel played as well. He scored as Edinburgh went down 3–4 to a strong Aston Villa side.

Celtic had a strange season in 1944–45. They started off badly, but rallied to play some brilliant and recognisably Celtic football after the New Year until they failed to deliver at the end. Delaney suffered a series of injuries from which he was now, of course, taking longer to recover. On 3 September 1944 it was the fifth birthday of the war, but the 30th of Jimmy Delaney. It might have been assumed that his playing career was meandering ever so gently to its conclusion. This was far from the case – there were more than 12 years still to go.

A young man called Bobby Evans played in the second game of the season at outside-left, as Celtic beat Albion Rovers 1–0. Although Jock Stein bottled up Gallagher in the middle, both wingers, Delaney and young Evans, were immense. Delaney, however, to his chagrin presumably, was obliged to move inside to allow the injured Bobby Hogg to limp on the right-wing. This was a fairly common move in the pre-substitute days. If a player could walk at all, he was normally put on the right or left wing as nuisance value if nothing else.

Unaccountably, Celtic played two dreadful games in early September after their supporters had conned themselves into thinking that the team had turned for the better. First, an inept defensive performance allowed Hamilton to beat them 6–2 and then Rangers came to Parkhead and before 45,000 beat them 4–0 with Celtic players and fans visibly giving up midway through the second half.

Not for the first time the finger was pointed at Jimmy McStay by angry fans. There seemed to be no rhyme or reason for the team's inconsistency other than the hoary old one of 'wartime circumstances'. This was only half true. Celtic, like everyone else, suffered from what was going on. But Rangers had done what Celtic did in World War One by ensuring that their men were working in reserved occupations and doing their best to make sure that they were available to play for them. Willie Maley had done this brilliantly through his contacts between 1914 and 1918. But Jimmy McStay was no Willie Maley.

On 16 September 1944, Celtic beat Dumbarton 3–0 at Boghead before once again collapsing to Clyde. Clyde were a consistently good side during the war years, but would have been surprised to be four goals to the good at Parkhead before Delaney introduced a modicum of sanity to proceedings with two late goals. Meanwhile, in Europe what became known as 'the bridge too far' was going on. This was an attempt to capture Arnhem. Had it worked, it would have shortened the war by many months and possibly even finished it by Christmas 1944, but it was a colossal failure and cost many lives.

Delaney was tried in the centre-forward position for a couple of games, but pulled a muscle in the second of them, a 3–4 defeat to Morton at Cappielow, thus missing three games in October. One of them was the Glasgow Cup Final and another (more gnawingly for Delaney perhaps) the international at Wembley on 10 October. He must have felt fated never to play at Wembley, for he had missed 1936 and 1938 and then the problem with insuring his arm had meant he missed the early wartime games as well. On this occasion it was perhaps as well, for England beat Scotland 6–2. However, Delaney's Wembley moments would come.

On his return to Parkhead, the indifferent form continued. November had its high spots, notably a brilliant header to score against Falkirk – a consolation goal – and then on 25 November at Sheffield he was given a game for Scotland in an unofficial international against the RAF. Scotland won 7–1 in front of 40,172 at Hillsborough and Delaney is reported as running rings round the RAF defence, which contained many men who would have been full internationalists in peace time. Celtic, however, lost that day to Hearts and were now 11th out of 16 in the Southern League.

McStay's skin was saved by a turnaround in form which began on the first Saturday in December and continued for the rest of the League season. Altogether, 14 games were won and one was drawn. Had this form been shown in the early part of the season, Celtic would have won the Southern League. As it was, they finished seven points behind Rangers, but the honours belonged to Celtic. They even managed to win the New Year's Day game at Ibrox. It was a fortuitous goal scored early in the second half by left-half George Paterson which won the day, but a feature of the game was the way in which Delaney repeatedly got the better of Jock Shaw.

It would have to be admitted that not all the opposition was of high quality, for some of the poorer teams often struggled to get 11 men on the field – a phenomenon that grew more marked the longer the war went on. Loudspeaker appeals for anyone who had played junior football were not unknown, and a further sign of wartime football was seen in the quality of refereeing. Men who were blatantly too old or manifestly unsuited for the task appeared with a whistle and genuine questions were often asked about a man's eyesight – or even, in the case of Mr M.C. Dale, his sobriety.

Celtic at last seemed to have got it together, just as peace was appearing on the horizon and the Allies reached German soil. Yet the cynics remembered the previous year and said that there was a similar phenomenon of Celtic doing well in the League once the cause was lost and then, when the Cup tournaments came at the end of the season, their form deserted them.

This was exactly what happened in 1945, but before then Delaney had another call to international duty. This time it was to Villa Park, Birmingham, on 3 February where he and Willie Fagan, who had played off and on with Celtic before and during the war, formed a potent right-wing combination.

Sadly, however, Scotland were again on the losing side, going down narrowly 2–3. This time it was Stan Mortensen who did the damage for England, but Delaney did score one of Scotland's goals, the other coming from Jock Dodds of Blackpool.

His goal is well described by Capel Kirby in his report of the game in the *News of the World*: 'Surprisingly enough he beat Swift with a slow but well directed left foot shot from the inside left position to which he had run to receive Dodds' centre.' Had Mr Kirby watched Celtic a little more often he would have been less surprised at Delaney's ability to score goals from all over the field. Earlier, Delaney's powerful shot had scraped the bar, and late in the game Delaney inspired Scotland, but the winner came at the other end.

Celtic played in the Southern League Cup in spring 1945 in a group containing Clyde, Falkirk and Partick Thistle. Celtic had twice drawn with Clyde and beaten the other two teams, when they attracted a crowd of 20,000 to Brockville. The atmosphere was tense, but Celtic's downfall came when, for the second time that season, Delaney pulled a muscle and had to limp off at half-time. Celtic lost the game 0–1 and went on to lose the next game as well, but for Delaney the consequences were altogether more serious, for he was now out of contention for the whole of April. Willie Waddell of Rangers played for Scotland on the right wing on 14 April at Hampden, a game that turned into a rout as England won 6–1.

On 30 April, the Russians captured Hitler's bunker a matter of hours or possibly even minutes after he committed suicide and Berlin surrendered to the Russians on 2 May. Germany itself surrendered to the Western Allies on 7 May. Tuesday 8 May would be designated VE Day and on that day crowds in front of Buckingham Palace saw the King wave to them and Churchill declare that 'In all our long history we have never had a greater day than this.'

But things were not so good at Parkhead for Delaney. He was now fit, but not in the team. It seems that Delaney, increasingly worried by the repeated injuries from which he was suffering, and concerned about his future, asked the club for a benefit. He had, after all, been with the club since 1934 and this was the end of his 11th season. It was by no means an unreasonable request, but the directors turned it down. Not only that, but McStay, it appears, was instructed by the directors to keep him out of the team.

This was crazy. McStay, who would himself very soon be shown the door, would never presumably have dropped Delaney for footballing reasons. What did the directors want – to teach him a lesson for his impertinence? Delaney was a man who had Celtic written all over him until the day that he died. As it was, Delaney was manoeuvred into asking for a transfer. It too was refused. What was going on? The only explanation does indeed seem to be that the directors in their folly were attempting to teach Delaney a lesson. Such folly cost Celtic the Glasgow Charity Cup. VE Day, which should have been a day of great rejoicing for everyone, saw Delaney in despair and he did not play in the Victory in Europe Cup game against Queen's Park the following night, which was won by Celtic on corners – one of the club's few wartime successes. Indeed, the breach might have been permanent, had the newly formed Supporters' Association not mediated. As it was, Delaney was accepted back to play (badly) in two games in the Summer Cup.

This was the forerunner of things to come between Delaney and the team that he loved. In summer 1945, it caused a certain amount of cloud over the end of the war and perplexed the men in khaki, who were looking forward to coming home and seeing Jimmy Delaney in action once again. But by the start of the 1945–46 season, things would have yet again changed; changed utterly.

A fine picture of Jimmy in 1936.

Celtic with the Scottish Cup in 1937. Back row, left to right: Geatons, Hogg, Kennaway, Morrison, Buchan, Paterson. Front row: Manager Maley, Delaney, McGrory, Lyon, Crum, Murphy, trainer McMenemy.

A cartoon of Jimmy.

A very young Jimmy Delaney (third from right in the front row) in a representative game, possibly Glasgow v Sheffield at Parkhead in 1935.

Celtic's team of 1938 which won the Scottish League and the Empire Exhibition Trophy. Back row, left to right: Geatons, Hogg, Kennaway, Morrison, Crum, Paterson. Front row: Delaney, MacDonald, Lyon, Divers, Murphy.

insi......... In h.. junio: ..s G......
prefer..... to be ... the ...cking line. Has appeared in both wing half positions ...ith the Rangers but excels on the left. A graduate of Glasgow University and is in the Scholastic profession. Honours:—England (4), Wales (4), Ireland (2), English League (4), Irish League (2), Austria (1), Germany (1).

JAMES DELANEY (Celtic)—Outside right. Height, 5 ft. 8 ins.; weight, 10 st. 8 lbs. Born in Cleland. Is still able to hold his place. Learned his football with the village club in Cleland and joined the Celtic in 1934, when they experienced difficulty in finding a successor to Bert Thomson. Sometimes Napier was outside right, but gradually Delaney, tried in various positions, made good on the right. Now the S.F.A. have given the Cleland youth the place assigned Charlie Napier last season against England. Napier is now with Derby County. Every player has a bit of luck some time. As Bobby Main of the Rangers was unfit, Delaney got his place over Munro (Hearts) in the match at Hampden Park, on August 25, 1935, between Scotland and England, in aid of King George V's Jubilee Trust Fund. His dash at goal enabled him to score both goals for Scotland against Germany this season, a feat that influenced his selection against England. Honours:—Wales (1), Ireland (1), Germany (1), England (1), English League (1), Irish League (1).

TOM WALKER (Heart of Midlothian)—Inside right. Height, 5 ft. 8½ ins.; weight, 11 st. 7 lbs. Born in Livingstone. Is reckoned to be the greatest inside forward the Hearts have had since the illustrious Bobby Walker; the best of ....forwards. ...ed in Scotland. .....eer .....ht it is to

The relevant extract about Jimmy from the programme for the Scotland v England international of 1937, which produced Hampden's record attendance.

Celtic off duty in 1937. Jimmy is on the left of the second row, behind Manager Willy Maley.

Official Programme

International

SCOTLAND

v.

WALES

TYNECASTLE PARK

Edinburgh

Wednesday 9th November 1938

Kick-off - 2.45 p.m.

Price 3d

Adshead, Printers, 34-36 Cadogan Street, Glasgow

The programme for Scotland v Wales in November 1938. Scotland won the match 3–2.

The young Jimmy Delaney is second from the right of this group.

Newlyweds! Jimmy and Annie in summer 1939.

April 1944. Field Marshall Montgomery is introduced to Scotland's team before the international at Hampden v England. Jimmy is fourth from the right. Notice the resemblance between Jimmy and Scotland's captain Matt Busby. Tragically, Jimmy's son Michael was fated to die that night.

Jimmy is in the front row (extreme left) in this picture of Celtic in 1945. Notice the shinguards! The manager is Jimmy McGrory and the trainer is Alec Dowdalls.

Chapter 5

Transfer and Victory
1945–1946

AROUND the end of July 1945, a year already rich in momentous historical events, two important changes occurred. One affected all of the British Isles, the other only Celtic fans. One was the arrival of the first-ever Labour Government that had a working (in this case an overwhelming) majority. The election had been held on 5 July, but counting had to be delayed for three weeks to allow for the soldiers' votes arriving from overseas and then being distributed to their various constituencies. The result, which seemed to be a rejection of the hero of the hour, Winston Churchill, came as a shock to the world. Josef Stalin, for one, could not understand it. Neither could the Americans. Even in Britain itself, the middle classes reeled. 'They've voted for a Labour Government, but the people will not stand for it!' said one bewildered Conservative.

Yet there had been reasons for this change. One was indeed the soldiers' vote. All soldiers, after several years of 'bull' and the mind-numbing boredom of service life, had developed an intense hatred of the officer class, whom they identified with the Tories. Most soldiers had no real strong feelings against the Germans – but how they hated sergeants and sergeant majors! In addition, the Labour Party seemed to offer them the more likely possibility of an early demob. Back home, people had not forgotten the now discredited policy of pre-war appeasement and blamed the Conservatives for the unemployment of the 1930s and cynical disregard for health, social and educational issues. Labour on the other hand offered, and would successfully deliver, a National Health Service. The election victory was a landslide.

The Prime Minister was the small, meek-looking Clement Attlee, who appeared as if he should have been a bank clerk or a librarian rather than a politician. But he would turn out to be a mighty figure, harnessing and controlling disparate figures like the duplicitous Herbert Morrison, the bullish Nye Bevan and Glasgow's Manny Shinwell, who had been very much involved in the labour unrest of the Red Clydeside days. The result would not be seen for a few years yet, but the bad old days of poverty and want were now clearly numbered. There was a clear perception that the bad old days of the 1930s were not going to come back.

Nevertheless, to the eyes of Celtic fans (who usually voted Labour unanimously) even those momentous events took second place to what was happening at Celtic Park. This change was necessary, but done in a way which reflects little credit on the directors. Manager Jimmy McStay returned from holiday in Ayr the day before the General Election result was declared to discover newspaper billboards saying that he had been sacked. He immediately went to Celtic Park to find out what was going on. There he was indeed asked to resign.

McStay's departure caused little sadness among the fans. He had been a fine player and captain in the late 1920s and early 1930s, and he really did deserve a better chance than the wartime circumstances offered, but the fact remained that he had been a failure. It is to the man's credit that he remained on good terms with the club and with his successor, his old teammate Jimmy McGrory, even scouting for the club in later years. He remained Celtic to the core until his death in early January 1974. He was the great-uncle of Paul and Willie McStay, who played for Celtic in the 1980s.

Jimmy McGrory had been manager of Kilmarnock before the war and he was a popular choice with Celtic players and fans. Delaney must have wondered how he would get on with his new boss, who of course in 1936 had been his friend and teammate in one of Celtic's greatest-ever teams. Certainly, Delaney was aware that there would be an immense amount of work for McGrory to do. No easy answers would necessarily be forthcoming and McGrory's solutions would have to be long term.

This immediately raised a question about Delaney's future at the club. He would soon be 31 and there was still the niggle of the lack of a benefit match, which had caused dispute and resentment in May. Delaney found himself torn between his love of the club, their supporters and the very concept of Celtic on the one hand and his contempt, distrust and suspicion of those currently in charge of the club on the other. He was hardly the first or the last Celtic player to have this dilemma! His old manager Willie Maley would have sympathised, but how would Jimmy McGrory react to all this?

Wartime arrangements would continue for season 1945–46: no official internationals and no Scottish Cup, although there would be a Victory International Tournament and a Victory Cup. The League would still be unofficial, but it would now be called the Scottish League again, for Aberdeen were invited to join the Glasgow and district caucus which had made up the Southern League. It would be 1946–47 before peacetime arrangements could properly be made. In the meantime, spectators would have to make do with seeing their favourites in ragged or faded jerseys (clothes were still rationed) and some of the footballs themselves looked as if they had seen better days. If they burst (as happened with the old heavy leather casing surrounding a bladder) there was often a frantic search for a replacement, and the away team was duty-bound to bring a spare ball with them, just in case the home team's supply had run out.

The war was still going on. There was sporadic fighting in the Balkans and in Greece, and the Japanese issue would only be resolved in early August by the dropping of two atomic bombs on Hiroshima and Nagasaki. Ironically, horrific though those events were, they probably saved lives – certainly in the West. The invasion of Japan by the American, British and Commonwealth forces would surely have cost a lot more casualties.

Thus, at the start of season 1945–46 began the 'atomic age' and the Cold War with the world nominally at peace (and very grateful for that) but knowing that one bomb could now in all probability destroy thousands of years of history and civilisation. It would be some time, however, before people began to worry about this. For the moment, the predominant emotion was relief mingled with pity and horror at the sufferings of those unfortunate enough to have been captured by the Japanese.

Delaney played for half the 1945–46 season with Celtic. It was clear from an early stage that there was no great improvement in Celtic's performances, with inconsistency being the order of the day. In the early season they lost twice to Rangers in the League and the Glasgow Cup and the tendency for the defence to give away suicidal goals meant that games which should have been won, were in fact drawn.

Delaney was a part of this general inconsistency. Those who came to Parkhead, not having seen him since the day he broke his arm on 1 April 1939 – six years ago and a whole world away – would notice that he lacked none of his old trickery, his crossing ability and, amazingly, his speed. He had lost even more hair, of course, but there was still that youthful face, boyish enthusiasm and the love of the game. Yet there were times when he did not impose himself on the game as he used to; times when he sank to the same level as everyone else in that indifferent forward line.

It was as late as 15 September before McGrory won a game as Celtic manager, and that was against Hamilton at Parkhead with victory in doubt at 1–0 until Delaney's late clincher. McGrory had appointed Chick Geatons, another ex-teammate, as his coach, and that looked a good investment, for Geatons was a solid and reliable Fifer. Alec Dowdalls was now the trainer, but for all the knowledge and good will that existed among the backroom boys, there was still a sad lack of quality on the playing side. Apart from Delaney himself, there was goalkeeper Willie Miller, who was generally agreed to be one of the best of all Celtic's goalkeepers – and 'he got loads of practice wi' that lot in front o'im'. But there were few others that would have earned a place in the previous great teams of Willie Maley or the subsequent ones of Jock Stein. Willie Gallacher, son of Patsy of Celtic, and Jackie Gallacher, son of Hughie of Airdrie, Newcastle and Chelsea, tried manfully but in both cases clearly lacked the ability of their illustrious fathers. And yet one always felt that as long as Celtic had Delaney something could happen.

Delaney was injured against Hibernian in early November, missed a couple of games (and a potential Victory International cap against Wales) and then came back for the Morton game on 24 November. This was a poignant game for Celtic because the flags were at half-mast for the death of the great Jimmy Quinn, who had died in Croy in midweek. Quinn had been very helpful and supportive to Delaney in his early years with the club and Delaney would often deliberately model himself on the humility and modesty of the great Jimmy. Their backgrounds were almost a carbon copy of each other – both born of an Irish family in a small coalmining village and both particularly loved by the support who recognised them as one of their own.

Sadly, Delaney injured himself yet again in the game against Morton. He had scored Celtic's second goal – a typical Delaney goal, running in from the wing – but then was injured in an accidental clash with a Morton defender. He was seen to limp towards the end of the game and he was out until the week between Christmas and the New Year, when Celtic finished off their miserable year of 1945 by going down 3–5 to Hearts at Parkhead.

By now money was beginning to dominate things again. There had been a threat of a general strike by Scottish football players on New Year's Day for more money, and in the circumstances Jimmy felt justified in asking for an increase on his wartime wages of £2. Even a return to the pre-war wage of £4 or perhaps just £3 would have kept him happy. He knew that manager McGrory sympathised, as did Chick Geatons, but chairman Tom White was adamant. This affair was kept quiet for a while as it lingered on through January 1946, during which time Delaney's Celtic form obviously and visibly slumped. But on 26 January, before a game at Brockville in which Celtic went down 4–2, Jimmy made a dignified and private request for a transfer if his reasonable wage request was not met.

This request was far from a petulant demand of 'I want more money'. It should be seen in the context of the new optimism of the working class brought about by the arrival of 'their' Government. It is also true that, although there were shortages and rationing for various goods (and there would be for some considerable time), there was actually no lack of money. People's standard of living had increased dramatically during the war years with everyone having a job, and soldiers coming home from the Forces had usually earned enough money to keep them going for some time. True prosperity was certainly some distance away, but expectations were rising.

In the middle of all this, a clear indication of the value of Jimmy Delaney came on 23 January 1946 when, in the first international since hostilities ended (still sadly described as an unofficial international), a grateful Belgian side came to Hampden and drew 2–2 before 49,000. Delaney scored both Scotland's goals from the centre-forward position – Gordon Smith was on the right-wing. Surprisingly, though, Delaney was not chosen for the next game against Ireland in Belfast. The right-wing position went to Willie Waddell of Rangers, possibly because of the ongoing problems that Delaney was having with Celtic or, more likely in the eyes of the cynics at any rate, because the Orange crowd of Belfast wanted to see Willie Waddell. It was an argument that Delaney himself apparently saw the strength of.

The Celtic board meanwhile had a knee-jerk reaction of putting Delaney on the transfer list and then, as if to prove the point that they did not need Delaney, they bought an inside-forward called Tommy Bogan from Hibernian. Delaney would later team up with Bogan in his Manchester United, Aberdeen and Falkirk days. At the same time a bland statement was issued to the effect that 'There is no friction of any kind between Celtic and Delaney' – a statement that was in fact correct because the last thing on Delaney's mind was to cause trouble for his beloved Celtic.

It was, of course, the Celtic board that were bringing trouble on themselves – hardly for the first or last time in their history. It is not clear what Jimmy McGrory thought of all this. McGrory was invited to talk to the Supporters' Association on Sunday 3 February 1946, the day after a game against Hibernian in which Tommy Bogan had played but Delaney did not and Celtic lost 0–1. He agreed to do so, but stated that he would not answer questions on the ongoing Delaney situation. McGrory duly talked all about his early life, his career, Patsy Gallacher, Willie Maley and others and expressed hope for the future, but did not mention Delaney.

Meanwhile, Glasgow was seething with rumours. Any team in the British Isles that one cared to mention was offering Delaney a king's ransom. Shamrock Rovers, for example, were reported, according to the gullible, to be offering Delaney a ridiculous £25 per week. Hibernian, Aberdeen, Tottenham Hotspur and Sunderland were all supposedly interested, but the one name that would not go away was that of Manchester United.

At this point Matt Busby, the recently appointed manager of Manchester United, who had been monitoring the situation all along, became involved. Sometime during that week Rex Kingsley, the *Sunday Mail* journalist, brokered the arrangements and acted as a primitive kind of agent as he drove Busby from Glasgow Central Station to meet Delaney. Busby and Delaney were already friends and both were Celtic daft until their dying days. The two men agreed a package about terms and then an official approach was made to Celtic. A fee (supposedly £4,000) was agreed and with surprising suddenness Delaney became a Manchester United player on Friday 8 February 1946.

It is stating the obvious to say that Celtic supporters were upset by all of this. It was possible to justify the action of the Celtic board. Jimmy had played for Celtic for a long time (since 1933) and, in the Scottish phrase, 'didnae owe them onything'. He was now 31 and perhaps his best years were behind him. The money could be used to help new manager McGrory to develop a young side. Celtic had depended on Delaney for too long and he was now ageing and increasingly injury-prone.

These arguments were used by some supporters, but the opinion of the majority was that it was absolute madness and despicable money-grabbing to get rid of their star man and one of only three players left from the great Empire Exhibition team of 1938 – Bobby Hogg and George Paterson were the others. Delaney was a class act and could have helped the development of youngsters as Celtic strove to come to terms with the new post-war situation. The future would have been more secure if an old hand like Delaney had still been there.

The story is told of the soldier returning from the war, at last demobbed in February 1946. On the long journey home through Europe to the home that he had not seen for three and a half years, he noticed newspaper bills saying 'Delaney Goes To Manchester'. When the train eventually arrived home, there was a reception committee of father, mother, sisters and friends, rightly and fiercely proud of the part that the soldier had played in saving the world from barbarism and tyranny. Flags waved and his mother ran to kiss him as he got off the train. He responded, but when he turned to his ageing and crippled father, the first question was 'Is it true they've sold Delaney?' The response was 'Aye, and he missed a penalty in his first game for Manchester United!'

Delaney himself was devastated by this turn of events. His gentle appeal for a wage increase had set in motion a chain of events which he could not moderate or control. If only the directors had not been so pig-headed and stubborn. If only they had been Celtic supporters instead of businessmen obsessed with balancing books. If only his friend Jimmy McGrory had been there a little longer, had been a little stronger and had put the foot down a little more firmly. If only...

Although he was unhappy about leaving Celtic and his family and friends in Cleland, Jimmy had the feeling that he was moving to a place with a future. His glittering, romantic, brilliant and tragic career with Celtic was over. It was perhaps time to try something else in the company of his friend, fellow Scotsman and fellow Celtic supporter, Matt Busby. It was almost like a Celtic in exile situation, not entirely dissimilar to the millions of Scottish and Irish families who had been compelled to move to the New World in the Diaspora of the 18th, 19th and 20th century. The future now lay beyond the wave, but the heart remained at home.

This was all very dramatic, but a scarcely less important event occurred in Delaney's life on 13 April 1946 when Scotland played England at Hampden Park in the Victory International. Sadly, this is not an official international, for they only recommenced the following season, and no official caps were awarded. This should not, however, in any way diminish how important the game was in the British psyche.

Before the war, there had been huge crowds (notably in 1937 and which was almost equalled in 1939, 1944 and now 1946) to see this international fixture, which was regarded not entirely without justification as the most important game in the world. Feelings about Scotland v England had not gone away, even though men on both sides had been comrades in arms against the power of the Nazis. Indeed, such feelings had been intensified in the war years, which for many supporters had been the only time in their life that they had had the opportunity to meet people from the other country. Friendships were forged and World War Two had been a great triumph for the two nations working together. But football still divided.

Yet the division was amicable and nothing like as intense, for example, as the Celtic v Rangers divide which had on one occasion in 1941 seen a stone throwing riot in Glasgow as bombs were dropping a few miles away in Clydebank. Violence was not a phenomenon associated with Scotland v England games – not least perhaps because Scotland often got the better of England in the years between the wars, winning the Hampden fixtures in 1921, 1925, 1929, 1931, 1933, 1935 and 1937. Results during the war had favoured England, but those were unofficial and did not count, said the Scots.

There was a glorious feeling of optimism in Glasgow and Scotland. The war was over, a Labour Government was in power and pledged to improve the lot of the working family, and football was back. A year previously, Hitler had still been holding out in his bunker, thousands of British prisoners of war were still suffering unspeakable horrors in oriental prison camps and nobody had ever heard of an atom bomb. In addition, England had beaten Scotland 6–1 at Hampden in a wartime international. But this was now a whole new scenario. Vera Lynn had predicted there 'would be fun and laughter and peace ever after' the war. She had crooned, 'Johnnie would go to sleep in his own little room again'. The new era was beginning.

Jimmy Delaney was chosen in the centre-forward position, rather to the surprise of the punters. He had played there – indeed his last two games for Celtic at the end of January had seen him in the centre – but right-wing was his usual position. Busby had not yet tried him in that position for Manchester

United. Yet Willie Waddell could hardly have been denied his place on the right wing. Cynics said that this was an attempt to keep both halves of Glasgow happy. The Rangers fans would be happy and the Celtic support would be placated. Even though Jimmy no longer wore the green and white, he was still considered to be a Celtic man.

The game was much anticipated and discussed – the whole of Scotland talked about little else. The gradual improvement in transport, particularly the railways, meant that people with lots of money in their pockets could travel to Glasgow to see the game. From early on that spring day, trains rolled in to Buchanan Street, Queen Street and Central Station disgorging tartan-bedecked fans. Often it would be a family affair with women going shopping – although, with the rationing still in force, the opportunities for this would be limited – while the men would walk the streets, and have lunch and liquid refreshment, all the time smoking interminable cigarettes before heading for the game. The English fans were welcomed and hands were shaken, while good-natured banter and badinage would be exchanged. 'Where are you from, mate?' 'Aberdeen.' 'I knew an Aberdeen man in the RAF. Do you know 'im? His name's Jock Smith.'

The way to the game was colourful with lots of tartan rosettes, and accordion players entertaining the crowd with *Loch Lomond*, *Ye Banks and Braes* and *Mary, My Scots Bluebell*, as well as the wartime favourites of Vera Lynn like *We'll Meet Again*. Newspapers were on sale with pictures of the players. 'Sooveneer Speshul' trumpeted the sellers, often a man with one arm (possibly the other one lost in one of the world wars) who amazed everyone with his dexterity in giving a paper, taking money and giving back change all with one hand. Everybody walked to the game with a spring in their step, proud to be Scottish, proud even to be British and very glad to be at peace. The war wounded were treated with respect and helped to a privileged position on the terracing, if they had not been allocated a place in the special enclosure for the injured. The blind had their own special seats in the stand where a volunteer would deliver a commentary.

For those not at the game, the radio or the wireless assumed enormous attention. World War Two had seen the triumph of this medium, as bandleaders like Tommy Dorsey, singers like Vera Lynn and comedians like the Crazy Gang had kept the home fires burning. Churchill himself had been the master of the radio and the BBC had been looked upon as the voice of the free world with its regular, reliable and optimistic news. Football had been on the radio as well, but never had there been the attention paid to games as there was to this one. Batteries were charged up on the morning of the game and neighbours invited in to listen. Boys playing their own game of football in the street suspended operations to come in and listen to the match.

The weather was reasonable and the game itself attracted 139,468 in demob suits, utility clothing and some still in military uniform. More than a few Americans, Canadians and Australians (and even some Italian and German prisoners of war who had chosen not to go back) appeared to see what this passionate Scottish game of football was all about, for the 'Jocks had talked about little else'. Women wore pillbox hats with flowers and berries on them, and stockings with seams down the back. If they could not afford or get hold of these nylons, they would even paint a seam down the back of their legs. Everyone was eager, happy, excited and enthusiastic. There was community singing, pipe bands and the National Anthem was either sung lustily or greeted with the most polite respect.

The teams were as follows. Scotland: Brown (Rangers); D Shaw (Hibernian) and J Shaw (Rangers); Campbell (Morton), Brennan (Newcastle United) and Husband (Partick Thistle); Waddell (Rangers), Dougall (Birmingham City), Delaney (Manchester United), Hamilton (Aberdeen) and Liddell (Liverpool). England: Swift (Manchester City); Scott (Arsenal) and Hardwick (Middlesbrough); Wright (Wolverhampton Wanderers), Franklin (Stoke City) and Mercer (Everton); Elliott (West Bromwich Albion), Shackleton (Bradford City), Lawton (Chelsea), Hagan (Sheffield United) and Compton (Arsenal).

The referee was P. Craigmyle of Aberdeen.

Unfortunately, the game was a disappointment. The score was 0–0 and the game was meandering towards its dismal conclusion. 'Nae goals, nae fitba' was a Scottish truism. There was a feeling of anti-climax. A few chances had come at both ends but the goalkeepers were well in control, particularly Frank Swift of England with his dominance of the penalty area. Yet Frank had had his problems with Jimmy Delaney. Frank was notorious for having a very low trajectory in his clearances and kick outs. In the days before the back-pass rule was introduced in 1992, a defender under pressure from the likes of Delaney would frequently pass the ball back to the goalkeeper. He would pick the ball up, advance a few steps and send the ball upfield. Knowing that Swift's kick would be a low one, Delaney closed in on him and on several occasions almost panicked him into making a mistake.

There was also one bizarre incident early in the second half, when Dennis Compton, who would soon become more famous as a cricketer, batting for Middlesex and England, collided with a Scottish defender and a corner flag at the King's Park End of the ground on the left. The flag post was broken and an opportunist souvenir hunter ran on and stole part of the flag post! Clearly, the stump of the post would be dangerous to players, so there was a delay while a substitute corner flag was found. Luckily, corner flags were not apparently on the ration, like food and clothing, and the game was able to continue.

The game itself was a dull stalemate with the defences of both sides able to counteract the flair players in the attacks of the other. A draw would be a fair result, reckoned the Scottish fans. In fact the Scottish fans would be reasonably happy, for wartime internationals had been predictably and repeatedly dreadful, apart from one in 1942. At least 0–0 was not the cataclysmic outcome that might have wrecked many a soldier's homecoming.

But the game was not over. Scotland won a free kick about halfway inside the England half on the left side of the field when George Hamilton of Aberdeen had been fouled. It was taken by Jackie Husband, the excellent Partick Thistle left-half, who was famous for his long throw-ins and the pinpoint accuracy of his free-kicks. This one, however, seemed to have been hit too hard to present any immediate danger to the England defence, who visibly relaxed as the ball came across to Willie Waddell of Rangers. Willie turned the ball back, found the inrushing Delaney and hit the ball past Frank Swift to unleash a veritable orgy of celebration all round the park and all over Scotland. Referee Peter Craigmyle from Aberdeen clearly savoured the moment. It was his habit to pause in such circumstances, while everyone looked at him to see if there had been some infringement, before he pointed majestically up the field to indicate that a goal had been scored. On this occasion he made the most of it, but the effect was lost somewhat, for his linesman had begun to run up the field and, in any case, the nation had already begun to celebrate long before Craigmyle himself ran up to the centre spot.

The crowd erupted in the way that 1940s crowds did as everyone grabbed one another, hugged total strangers and screamed 'Goal!' into each other's ears as if they had not grasped that fact. As it was a fine spring day, the dust from the cinders rose as the crowd danced their joy. A few minutes later there was another outburst of frenetic and maniacal emotion as Craigmyle, again savouring the moment, pointed melodramatically (after allowing the game to continue longer than necessary just so that more people would look at him) to the pavilion for full-time.

There is a story about this goal. The author cannot guarantee its authenticity, but it is a family folktale and firmly believed – and indicative of how much football meant to the Scottish nation in 1946. Imagine the scene in a respectable Scottish working-class household. The mother of the family has saved up her coupons and managed to get sausages for tea. She is cooking them, humming happily to herself, rejoicing in the recent return of her son from faraway fields of glory like Mersa Matruh and Monte Casino. The hero of this hour is sitting in the living room along with the father of the house, a hero of an earlier war and now sadly crippled. Father and son are listening to a commentary of the football.

The old radio, now somewhat worn but with its batteries recently recharged, has done yeoman service over the past few years assuring the population that 'we shall go on to the end', 'a bright gleam has lit the helmets of our soldiers' and 'this morning Allied forces have made several landings on the Normandy coast of France'. It is now used for more peaceful purposes, with Raymond Glendinning talking about men like Frank Swift and this man who seems to mean so much to her husband and son – Jimmy Delaney, late of Celtic and now of Manchester United fame.

Suddenly, a great cry is heard. Fearing for her husband's health, she rushes through to find father and son in a 'danse macabre' of joy, for Jimmy Delaney has scored. Raymond Glendinning is shouting 'Yes it's Delaney – Jimmy Delaney! Jimmy Delaney of Scotland.' Mother, delighted that that is all that has happened, returns to her sausages, benignly shaking her head about the passion for football. She sees something magical, however, for the sausages are standing up and cheering, nodding to each other and saying 'Delaney! Delaney!' before settling down for the rest of their sizzle.

In 1946, before the advent of television (it had started in a limited way in London in 1936, but had been closed down for the war and only reached Scotland in 1952), there was no way of seeing that goal until the Pathé or Gaumont newsreel came to the local cinema. It would have been listened to many times as the radio would play the commentator's description of it again and again, and it would be read about in the many newspapers which flourished at that time. There would be still pictures, but seeing it actually happen was far more elusive.

People would go to the pictures, an industry which had flourished during the war and continued to do so for many years afterwards, just in order to see that goal. It was worth sitting through Errol Flynn or Merle Oberon, the advertisements for ice cream and the crowing of the cockerel which signalled the start of the newsreel. On the newsreel there would be information about the post-war rebuilding of Britain and Europe, the trial of Nazi war criminals, the King (a dignified but clearly unhealthy man) opening a hospital and then the moment everyone had come to see – a brief flicker of the Delaney goal. 'Husband takes the free-kick, Waddell knocks on, Delaney rushes in – and all Scotland goes mad.' The cinema resounded to clapping and cheers, and then the audience would settle down to watch the film or to their courting in the back seats.

However, Scotland and Delaney were not yet finished in 1946. Even more joy was to come. Switzerland came to Hampden on 15 May and were beaten 3–1 in front of a huge crowd of 113,000. This was large in any circumstances but even more so as it was a Wednesday afternoon. The forward line of Waddell, Thornton, Delaney, Walker and Liddell 'sparkled throughout' as Billy Liddell scored twice and Jimmy Delaney scored the other. It was now clear to all that the war was indeed over and that football was back. Johnnie could indeed 'go to sleep in his own little room again'.

Chapter 6

Manchester United
1946–1950

THE CONTENTION that Manchester United are one of the greatest football teams in the world would find few people to dispute it. Today their stadium is vast and their support is the biggest in the United Kingdom – although in worldwide terms, possibly not quite as large as that of Celtic, such has been the effect of the Irish and Scottish Diasporas. They have dominated the English Premiership since its inception in the early 1990s, although in recent years they have lost out to the London clubs, Arsenal and Chelsea. Their players are well known throughout the world and there can be little doubt that they are one of the best-known institutions in the world. A visit to Dublin, for example, will prove that it is difficult to walk down O'Connell Street without seeing several football tops belonging, sadly, not to Shamrock Rovers, Shelbourne or St Patrick's but to Celtic and Manchester United.

Since World War Two, the history of Manchester United is littered with legends, legendary characters and legendary happenings – good and bad. There was notably the tragedy of the Munich Air Crash in 1958, which saw the premature death of talented young men like Roger Byrne and Duncan Edwards. Happier events were the winning of the European Cup in 1968 and 1999 and their consistent success in the Premiership in recent seasons under Alex Ferguson. Like Celtic they have occasionally suffered from inept directors, notably in the 1980s when they consistently failed to come to terms with the League dominance of Liverpool, and one or two managers who have left with major question marks hanging over them. The football world was shocked when relegation came their way in 1974. On the other hand, there have been Denis Law, Bobby Charlton, George Best, Ryan Giggs, David Beckham, Roy Keane, Alex Ferguson and many others who have made United a perpetual topic of conversation not only in the British Isles but throughout the world.

There are many similarities between Manchester United and Celtic. Both teams have huge support and tend to be associated with brilliant players and glorious triumphs, albeit sometimes isolated ones. There tends to be a huge dichotomy about them; they are either loved or hated. In the same way that Celtic fans often feel that supporters of Motherwell, Hearts, Kilmarnock and others will side with Rangers rather than themselves when the chips are down, so too is there a tendency for any defeat of Manchester United to be received with greater joy among the average fan than reverses for anyone else.

Like Celtic fans, Manchester United supporters do not all live in the immediate geographical area of their ground. People will travel from all over England, Scotland and Ireland to see their home games, and any game that involves the Old Trafford men will excite and provoke arguments wherever the game is played. Their games can now of course be watched throughout the world via satellite television and, if anything, love for the club seems to be growing.

But it was not always so. Between the wars, for example, United were no strangers to the Second Division and were always a big city team which failed to live up to the expectations of their supporters. Even today, it is noticeable that although they have won the Premiership more often than other teams in recent years, over the course of history they have been champions fewer times than the likes of Liverpool or Arsenal. They have won the English Cup the most times (11 in all and seven times since 1983), but it is rather surprising to find out that the European Cup has only found its way to Old Trafford twice – something that will hurt Manchester United supporters, especially as rivals and neighbours Liverpool have now carried off the trophy five times.

Before World War Two, United had won the English League in 1908 and 1911 and the English Cup in 1909 in the halcyon days of the mighty Welshman Billy Meredith, but since then their great support had been starved of the success that near-neighbours Everton and Manchester City, for example, were accustomed to. Anyone who was asked to name the biggest team in England in the 1930s would have come up with Everton, perhaps, or Arsenal. Manchester United would have been a long way down the list – possibly even below the name of Manchester City. The question 'What is Old Trafford?' would possibly have elicited the response 'the home of Lancashire County Cricket Club' before 'the home of Manchester United'.

It was Matt Busby who changed all that. His recognition as the father of Manchester United is well deserved, for it was his appointment in February 1945 that awoke the sleeping giant which lived at Old Trafford. Or rather it did not, for the sleeping giant that was Manchester United in 1945 did not even have a home. Old Trafford had been badly damaged by *Luftwaffe* bombs in March 1941 and would not reopen for football until 24 August 1949. Home games had to be played at Maine Road, the home of their rivals Manchester City.

Matt Busby had many similarities to Jimmy Delaney, his first signing. In the first place there was a definite physical similarity, with a receding hairline and broad face. They both came from Lanarkshire and they were both Celtic daft. Busby would have loved to have joined Celtic, but the invitation never came.

Before the war Busby had played as a right-half for Manchester City and Liverpool, and had earned one Scottish cap. Sadly for Busby it was an unfortunate day for Scotland as they lost 2–3 to Wales in 1933, and he was never asked again in peacetime. But he did play in a few wartime internationals, often as captain, and it was there that he met and played alongside Jimmy Delaney, with whom he developed a great affinity. His appointment as Manchester United manager in February 1945 was to take effect whenever he was demobbed (effectively October 1945) and was the great decision that made Manchester United a world superpower. There are great parallels with the decision of the Celtic board to appoint Jock Stein in 1965, yet another man from the coalfields of Lanarkshire.

Busby inherited an ordinary team, for wartime conditions were chaotic and haphazard. The same could be said of the country at that time in 1945. The war had been won, but it would be some time before the benefits were seen. Nevertheless, the country was blessed by men of vision and of great political will who, within a decade, would change the face of the country as milk was put into babies, and health and housing were gradually brought up to an acceptable standard. The Labour Government would do that job, saying a final farewell to the horrific conditions that had remained in this country since the Industrial Revolution. Matt Busby would slowly set about doing the same for Manchester United and their huge band of frequently disappointed followers. The bad old days were behind them; the way was forward.

It was for these reasons that Busby signed Delaney. In early 1963, 17 years later, another Celtic man called Pat Crerand would follow the same path and for the same reasons – the Celtic management would not pay him what he thought was a fair rate for the job that he could do. Jimmy and Pat would both find Matt Busby a man of their own kind, a man who knew how to manage players, and both Jimmy and Pat were destined to become part of great teams, albeit in totally different circumstances.

Many Manchester United fans would have queried the value of signing Delaney. He would have been very well known, for he had been much talked about by Scottish soldiers in the British Army, but at the age of 31, it would have appeared that Delaney's best years were behind him. He was definitely injury prone, it was believed, and he earned the nickname 'Old Brittle Bones' – something that was grossly unfair, for he had had only one real fracture of a bone, admittedly a very bad one, in 1939. He certainly looked old with his lack of hair and he had spent the war playing in a poor team in a poor grade of football in Scotland. On the other hand, he had played several times for Scotland before the war and had played in the Empire Exhibition Trophy winning team of 1938.

In February 1946, Manchester United were already out of the English Cup and about halfway up the Football League North, as it was called in this, the last season of wartime football before the League began properly the following year. A day after his transfer, on 9 February 1946, Delaney found himself on the right-wing against Liverpool at Maine Road before 33,000 fans, and he played well as United won 2–1. United's team was: Tapkin; Whalley and Walton; Warner, Chilton and Cockburn; Delaney, Hanlon, Smith, Carey and Wrigglesworth. The only blot on his copybook was that he missed a penalty.

Several of the great team were already in position, notably the Irish international, Johnny Carey (another lookalike for Delaney and Busby when his hair began to disappear) and the centre-half with the unlikely name of Allenby Chilton (named presumably after the famous general of World War One). Gradually other great names were assembled over the next few seasons and the first of Busby's many great sides would emerge.

It was the habit in 1946, as it had been for a few seasons in the 1920s, to play games against a particular team back to back, so the next game a week later was also against Liverpool, this time at Anfield. Delaney is mentioned as starring in this game for he laid on a couple of goals for Jack Rowley in the comprehensive 5–0 drubbing of the Merseyside club. His first goal was against Bradford on 30 March and he scored another couple before the end of the season. When the season ended on 4 May, Manchester United had reached fourth place and Delaney had only twice been in a losing side.

Busby had given Delaney a couple of games in the centre-forward position when injury and unavailability forced him into it, but Jimmy felt able to tell Busby (in a way that he certainly would not have felt able to do with Willie Maley or even Jimmy McStay) that his best position was on the right wing. In fact there was little argument about it and for the next four seasons he would play virtually nowhere else for Manchester United.

Manchester, like the rest of Britain in 1946, was still recovering from the war, but the revival was underway. This age is often referred to as an age of 'austerity', as if people were poor, but this is not really so. There were shortages – some foods stayed rationed, as did clothes – but there was a return to full employment. The cries of poverty and hardship often came from the middle classes, who for the first time in history found themselves living in a time of economic stringency under a Government which was not exclusively devoted to their interests.

Clement Attlee was a small, nondescript man. 'A sheep in sheep's clothing', 'a modest man with a lot to be modest about', 'an empty taxi came up

Whitehall and Mr Attlee got out' were what his enemies said. However, he was proving himself to be Britain's best-ever Prime Minister, as mighty men like Nye Bevan, Ernest Bevin and Mannie Shinwell addressed themselves to the building of the promised New Jerusalem. It would take time, but the new generation of babies being born would grow up to be healthier and sturdier than ever before.

The Tory press, with the fury of impotence, tried to stir up trouble for the Government with talk of crises, both economic and energy, but the Government remained resolute in what it was going to do. In any case, the newspapers soon found that what their working-class readership was really interested in was football. More and more column inches were dedicated to the coverage of football, with far more pictures than before.

Television had not yet arrived as a mass media – only a small but growing minority in London possessed this luxury – but theatre, cinema and sport all boomed. Football attracted huge crowds, as it had done in the wake of World War One in the 1920s. Demobbed soldiers, so glad to be alive, thronged to the grounds. The referee was always in black, the ball was always brown and far heavier than in modern days, the goalkeeper always wore a thick polo-neck yellow jersey and European games had not been thought of, but football was the talk of the nation. Games were well attended in spite of the lack of adequate facilities. One or two disasters occurred through overcrowding, notably at Burnden Park, Bolton, in March 1946 when 33 people were crushed to death at an English Cup quarter-final between Bolton Wanderers and Stoke City. Toilets were a disgrace – barely existent for female supporters and a major health hazard for males – but nobody seemed to care.

One thing that the Scottish-born Delaney might have found difficult to comprehend in England was the fascination with and love of cricket, a sport that was almost as popular as football. In the winter of 1946–47, England had been invited to contest the Ashes in the sun of Australia and a squad of 17 lucky sportsmen had sailed away from England's dreary land, with all its shortages and rationing, just as the football season was beginning.

This tour was followed with rapt attention in England. People got up to listen to the 7am news on the BBC for details of the day's play and then grabbed an evening paper to read what E.W. Swanton was saying about the goings on. The fact that England, a woefully understrength side, were no match for Bradman's Australia did not in any way lessen the enthusiasm or love for the game, a passion which men like Busby and Delaney from the industrial central belt of Scotland may well have found puzzling.

Manchester United would not be able to reopen Old Trafford for several seasons. There were several reasons for this. Manchester United were themselves short of cash, but there was also a shortage of building materials and manpower. Understandably, the repair of a sports stadium had to take second place to the necessary building of houses. Bombs had damaged many homes, but this was not the main cause of the housing shortage. The main reason was that so much housing was classed, by strict Government inspectors, as unfit for human habitation and the word 'condemned' was used frequently of housing which did not come up to scratch. Some of these rat-infested slums had been unfit for human habitation for many decades, but the late 1940s was the first time that anyone did anything about it.

The lack of stadium did not stop Manchester United fans arriving in their droves for the first official post-war season. If anything, adversity seemed to be consolidating their love and affection for their favourites. Many of the supporters had spent their war years in prisoner-of-war camps, in the Western Desert, on the High Seas or on a Japanese railway line, yearning for such an opportunity. The season opened on 31 August 1946 when Grimsby Town came to Maine Road. The United team of Crompton, Carey, McGlen, Warner, Chilton, Cockburn, Delaney, Pearson, Hanlon, Rowley and Mitten won 2–1 in front of 41,000 fans.

Manchester United fans soon realised that their new Scottish manager was a winner and that he had made a great signing in fellow Scotsman Jimmy Delaney. They appreciated Delaney's speed, bodyswerve, determination and ability to resist temptation to retaliate when on the wrong side of coarse tackling. From newspaper reports, it is clear that people were still living in the aftermath of a dreadful war. For example, military imagery was very much to the fore: 'Delaney supplied the ammunition', 'Delaney brought up the heavy artillery' and even on one occasion 'Delaney's crosses were deadly bombs' – a piece of journalese that might be considered in bad taste now, let alone just after a world war in 1946.

United won their first five games before losing to Stoke in the Potteries on 21 September, in spite of a fine Delaney goal. They returned to form to beat Arsenal 5–2, a game in which 'Delaney was instrumental in ensuring that the Gunners were out-gunned', as the martial metaphors continued unabated.

United had a bad month in October and this may have been at least partially responsible for a major disappointment for Delaney. He was not picked for the first official international since before the war had started: Scotland against Wales at Wrexham on 19 October 1946. He would have been expecting to be chosen, as he was still the Scottish hero who scored in the Victory International the previous April. However, his place went to Willie Waddell of Rangers, an excellent winger and in later years a great friend of Jimmy's, in spite of their being on opposite sides of Scotland's divide.

Further disappointment came Jimmy's way a month later when he was not picked for the Ireland game at Hampden. This time his place went to Gordon Smith, a fine player in the fast-developing Hibernian team of that decade.

Jimmy began to feel that he had perhaps lost out a little in moving to England to Manchester United, who were not yet a particularly fashionable team. He was, however, far too much of a professional and indeed a gentleman to throw tantrums or issue stupid statements to the press about never wanting to play for Scotland again, as might have happened with less disciplined (and less talented) players in a later age.

Jimmy was injured and missed a couple of games in December 1946, but he returned by Christmas to play in the two games against Bolton Wanderers. United played Bolton away on Christmas Day before both teams travelled to Maine Road on Boxing Day for the return fixture. This quaint arrangement (a similar thing happened at Easter) prevailed for a few years and did a great deal for attendances. It was even the expected custom that a supporter would meet a supporter of the other team one day and then invite him for a drink or a meal the next. It did not always work and it is hard to imagine it happening now. United drew 2–2 at Burnden Park before 28,505 (the capacity was severely restricted in the aftermath of the previous March's disaster) and then beat them 1–0 through a Stan Pearson goal at Maine Road before an attendance of 57,186 on Boxing Day. Delaney was outstanding in both games.

January 1947 started well for Manchester United and Jimmy Delaney with two fine wins over Charlton Athletic and Middlesbrough in the League and a defeat of Bradford at the Park Avenue ground in the English Cup. Delaney is mentioned well in reports of these games. He did not score, but he supplied the other forwards with 'good quality service' so that they could do so. Things went a little wrong, however, on 25 January as United went out of the FA Cup to Nottingham Forest before 58,000 at Maine Road. Notts Forest were a Second Division team at the time and it was one of the many acts of giantkilling for which the English Cup is famous. Manchester United could do nothing other than hold up their hands and say that Forest were the better team on the day and that too many players had an off day, Delaney included.

This in no way lessened the disappointment that Busby must have felt. He thought that although his developing team still lacked the consistency to win the English League, they would be a good bet for the Cup. Delaney and Busby would hardly have been consoled when they listened to the results on the radio on *Sports Report* to discover that their other love, Celtic, had also been put out of the Scottish Cup at the hands of Dundee. Neither Busby nor Delaney, one feels, would have been in the mood for a Burns Supper that night of 25 January 1947.

As frequently happens in the wake of a Cup defeat, particularly an unexpected one, League form suffers as well. The next game saw a 2–6 defeat at Highbury (as Arsenal avenged the 5–2 result at the beginning of the year) in which the defence was minus Henry Cockburn and clearly had no idea how to cope with an Arsenal attack that knew how to run with the ball and pass at speed. This was followed by a miserable 1–1 draw with Stoke City at Maine Road in front of only 8,456 on Wednesday 5 February. As floodlights had not been installed yet, the match was played on a Wednesday afternoon, which explains the low attendance. And it was only a League game. The traditional excuses of auntie's funeral and hospital appointment could be used for a vital Cup replay; less so for a mundane League match.

The phenomenon for which 1947 became notorious then occurred – the bad weather. Great Britain was more or less paralysed as for day after day the country was blanketed with snow and ice. It was simply a bad combination of meteorological phenomena, but one or two minor groups came to the fore to cash in on the situation. One was the religious sect which told everyone that God was angry with Man for his sinfulness. There were also those who thought that the explosion of the atomic bombs in Japan in 1945, and one or two others which the Americans were trying out in the Pacific and the Russians were trying out in the Siberian wastes, were knocking the Earth off its axis and bringing us closer to the next Ice Age.

This winter was a lot worse in Scotland than in England. In Scotland the bad weather continued well into March, but in England it was not quite so persistent. Manchester United were able to resume playing on 22 February, admittedly on pitches that were sometimes dangerously hard (perhaps players were tougher then or referees more reluctant to call games off) and played from then on every week until the end of the extended season.

The enforced lay-off seemed to have done United a lot of good, for they played another 16 games and won 10, drew four and lost two. Delaney played brilliantly, adapting to the hard grounds a lot better than he normally did to the wet, heavy grounds, and teaming up well with Ronnie Burke, who was enjoying his purple patch and scoring goals regularly. Defeats of Everton, Wolverhampton Wanderers and Leeds (twice) put Manchester United in with a great shout of the League Championship but for Delaney personally, something else happened. He was picked to play for Scotland in the Wembley international.

Yet, although this was much to Delaney's surprise and delight (for he may have suspected that his international career was over), there was something strange about it – he was selected to play in the centre-forward position. This was indeed bizarre, for although Delaney was no stranger to the centre-forward position (not least the previous April in the Victory International at Hampden where he scored the famous winner), he had been playing successfully on the right wing all season for Manchester United. Both his managers, Willie Maley of Celtic (still very much to the fore in spite of his departure from Celtic in 1940) and Matt Busby of Manchester United, were in vociferous agreement that the right wing was his best place.

But the argument in favour of it was that Scotland was rich in right-wingers and that Gordon Smith of Hibernian was playing well in that position. This could not be disputed and the result was a typical Scottish compromise of playing a man out of position. One recalls the time in 1912 when Scotland took the field with three centre-forwards: Andrew Wilson, Jimmy Quinn and David McLean.

In the modern era this might not have mattered too much, but the late 1940s was a time when players' positions were far more rigid and pre-determined. Nevertheless, Delaney was thrilled to be playing for Scotland again, especially as it was his first game at Wembley. In 1947 the annual game between Scotland and England was the big fixture of the year, beating even the Cup Finals for interest. This was particularly true for that year as it was the first official Scottish visit to Wembley since the totally different circumstances of 1938. It was a tremendous experience for the Scottish nation, and many made the trek to Wembley while the rest sat glued to the radio, having made sure that morning that the accumulator batteries had been adequately charged up.

The game itself on 12 April 1947 was an anti-climax, finishing a 1–1 draw. Delaney did not have a particularly good game – but it was not a disaster either – and the draw was a fair result. Delaney enjoyed Wembley, the massive crowds and being introduced to Clement Attlee, the Labour Prime Minister. Attlee was notorious for being laconic and economical with his words, but he smiled as he met the man called Delaney of whom he had heard so much. After the game Attlee, an Englishman but well aware of the fact that Scotland voted Labour and with no desire to upset them, was asked whether he enjoyed the game and said 'Yes'. When pressed to elaborate, he said that 'both teams played well'.

In Delaney's absence, Manchester United had a disappointing 0–0 draw with Brentford that day. When Delaney returned, United had six games to play. He was outstanding as they beat Blackburn Rovers 4–0 on 19 April and then scored the game's only goal as they beat Portsmouth at Fratton Park. The crunch game was played at Anfield against Liverpool on 3 May. Liverpool were powered by Delaney's fellow Scotsman, the saintly Billy Liddell, who repeatedly got the better of Johnny Carey. Liverpool won the game with Albert Stubbins scoring in front of 48,800. Effectively it was this game which deprived United of the Championship, although they remained in contention until the very end.

Manchester United thus had to settle for second place in 1947: hardly a failure for Busby and Delaney, but a disappointment after such a vigorous late rally. For Delaney, there was further disappointment when he sustained an injury in the third from last League game on 10 May in a 1–1 draw with Preston North End. He might have been summoned to Hampden Park on that day along with Billy Liddell of Liverpool, because Great Britain were playing the Rest of Europe in an exhibition game, and for a while it looked as if Tommy Lawton would have to pull out. As it was, Lawton played in the centre-forward position, while Stanley Matthews played on the right wing. An impressive British performance led to a 6–1 win. Delaney's Manchester United colleague Johnny Carey from the Irish Republic was the captain of the Rest of Europe side. Sadly for Delaney, his injury prevented him from joining Scotland's tour of Europe.

With his wife and family (he had two children at this point – Pat and Kathleen) now settled in Manchester, Delaney would have been happy with life. He kept wondering and asking about Celtic, who had had a woeful season. They would be even worse in season 1947–48, but for Delaney and Manchester United, things were definitely on the up. Summer 1947 was as glorious as the winter had been bad and life generally was slowly improving for the people of Great Britain. Soon there would be a National Health Service.

The football season started again on 23 August, but Manchester United still had no home. There was still a problem with money (even allowing for the large crowds and the success of the previous year) but in any case, the construction industry might not have been able to undertake the work, for the priority was still housing. Slums and bomb-damaged housing had to be cleared up and new homes found for the people. The problem was not unemployment: it was not having enough workers to do all the jobs that were necessary. After the previous war, Lloyd George had conspicuously failed to deliver his 'land fit for heroes to live in'; this Government was at least making the effort.

The 1947–48 season saw the famous Manchester United forward line of Delaney, Morris, Rowley, Pearson and Mitten. Curiously enough, a glance at the early part of the season's results does not impress all that much. By 13 December, for example, only five games had been won, 10 drawn and five lost, and goals were not too frequent or plentiful. There were two spectacular six-goal sprees against Charlton Athletic and Wolves, and a 4–0 thrashing of Chelsea, but otherwise only twice did they score more than two. One of them was a 3–4 defeat to Grimsby Town and the other was a remarkable game at Huddersfield in which Jack Rowley scored all four goals in a 4–4 draw.

Delaney was consistently well thought of in newspaper reports. His nimble footwork was much praised, as was his speed, determination and crossing. He was an ideal team man as well: he was able to coax the best out of someone who was not having a good day and never caused any trouble within the team. A look of frustration was sometimes glimpsed when things did not go as well as he would have liked, but it was soon replaced by quiet determination. There was never a look of daggers at a colleague for a bad pass or the self-justifying, blame-it-on-someone-else looks and gestures, which were and are so much a part of the professional game.

One chapter in Delaney's life that was fated to end in season 1947–48 was his international career. He was picked to play in all three home internationals:

against Ireland in Belfast on 4 October, Wales at Hampden on 12 November and England at Hampden on 10 April. Scotland lost all three in what was one of their worst international seasons to date. Delaney himself did not star in any of these games. In the Welsh game he was once again played out of position at centre-forward, but few excuses are possible for either Delaney or Scotland in the other two games.

The England game at Hampden was a major disappointment for 135,376 fans. Scotland missed a few early chances when 'Delaney and Liddell looked in the mood', but England were quite simply technically superior to them and scored goals at crucial points of the game. Of the two right-wingers, there could be 'little denying that Stan Matthews was better than Jimmy Delaney' as a Scottish newspaper honestly put it. Jimmy would have some sort of revenge over his friend Stanley Matthews two weeks later in the English Cup Final, but 10 April belonged to England.

As Delaney shook hands with his English opponents in front of a stunned Hampden with some of the tartan tammies and rosettes streaming out of the ground and the remainder of the crowd in that sort of typically Scottish catatonic silence that betokens heartbreak, Jimmy might have realised that the game was up for him in international football. He was after all approaching his 34th birthday and had had a great innings for Scotland, having won 13 full caps, as well as war internationals and Scottish League appearances. Apart from his immortal Victory International goal, he would have good cause to remember with pleasure 'the goals that put Hitler off his tea' – his two goals against Germany at Ibrox in October 1936. But now, 12 years later, it was all over. He was not chosen for the Belgium game on 28 April or the European tour. However, his club career had a long way to go yet.

In December 1947, Manchester United had taken off. There were five straight victories in a row over the holiday time with the New Year's Day 5–0 win over Burnley, who were going strong at the time, a particularly impressive one. Life might have been different if they had beaten Arsenal at Maine Road on 17 January 1948, but they had to be content with a 1–1 draw. A crowd of 83,260 people attended this game, a record for a League match in England which still stands to this day and is unlikely ever to be broken. This is a powerful indication of the drawing power of the two teams and of the interest in football at the time. As Manchester United had lost to Arsenal at Highbury in September, it meant that Arsenal retained the initiative in the championship race, which they eventually won by seven points.

United lost other games, with the final blow coming on 10 April when they went down to Everton on the day that Delaney was in Glasgow playing in the ill-fated Scotland team against England. For the second year in a row, Delaney had to be content with his team being runners-up in the Championship race. If

United had played as well in the early part of the season as they did in the middle and towards the end, even the strong Arsenal team could not have withstood their charge.

If this was disappointing, there was ample compensation in the winning of the English Cup. This trophy is often called the FA Cup, a name resented by people who do not live in England, for there is the perfectly understandable feeling that as the Scottish Cup is for teams who play in Scotland, teams that play in England should play in the English Cup. In Delaney's case, there is an added reason why it should be called the English Cup – to distinguish it from the Scottish and Irish Cups.

The English Cup traditionally begins early in the New Year for top-division teams. Fortunately for United, this coincided with their surge in form; otherwise they might have gone out at the first time of asking on 13 January at Villa Park, Birmingham. Aston Villa scored one of the earliest ever goals in English Cup history in 13 seconds, while many thousands of the 58,683 crowd were still outside clamouring for admission at the seriously under-pressure turnstiles. But Delaney was at his inspirational best that first half and by half-time in this remarkable game Manchester United were 5–1 up, with Delaney having scored one of the goals. In the second half, Villa staged a spirited revival and scored three goals but United had added another and the game finished 6–4.

The Manchester fans rightly praised their mighty forward line of Delaney, Morris, Rowley, Pearson and Mitten. They all understood each other, could interchange when required – the famous Delaney ploy that he had picked up over a decade previously from Jimmy McMenemy – but played in the basic pattern of the time of the 'W', with the three prongs of Delaney, Rowley and Mitten running in parallel and being supplied by Morris and Pearson. They were all committed to the cause and all had the happy knack of being able to avoid serious injury, at least in this season. They played in every round of the campaign.

When it was announced on the radio, the draw for the next round paired Manchester United against Liverpool on 24 January 1948. Liverpool were last year's League champions, but their form had slipped a little after United had beaten them in the second game of the season and then drawn with them a week later. The match was a home game for Manchester United but, as Manchester City were also drawn at home, the game had to be moved to Goodison Park, the home of Liverpool's rivals, Everton. In these days, Sunday football was completely unthinkable and all games were played on Saturdays.

A crowd of 74,000 were reputed to be at Goodison that day, shoehorned into extremely cramped and dangerous conditions. United chose to play some of their best football that day and Liverpool were comprehensively dispatched 3–0. Morris, Rowley and Mitten scored the goals, but Delaney was the man who made it all happen for United.

More progress was made a fortnight later at Leeds Road, Huddersfield (another 'home' game for United), when Charlton Athletic, last season's winners of the English Cup, were disposed of with goals from Warner and Mitten. On 28 February, Manchester United were still at 'home', but this time at Villa Park for the visit of their Lancashire neighbours Preston North End. It needed to be a big ground, for 74,213 made the trip from Lancashire to the Midlands to see a great game in which United triumphed 4–2 with two goals from Stan Pearson, one from Jack Rowley and one from Charlie Mitten. Once again, it was Delaney who was the star – 'he of the nimble toes' as he was described in the press. Delaney laid on two of the goals and played a significant part in the rest of the play.

It was the team that won the Cup in 1946 which provided the opposition in the semi-final. Derby County appeared at neutral Hillsborough on 13 March and were comprehensively despatched 3–0 with all the goals coming from in-form Stan Pearson. It was once again a vintage performance by Jimmy Delaney. Jimmy himself said that it would be unfair to single anyone out, for this was a fine team and thoroughly deserving of Manchester United's first ever Wembley appearance and their first English Cup Final appearance since the Crystal Palace in 1909 – 39 years and two world wars ago. On that occasion, Billy Meredith had inspired United to beat Bristol City 1–0. Such was the impoverished history of the Red Devils before 1948.

It would be hard to imagine the thrill that affected all of Manchester in 1948 at the thought of that Wembley appearance on 24 April. In the early years of the 21st century, an appearance in the English Cup Final is big enough, even though it sometimes seems to be overshadowed by other competitions. Indeed, in the year 2000, Manchester United attracted a certain amount of criticism, not least from their own supporters, for neglecting the English Cup in favour of a money-spinning but insignificant trophy in Brazil. The decision was taken without the blessing of anyone and seems to have been made on the grounds of sheer greed. The tournament may have been called the FIFA Club World Championship, but it lacked the history of the oldest club tournament in the world.

If the English Cup is important now, how much more important was it in 1948? There were other ingredients as well. It was an all-Lancashire clash against Blackpool, it was only the third year after the war and it would be a great test of how Matt Busby's new Manchester United side would fare against the famous dribblers of Blackpool like Stanley Matthews and Stanley Mortensen. The 99,000 tickets fetched enormous prices – up to £1 for a 2-shilling brief – for this was the age of spivs and black marketeers. Television coverage had not yet really arrived for everyone and so it would be the radio for many supporters – not only in Manchester but in Scotland and elsewhere in the United Kingdom and beyond.

For Delaney personally, there were other issues. Wartime soldiers had argued the respective merits of Stanley Matthews and Jimmy Delaney as right-wingers. Matthews definitely had the better of the argument in the England v Scotland game on 10 April. Now, two weeks later, there was a rematch. Delaney was also aware that 24 April 1937, some 11 years previously, was the day that he won his Scottish Cup medal when Celtic beat Aberdeen in front of a record crowd. How appropriate it would be if he could win an English Cup medal on the same day. It was also his son Pat's eighth birthday.

In the build-up to the final, *Picture Post* magazine wrote a flattering feature on Manchester United. In an article called 'A Team that Deserves the Cup', it described them as:

> ...commonly thought of as the strongest and most attractive side at present on the go. United's style is the opposite of Arsenal's in so far as it is an aggressive, positive affair, based on constant methodical attack at high speed. It is not the bull-headed, blazeaway style the Wolves used to have in the days of the gland [sic] treatments. It is an ingenious, constructive business, centred on no fancy plan, but on the classical truisms of keeping the ball on the island, and keeping it low, and moving it quickly into the open spaces that lead to the other fellow's goal.

Delaney is described as 'The Evergreen. Still one of the fastest, cleverest, most dangerous of wingers.'

On the Saturday between the international and the Cup Final, Manchester United tuned up well by defeating Chelsea 5–0, with Delaney scoring one of the eight goals that he scored that season. He would have been forgiven though if his mind had occasionally wandered northwards to Dens Park, Dundee, where his first love Celtic were facing a crisis which could have led to relegation. A defeat would have imperilled their status. As it happened, they beat Dundee 3–2, having been 1–2 down for a while in the second half, and thus saved themselves. The cynics said that it was all fixed, and Dundee certainly did not give the impression of wishing to relegate Celtic and thereby lose money, but it was a nervous day for anyone connected with Celtic at that time.

The teams that took to the field on 24 April 1948, and were presented to the shy and stammering King George VI, were as follows. Manchester United: Crompton; Aston and Carey; Anderson, Chilton and Cockburn; Delaney, Morris, Rowley, Pearson and Mitten. Blackpool: Robinson; Shimwell and Crosland; Johnston, Hayward and Kelly; Matthews, Dick, Munro, Mortensen and Rickett. The referee was Mr Barrick of Northampton.

This Cup Final is frequently recalled as being the one with the most skilful football and the most chivalrous behaviour. Blackpool played in their tangerine strip and Manchester United in their change strip of blue.

At half-time it was 2–1 to Blackpool and hopes were high among Blackpool fans, and the many lovers of Stanley Matthews, that the 'wizard of the dribble' would get a Cup medal. Indeed, he had taken the free-kick which led to their second goal, although the final touch had been applied by Stan Mortensen, who was also a renowned dribbler. Blackpool's first goal was a penalty kick and Jack Rowley had scored United's goal after a defensive mix-up.

The second half saw a prolonged battle for supremacy, but gradually United gained the upper hand. In a purple spell between the 70th and 85th minute, Rowley headed home a free-kick from Morris, Pearson took a pass from Anderson to put United ahead and Anderson scored again after a quick one-two with Kelly to put United beyond reach.

Delaney, as in the 1937 Scottish Cup Final, had not stood out as being better than any of the rest of the team, but he had played his part in a magnificent day of football, and a magnificent day for Matt Busby and Manchester United. Indeed, it is the day that is often considered by Old Trafford historians to be the birth of Manchester United as a great power in the land.

The next few days passed like a dream for Jimmy as the team travelled back to Manchester, showing the Cup to delighted fans, and Delaney himself showed the medals to his family and friends, particularly his eight-year-old son, Pat. For all his love of Celtic, he would probably consider this to be the greatest single day of his life. 'The atmosphere's all different there, you understand...' he said in an interview with Archie McPherson years later.

Meanwhile, back home in Scotland, Celtic fans, although relieved at escaping relegation, cast envious glances at the teams who had won the Scottish honours – Rangers, East Fife and Hibernian – and cursed those who had allowed the mighty Jimmy Delaney to go. If he had been allowed to go because he was too old in 1946, how did he win an English Cup medal two years later?

There were two big sporting events in Britain in 1948. One was the Ashes series in which Australia, under the captaincy of Don Bradman for the last time, beat England comprehensively, and the other was the Olympic Games held in London for the second time. The organisers did a great job to produce the Olympics at such short notice and in such circumstances (it was claimed that the athletes brought their own sandwiches!), and the London audiences thrilled to the exploits of the Dutch housewife Fanny Blankers-Koen. The Olympics were widely broadcast on radio and even on television, although hardly anyone possessed a television set in 1948. Unforgivingly, and perhaps vindictively, the authorities did not invite the Germans to take part. Elsewhere, the National Health Service and the state of Israel were born.

The following football season was another good one for Manchester United, although ultimately disappointing in terms of winning honours. There was the inevitable feeling of anticlimax. For the third year in a row they finished second in the League, this time behind surprise winners Portsmouth, and they reached the semi-final of the English Cup. The team remained substantially the same as the previous year, although Johnny Morris was transferred to Derby County in early 1949 after a none-too-subtle disagreement with Matt Busby.

Delaney had another good season although he was intermittently troubled with injury. Yet the general play of the team was not quite as good as the previous season, for no more sinister reason than that all the players were now that bit older – Delaney, for example, was now 34. But he was fit. His enthusiasm for training was legendary and even on Sundays, when there was no official training, he would often be seen doing a little run round the area of his house after morning Mass.

Rigidly non-smoking (in the days when many football players were seen to smoke and even to endorse tobacco products) and virtually teetotal, Jimmy reaped the benefits of his lifestyle in the speed which he still possessed and the stamina which allowed that apparently slight figure to last 90 minutes on the most strength-sapping of pitches. His horrendously broken arm was a thing of the past (it was now a decade ago that it had happened, but it had troubled him now and again even after he resumed playing), apart from the psychological effect of the fear that it might happen again. But Jimmy always thought that the mind had to be trained in the same way as the body.

Finishing second in the League is of course no failure, but the position was not quite as good as it looked. It owed a great deal to a late surge in which United won four games in a row, including a victory over champions Portsmouth on the last day of the season, when Portsmouth were clearly in celebratory mode. If United had played as well as that throughout the season, the championship would have been theirs, but there were times, notably in the autumn and in the early spring, when form was less than totally satisfactory for championship aspirants.

The highlights of the League season included a 6–0 win over Preston North End at Deepdale at the end of October, but the best single game was at Maine Road against the previous year's defeated Cup finalists, Blackpool, when United lost 3–4. Delaney had a very good game that day and scored one of his four goals that season. The turn of the year saw United at their best with two very good 2–0 wins over Liverpool and Arsenal, but the transfer of Johnny Morris seemed to unsettle the side for a while and form suffered.

Although the team was not at its best, the performances of Delaney were consistently impressive, and he had a few hopes that he might yet earn himself a recall to the Scotland side. It is often felt that a winger can be 'read' as he gets older, that is the defender can work out in which direction he is to turn. In Delaney's case, though, this was not so. He could still shuffle, dummy, feint and glide past defenders in a way which perpetually delighted the fans.

The 1949 Cup campaign was a great deal less interesting than that of the previous year. United, for one thing, had a far easier passage than had been the case in 1948, starting off with a 6–0 beating of Bournemouth. This was followed by a prolonged struggle to get the better of Bradford Park Avenue, which took three games (Delaney missing two of them because of a leg injury). In the fifth round, Jack Rowley scored five against Yeovil Town and then there was an unimpressive 1–0 win over Hull City before the first really difficult team came their way in the shape of Wolves in the semi-final.

The first game was played on 26 March 1949 at Hillsborough and was a 1–1 draw, with Charlie Mitten scoring for United. Next week, however, saw Wolves win 1–0 at Goodison Park. Thus there was no Wembley Cup Final for Delaney this year. He would have cast a covetous eye at Wembley as well on 9 April, as United were drawing 1–1 with Chelsea, for Scotland were having a wonderful day beating England 3–1. But Delaney, a patriotic Scotsman and not given to jealousy, was genuinely delighted for the man who had his place, Willie Waddell of Rangers, and indeed for the rest of the Scotsmen.

It was a sobering, but still satisfactory season for Delaney and Manchester United. Importantly for the club, the financial side of things had improved and the club would be able to move back into their Old Trafford ground from the start of the following season. Busby had now established himself as a fine manager, and had declined offers to leave United to manage Tottenham Hotspur and, bizarrely, the national side of Italy. Being runners-up in the League Championship for three years in a row was a success in England: it would not have been considered so in Scotland.

Delaney would have one more complete season in England before he returned to Scotland. At long last he played a home game on 24 August 1949 when 41,748 saw Manchester United beat Bolton Wanderers 3–0 at Old Trafford. Old Trafford was like the cities of Cologne and Coventry in that it emerged from its World War Two battering in a better shape than it had been before. Although it was nothing like the fine stadium that it is in the 21st century, it was acknowledged as being noticeably ahead of other grounds at the time for spectator comforts, and also a mighty sight better than what it had been like before the *Luftwaffe* had done it an unwitting good turn.

Delaney played well in the Bolton game. Indeed, United were off to a bright start, raising all sorts of hopes that after three years of finishing second, this might at last be the year in which they lifted the Championship. By the beginning of September, when United defeated rivals City 2–1 in the first Old Trafford derby for many years, United had played five games and won four of them. But this was followed by a succession of draws and defeats in October and a couple of other defeats in December, which seemed to knock them out of contention.

Briefly in March a spectacular 7–0 thrashing of Aston Villa raised hopes again, but form went out the window in April as the postponed games were being played off and Manchester United ended up fourth. Yet they were only three points behind winners Portsmouth, in what had been a very open championship. Had the crucial game against Portsmouth at Old Trafford on 15 April gone the other way, life might have been totally different.

There were increasing signs from Delaney that he was now finding the pace in this League to be a little on the tough side, as was likely to happen to a 35-year-old. On occasion he lacked not the pace, but the actual turn of speed that used to be so successful at catching defenders off guard. Delaney in fact played in every one of the 42 League games, and several times he appeared to be carrying an injury, when wiser counsel might have suggested a rest. But Busby retained total faith in him, as did the Old Trafford support.

For a considerable part of the season, Delaney had alongside him at inside-right another ex-Celtic player by the name of Tommy Bogan. Tommy had played the first two post-war seasons with Celtic, but had never really lived up to expectations, nor had he ever given the impression of being totally happy. After a season at Preston, Busby had picked him up to replace Johnny Morris, but Bogan was a little short of that ability. He was an earnest player, but never of the standard required by a team that expected to be challenging for honours. However, the tendency for Bogan to follow Delaney around would continue when he returned to Scotland.

The English Cup once again produced its excitement and its pain. Weymouth were competently despatched, then there was a struggle to beat Watford at Vicarage Road, before United found themselves drawn against Portsmouth, last year's Championship winners, and fated to do the same in the 1949–50 season. The game on 11 February at Old Trafford before 53,688 supporters was an absolute thriller on heavy ground which ended up 3–3. The following midweek at Portsmouth, in front of an astonishing crowd of 49,962 (including an amazing number of fans who had travelled down from the north on a Wednesday afternoon), Jimmy Delaney put United on their way to a 3–1 win with a fine goal.

The Cup run came to a halt at Stamford Bridge on 4 March in the fifth round before another massive crowd of 70,362. Northern teams do not always do well in London and, on this occasion, it was simply the case that United froze and that Chelsea played better. The trains back to Manchester that evening were silent places, for there had been a genuine belief that this could again be United's year. Arsenal ended up as the winners of the English Cup in 1950, beating Liverpool 2–0.

On the broader front, two significant things happened. One was the General Election of 23 February 1950, when the Labour Government retained power, albeit with a hugely reduced majority. The other was the outbreak in June 1950 of the Korean War, when the Communist government of North Korea invaded the South with little moral justification other than a desire to unite the country. The United Nations immediately authorised the use of force and the US and Great Britain were very much involved, while the Soviet Union and China backed up the North. It was one of the times when the Cold War turned very hot indeed.

On 3 September 1950, Jimmy Delaney was 36. Unfortunately, he celebrated his birthday while he was out of the team injured. He had played in the first three games of the season: a 1–0 win over Fulham, followed by defeats to Liverpool and Bolton Wanderers. He was injured in the third game and was now very aware that an injury was taking much longer to heal. He missed four games before returning on 13 September.

Delaney had been very happy at Manchester United, and his wife Annie more so. They had plenty of friends and being Scottish in Manchester was not exactly living in an alien land. But Jimmy began to feel that his career might be coming to an end and began to pine for home. He wanted to return to Scotland. He would of course have loved to put on the green-and-white jersey of Celtic once again, but no approach was ever made from his erstwhile teammate Jimmy McGrory. Yet he felt that he might still be of some use to a Scottish team. He had done well with Manchester United and with Matt Busby, but he felt that getting out when he was winning might be no bad a thing.

The fine forward line of 1948 was beginning to break up. Morris had departed in 1949 and then left-winger Charlie Mitten amazed everyone by going to play in Colombia. Busby in any case made no secret of the fact that he wanted to build another team with the emphasis on youth – they would eventually be called the 'Busby Babes' – and possibly Delaney felt that it was a good idea to go before he was pushed. It is always a good idea to have people asking 'Why?' before they ask 'Why not?'

The team's form was inconsistent after Delaney returned. An excellent 4–1 win over Everton had to be balanced with a 0–3 loss to Arsenal at Highbury, and it was beginning to appear that yet again this would not be United's year. Delaney was disappointed in his own form and it did not help that he was unsettled and unsure of his future.

In football, as in every walk of life, there is a network of information passed on to people in the game, sometimes by direct contact, sometimes by the agency of a newspaper reporter. The fact that Delaney was becoming more and more unsettled at Old Trafford began to be hinted at in the press and astute managers would get their tips from reliable sources. Somehow or other, David Halliday of Aberdeen became aware of Delaney and contacts were made.

Busby considered the situation. He did not like the idea of losing Jimmy, whom he always looked upon as a friend, but on the other hand, Jimmy was not getting any younger and Aberdeen were offering £3,500. Jimmy also thought about the offer. Aberdeen was in Scotland, but still far from his Lanarkshire home. Aberdeen though was a fine city, mercifully free from the sectarian nonsense that befouled West Central Scotland, and Halliday was persuasive. Indeed, Aberdeen were a fine team, consistently doing well in the League. They had won the Scottish Cup in 1947, had a large support and were offering a wage which was not that much less than Manchester United were offering him.

Jimmy decided to go north. His last game for Manchester United was a 0–1 defeat by Chelsea at Stamford Bridge on 11 November 1950. His departure was looked upon as inevitable, but very sad as well, by the thousands of Mancunians whose post-war life had been brightened by Jimmy Delaney. Matt Busby would say that Delaney was 'just about one of the best signings that any football manager could desire. He was one of the main reasons for the emergence of Manchester United as the most successful team in post-war football. Not a bad effort considering the deal cost United no more than £500.' Busby's statement of 'no more than £500' is considerably at odds with the normally quoted £4,000, but Matt would have his own agenda in claiming he got Jimmy on the cheap.

Another tribute comes from Johnny Carey, who said that whenever he wanted a breather he would work the ball up the right-wing and give the ball to Delaney. 'That done, I could take a rest for five minutes while "Baldie" waltzed round the place for a time.' Jock Stein would frequently urge his Lisbon Lions to use Jimmy Johnstone for a similar purpose.

Chapter 7

Aberdeen and Falkirk
1950–1954

ABERDEEN, the Granite City, is little given to enthusiasm or hysteria about football. Football was late arriving in the city and the current Aberdeen Football Club was founded in 1903, a lot later than most teams. In addition, there had never been any great Irish influx into Aberdeen, which meant that, unlike Glasgow and to a lesser extent Edinburgh and Dundee, there was no great Catholic-Protestant divide.

Aberdeen Football Club has possibly suffered as a result of its isolation, and also because of distance as the nearest rival was Dundee, some 60 miles away. On the other hand, the club does have the undivided love and affection of the whole city, although it is an affection that lacks passion. There is a comparative lack of fervour associated with football and the city of Aberdeen. Jokes are made about sweet papers rustling when the team are doing well and the crowd are getting excited.

Delaney had played against Aberdeen with Celtic, notably in the 1937 Scottish Cup Final. Since then a great deal of water had flowed under the bridge. Aberdeen had won the Scottish Cup themselves in the first post-war tournament of 1947 and they had changed their colours from black and gold to red. However, they still awaited their first League Championship.

It was not that they had been without great players in the past – Jock Hutton, Donald Coleman, Frank Hill, Willie Mills and Matt Armstrong to name but a few – and they had had fine managers in Jimmy Philip and Paddy Travers. But their very distance from everyone else meant that they always felt at a disadvantage while travelling to Glasgow, which they had to do about four or five times per season. The huge following for the black and golds for the 1937 Scottish Cup Final had taken everyone by surprise, but it did show the great, if possibly latent, interest there was in football in the city.

Everything to do with football does tend to be on a lower key in Aberdeen than elsewhere, but even so the front page of the *Aberdeen Press and Journal* on Thursday 16 November 1950 contained a small note about the signing of Jimmy Delaney. Norman McDonald, the journalist of the *Press and Journal*, had one of those days when he clearly knew that everyone in the city would be reading him. With page four virtually to himself, he expatiates at length about Jimmy's career with Celtic, Scotland and Manchester United and gives a virtual blow-by-blow account of the transfer negotiations.

The deal had been a well-kept secret but, after many telephone conversations, manager Davie Halliday slipped away in conditions of the greatest secrecy on an early morning train from Aberdeen to Manchester on Tuesday 14 November. He telephoned news of the successful negotiations on the Wednesday. Delaney arrived on the Friday and was in the team for the visit of Falkirk on 18 November 1950.

The team for Delaney's Aberdeen debut was: Martin; Emery and McKenna; Anderson, Young and Harris; Delaney, Yorston, Hamilton, Baird and Pearson. The very thought of Jimmy Delaney in the team motivated more people than normal to trek along King Street and the large crowd of around 15,000 saw Aberdeen win comfortably 5–1 with Delaney laying on a goal in the opening minute and being involved in the build-up for another two. Norman McDonald was jubilant: 'There is still a lot of artistry about Jimmy Delaney. The Pittodrie club seem to have done a good stroke of business.'

Delaney played less well in his next game against the excellent Raith Rovers at Stark's Park, Kirkcaldy, when 'he flashed into the picture once or twice in the second half, but generally McNaught had him under close surveillance' in a 1–0 victory for the home side. It would take time for him to adjust to the new conditions. His family moved to Aberdeen in late 1950 and the Delaneys settled in Cairnfield Place, Aberdeen, in a flat supplied by the club. Their next-door neighbour would be George Hamilton, Aberdeen's famous inside-forward, who had won the Scottish Cup with them in 1947 and who would eventually win five caps for Scotland. He had also played alongside Delaney in the 1946 Victory International. Very soon, Delaney would justify his £3,500 price tag in the excellent forward line of Delaney, Yorston, Hamilton, Baird and Pearson.

December 1950 saw two things dominating the headlines in the *Press and Journal*. One was the Korean War, with its unacceptably high casualty levels. This war, which had broken out suddenly on 25 June 1950, had now been in progress for six months and the United Nations troops were not enjoying consistent success. The going was tough in difficult conditions for western soldiers. The war did not enjoy universal support in Great Britain and there was always the ever-present threat of another atomic bomb.

The other event that dominated the Aberdeen headlines was the happier one of the Dons' charge for the Championship. Clearly, with Delaney on one wing and Tommy Pearson on the other, they were going to take some stopping. The weather was bad, but the Dons always managed to get their games played with a 2–0 win over Hearts and 4–2 over Motherwell. Then, on a particularly difficult pitch at Cappielow in Greenock on 16 December, the Dons, playing in rubber soles, scraped it over Morton. James Forbes, deputising for Norman McDonald in the *Press and Journal*, said that the 'rubber shod Aberdeen quintette could pick their way forward slickly and with fast open passes. Delaney never shirked the hefty tackling of left flank defenders.' Aberdeen won the game 2–1 to put them into serious contention at the top of the League.

The Dons unaccountably drew their next two games. There was a 1–1 draw against Airdrie at Pittodrie a couple of days before Christmas, a performance so dire as to induce barracking (a sad but by no means uncommon Aberdeen phenomenon), and a goalless draw at East Fife on 30 December. However, the other teams were also having their moments of weakness and when Aberdeen beat Dundee 1–0 at Pittodrie in front of a 30,000 all-ticket crowd at Pittodrie on New Year's Day, Aberdeen were briefly top of the League. Delaney won a corner late in the game. He took the corner himself, the ball 'danced in the goalmouth for a few seconds' and George Hamilton fired home to give the Dons pole position.

It was short-lived. The following day, they went to Easter Road and collapsed 2–6 to the Hibernian team which would win the League that year. In a metaphor appropriate to the Cold War times, the *Press and Journal* enthuses about the 'atomic football' of Hibernian, even though Delaney 'twinkled occasionally'. On Saturday 6 January, a timid performance earned them a draw with St Mirren at home – and the wrath once again of their own supporters and the *Press and Journal*.

On 13 January 1951, 60,000 were at Parkhead. Games between Celtic and Aberdeen normally attracted big crowds in those days, for Aberdeen had a deserved reputation for playing good football. In addition, there was a long tradition of Celtic and Aberdeen fans getting on well together when Celtic went up north. This match would have an additional element. It would be the Celtic crowd's first chance to see Delaney in action since his return to Scotland. Delaney was made captain for the day in a fine theatrical gesture by Davie Halliday and he was greeted with genuine enthusiasm and love by the crowd who used to adore him. As he took up his position on the right-wing in front of the Jungle the applause intensified. When Alec Rollo tackled him heavily, the Celtic player was booed heartily by his own supporters. They would react in a similar way to Frank Meechan a few years later when Delaney was with Falkirk. This was no way deal with as illustrious a Celt as Jimmy Delaney!

The game was a good one, with the teams locked at 2–2; Aberdeen having equalised Celtic's two early strikes. It was then that Celtic supporters were put to one of their sternest tests. Delaney picked up a pass from George Hamilton and scored a goal to put Aberdeen 3–2 up. It was not without a touch of luck, as it took a deflection off Jimmy Mallan. The crowd went silent, as home crowds do when a goal is scored against their favourites. But then came the realisation that it was Jimmy Delaney who had scored the goal. A few fans began to applaud, then more, and finally the whole Parkhead crowd joined in what was possibly the loudest cheer ever for an opposition goal.

The Dons went on to win the game 4–3 and another win in Glasgow the following week, 2-0 against Clyde at Shawfield, where Delaney made a brilliant goal for Hamilton, put the Dons back into title contention. Sadly, a defeat from Rangers at Pittodrie, a draw at Brockville (although Delaney scored a late goal which was mysteriously disallowed) and a home defeat by Raith Rovers put paid to title ambitions.

Injuries to Alec Young, Archie Baird and Tommy Pearson were a factor in this fall from grace, but there was still the Scottish Cup. Inverness Caledonian provided few problems in the first round before the Dons really turned it on to defeat Third Lanark 4–0 at Pittodrie on 10 February. All the forwards were in a 'rollicking mood' and Norman McDonald was once again going into overdrive in the *Press and Journal* about Aberdeen's two wingers. 'Pearson is the subtle and thoughtful ball player. Delaney is the speedy, direct and dashing type.'

This fine win over Third Lanark set Aberdeen up with the game of the season in the quarter-final; a trip to Celtic Park. A crowd of 75,000 appeared there, with Aberdeen supporters somewhat under-represented. The *Press and Journal* said 200 (presumably it meant 2,000), but even so that is a very small proportion of 75,000. Two days before the game, Davie Halliday had signed another ex-Celt and a comrade-in-arms of Jimmy Delaney in his Manchester United days. This was Tommy Bogan, whom Delaney had presumably recommended. For this match, Tommy would play in the centre to replace the injured George Hamilton.

For one reason or another, Aberdeen simply collapsed against a much-improved Celtic team and were lucky to get off with a 0–3 defeat. Delaney played 'with any amount of dash, but little subtlety' and in desperation was even tried in the centre at half-time in a tacit admission that Tommy Bogan was struggling. It was a bitter blow for Aberdeen, especially as their title challenge was now evaporating in front of their eyes. They had hoped to do better in the Cup: having won the trophy in 1947, they felt they could do it again.

It was some 10 days after this defeat that the rumours began to circulate about Delaney asking for a transfer. There was indeed some substance to this story, but Delaney himself stated that reports of him having asked for a transfer were 'exaggerated'. The problem was that he and his family were finding it difficult to settle in Aberdeen, a city with a totally different culture from that which they had been used to in Lanarkshire and Manchester. There was no real problem with the flat in Cairnfield Place: it was simply that he would prefer to live closer to his extended family in the west of Scotland. In addition, he knew very well that the life of a professional footballer is by nature a fickle one, and that it would be folly at his age to think of his stay in Aberdeen as a permanent or long-term one. He asked the club if he could live in Lanarkshire, train with someone in the west of Scotland (Celtic presumably) and travel to Aberdeen for home games.

The *Press and Journal* of Tuesday 20 March is interesting. It reveals, for example, that Delaney had stayed with his family in Cleland after the game against Motherwell at Fir Park on Saturday night instead of coming back to Aberdeen. There is also a picture of him with training gear coming out of 'Parkhead'. But does it really mean Parkhead? Was it simply an understandable Freudian slip for Pittodrie, which the proofreader had not noticed? Or had Delaney already been training at Parkhead? (The picture itself gives no clear indication which ground is being referred to.)

The idea of a player training at a ground other than that of his employers was not unheard of in the early 1950s. Housing was not as available as it is now. Later in the year, Tommy Bogan would make a similar request. No one seemed seriously to suggest that Delaney would be a 'spy' and pass on Aberdeen's secrets to Celtic, and Delaney could certainly be relied upon to train conscientiously, for he remained an obsessive fanatic in that respect all his life. However, Aberdeen's directors insisted that Delaney and others stayed within a reasonable distance of Aberdeen – possibly Stonehaven or Banchory, for example, if he did not like the city of Aberdeen itself.

Delaney was now backed into a corner and did indeed ask for a transfer, but was distinctly half-hearted about it and possibly accepted that Aberdeen had a point. In any case, perhaps, one had to give things time, and in the meantime, there was no doubt that he would remain fiercely committed to the Dons. No enquiry for his services seems to have come from anyone else at this stage, although many of the green and white persuasion remained optimistic that, even at this late stage of his career, the call might yet go out from down Parkhead way.

Aberdeen's season now fizzled out. Delaney scored a good goal against Morton on 31 March and made another, and then in the Pittodrie rain against East Fife on 7 April, as the team went down 1–2, Delaney scored what looked like a valid equaliser, but found it chalked off. The final two games against Hearts and Third Lanark were 'listless and uninspiring' defeats, but several things would have cheered up the Delaney family in April 1951. Jimmy was retained by Aberdeen, Scotland beat England 3–2 at Wembley and Celtic won the Scottish Cup for the first time since Delaney's medal in 1937 by beating Motherwell 1–0.

As the city of Aberdeen settled down to its summer of cricket – crowds at Mannofield in the late 1940s and early 1950s were often not far short of those at Pittodrie – Jimmy seems to have decided that he would give it another go with Aberdeen. He was certainly much loved by the support, whose adulation of him was possibly less effusive and obvious than it had been at Celtic and Manchester United, but no less real. Yet he would be 37 in September. It did not take a genius to work out that the clock was ticking, certainly for football at the top level.

When the season started on 11 August 1951, Delaney was fit and ready and running about like a man 15 years younger. Sadly, he did not look like that age, for no one could disguise his bald head, which was often the subject of basically kind comments by the support. A 'loon' (boy) for example chatting up a 'quine' (girl) would try to be 'as smooth as Delaney's heid' rather than the more vulgar 'baby's bottom'.

The League Cup section was a disaster for Aberdeen. The Dons had done tolerably well in this tournament in the past, winning it in the unofficial season of 1945–46 and getting to the final in 1946–47, but this year they lost four games and had only one memorable night. This was Wednesday 29 August when Delaney, playing in the centre-forward position, destroyed Rangers at Pittodrie by scoring the first goal with a 'cute flick from the outside of his left foot' and set up Hay for the second. The forward line that evening was Bogan, Yorston, Delaney, Hay and Hather, and Delaney led the line 'with dash and the careless abandon of youth'.

The word 'mercurial' was frequently applied to the Dons by the ever-faithful Norman McDonald of the *Press and Journal* that autumn. Delaney scored from the centre-forward spot against St Mirren, then he was injured in the face in a 4–4 thriller with Hibernian but recovered promptly. Next, in a heartening 3–1 win against rivals Dundee, 'there was no more whole hearted player than Delaney'. However, he injured his knee in that game, missed the next one and played the game after that when not fully fit. This was a 1–4 home defeat against Airdrie which the *Press and Journal* freely described as 'awful' and noted sadly that the 'boo boys' were back in strength.

But it was not all bad for Delaney. In the midweek after the defeat of Dundee on 27 September 1951, Annie produced a baby boy. This was John, a younger brother to Pat and Kathleen.

Delaney is described as 'hard running' in an otherwise punchless 2–1 victory against Queen of the South at Palmerston Park in mid-October and he scored the fourth goal in a 4–2 win over Partick Thistle in November. The following week, on 17 November, against Stirling Albion at Annfield, Delaney inspired the Dons to a 4–0 victory and was described as being in a 'most dashing mood' and the 'liveliest of the five forwards'.

Meanwhile, things had changed in Britain. The Labour Government had come to an end on 26 October 1951 when Winston Churchill and the Conservative Party won the General Election with a small majority. Although more people voted Labour, the Tories won more seats. It would be to Churchill's credit that he would do nothing to dismantle Labour's National Health Service or welfare state, but in other areas there would be changes.

Things were changing in Scottish football as well. The *Press and Journal* reported a strange occurrence on 7 November 1951 at Ochilview Park, Stenhousemuir, when the local team lost a friendly 5–3 to Hibernian in what was claimed to be Scotland's first-ever match under floodlights. This was not quite true, as Celtic and Clyde had experimented with primitive floodlights as early as the 1890s, but nothing had come of them. Even in faraway Aberdeen people were impressed, but questions were raised about whether it could ever catch on.

Delaney's move away from Aberdeen came quickly. Although some of the fans had begun to hope that he would stay for years, the more realistic of them accepted that age and injuries were beginning to be a problem at Division A level. They would not therefore have been taken totally by surprise by the news on 5 December that he was moving to Falkirk in Division B. Contacts had obviously been going on behind the scenes for some time and it was no secret that Jimmy liked West Central Scotland, but for most of the city it was a disappointment. 'We wish him well' said the *Press and Journal* laconically, and commented little more about him in the future.

The *Falkirk Herald*, on the other hand, was jubilant on 8 December 1951 with the news that Jimmy Delaney was coming to town. It was claimed that £4,000 changed hands for Delaney – the 'exact amount that Manchester United gave Celtic in 1946' – and Delaney, 'so unhappy at Aberdeen that he asked for a transfer after four months', according to the writer of the *Falkirk Herald*, would have been very willing to go to England. Hull City in particular were very interested in him, but he was prevented by a regulation from returning to England as he had already received some money from the Provident Fund when he left Manchester United. All these and many more stories reveal that the football correspondent of the *Falkirk Herald* (who does not give his name) was a very excited man indeed.

The facts of the case do not necessarily agree with the euphoria of the *Falkirk Herald*. The correspondent's estimate of the transfer fee is possibly suspect and the real reason for Delaney's move was nothing other than a feeling that his career was coming to an end at the high level of Division A. There was also a desire to move back closer to home in Cleland, as well as his close friendship and high regard for Falkirk's manager, Bob Shankly, the brother of Bill Shankly, who would in later years do so much for Liverpool. Bob himself would be the manager of Dundee when they won the League Championship in 1962.

Shankly possibly envisaged Delaney as a mentor figure for developing youngsters such as Angus Plumb. Jimmy was already famous for his ability to get on with youngsters, for his encouragement of them and particularly for his example in his total (and sometimes obsessive) dedication to fitness and his never-say-die attitude to which youngsters like Plumb would respond. A match was never lost, according to Jimmy, until the referee blew his final whistle. Such a man would make a fine coach, as well as a good player, reckoned Shankly.

Falkirk were in need of some pre-Christmas cheer that December. They were a team with a praiseworthy if not entirely glorious past. They had won the Scottish Cup in 1913 and had been second to Maley's Celtic in the Scottish League in 1908 and 1910. In recent years they had reached the final of the Scottish League Cup in 1947. However, they were relegated to Division B in summer 1951, a fate that they had taken some time to come to terms with. Falkirk and Clyde (with whom they had been relegated) were at the top of the League fighting off the challenges of Kilmarnock and Dundee United, but both the club and their fans were missing the big occasions when Celtic and Rangers came to town – and the big money that they brought with them. The purchase of Jimmy Delaney, perhaps even on a short-term basis, was obviously designed to bring the Bairns (as Falkirk inhabitants were known) back among the big boys.

Recalling that they had enjoyed the services of a previous ex-Celt in Patsy Gallacher in the late 1920s, the fans of the Bairns were clearly looking forward to seeing Jimmy Delaney. The *Falkirk Herald* said that he was 'a personality' and hoped that he would make them more than 'just ordinary'. He was perfectly fit, in spite of his 37 years and bald head which made him look even older, and went straight into the team, which was: Scott; McDonald and McPhee; Gallagher, Wilson and McKenzie; Delaney, Dunlop, Plumb, Wilson and Brown.

Delaney's debut game was at Station Park, Forfar, on 8 December 1951. This was a boost to the ailing finances of the small Angus team as well, and the crowd reached almost 2,500 – a quarter of the town's population. A considerable number of the fans chose to stand beside where Falkirk's right-wing was and then moved round to the equivalent place on the other side of the pitch at half-time. This gave them the best view of the tricks of Delaney, whose very name still inspired such awe.

Delaney was closely marked by Forfar's defenders, but still played well enough to convince the man from the *Falkirk Herald* that he remained a 'grand winger'. Falkirk were two up at one point, but as Delaney and others tired on the heavy December ground, Forfar pulled two back. Delaney was put into the centre in an attempt to score the winner, but the game finished 2–2. It remains one of the few times in Forfar Athletic's history that an opponent was cheered as he left the field!

It is an odd coincidence that 8 December 1951 was also the debut for Celtic (against St Mirren at Parkhead) of a man who had played for Albion Rovers against Delaney and whose career was now being resurrected after a none-too-successful spell in Wales. He and Delaney would always have a strong mutual admiration, although their paths had seldom crossed. He was, of course, Jock Stein.

The following week saw Kilmarnock come to Falkirk's home ground of Brockville. The *Herald* was not too impressed with Delaney's performance in the 3–3 draw. He 'helped to pull the game out of the fire with a timely goal but did nothing for anyone to get ecstatic about'. On 22 December it was dark and miserable when the next match kicked off at 2pm. Indeed, it was dark and miserable for Delaney, who was injured early in the game but soldiered on, and might, if fitter, have won the day for Falkirk against Dumbarton. The crowd was a creditable one of about 5,000.

Delaney's injury kept him out of the New Year fixtures, but no doubt it gave him a good opportunity to settle himself and his family in Grangemouth, where they would stay for the duration of his Falkirk years. On 19 January 1952, Delaney played on the left wing against Hamilton, but he is not mentioned in the report, an indication that his role was distinctly ordinary. He missed the next game before playing in both Cup games against local rivals Stirling Albion.

Black armbands, a minute's silence and genuine grief among the crowd marked the first game at Brockville on 9 February. This was to commemorate the passing of King George VI who had died in midweek. Delaney had been introduced to the King at Wembley in 1948 and had been impressed by the man's genuine love of football. Sadly, the King's stammer had prevented him communicating too much, but Delaney had a tremendous respect for the man who had done so much for his country in difficult, and even heroic, times.

Delaney scored a penalty in the first game against Stirling Albion and then the *Falkirk Herald* claimed that Delaney's 'drive' won the day in the replay at Annfield on Wednesday 13 February – Delaney's drive from 10 yards gave Falkirk the equaliser and then it was his 'drive and enthusiasm' which won the game, as Falkirk snatched their late winner.

The next few games saw Delaney at inside-right and late February was a very successful time for both Falkirk and Jimmy. The *Herald* damned with faint praise about a 5–1 win against Arbroath when it said that Delaney had 'a really serviceable game', while the *Dundee Courier* said he was 'outstanding'. But when Falkirk reached the quarter-final of the Scottish Cup with a 3–1 win at Boghead over Dumbarton, the *Herald* pulled no punches and led with the headline: 'Delaney Inspired Cup Triumph'. Against St Johnstone he scored with a header. Clearly, Delaney was now doing what he had been brought in to do: namely to get Falkirk back into Division A.

Before promotion could be achieved there was the welcome diversion of the Scottish Cup on 8 March. The quarter-final draw had paired the Bairns with Third Lanark, a Glasgow team which went out of business in 1967, but who in 1952 were still a respectable Division A outfit. Indeed, the 'Hi Hi His' (as they were called) had put Celtic out of the Scottish Cup in January. Possibly about 3,000 Bairns travelled to Cathkin Park (not far from Hampden) to see this game, but they returned heartbroken as Falkirk went down 0–1. Delaney, still at inside-right, played well, but missed a chance himself as did several of the other forwards.

The cliché that the team could now concentrate on the League now became true. In truth, Falkirk did not have a great side, but they were good enough for promotion, especially with the old schemer Jimmy Delaney on board. A 1–0 win at Alloa was acceptable, but then Delaney put Falkirk within a whisker of promotion with a 6–0 thumping of Forfar at Brockville. A win over Kilmarnock on 22 March would have earned promotion in second spot, but the team lost 1–2 at Rugby Park. The team bus, however, was cheered by the news on the radio that they were indeed back in Division A, as Dundee United had gone down to Dumbarton.

This was definitely promotion via the backdoor and the *Falkirk Herald* was none too enthusiastic, pointing out that the squad would have to be strengthened for Division A. The newspaper also asked the pertinent question of whether Delaney would have the ability to stand up to the pace of Division A, bearing in mind that he had left the top division earlier in the season because he found the pace too much. Delaney would have read that, for he was always very interested in what the press said about him, and determined that, come what might the following season, he would be fit.

Falkirk still had a chance of actually winning Division B, a chance greatly increased on 5 April when they beat fellow promotion-winners Clyde 2–1. It was a foul day with wind and rain, but Delaney 'the schemer' (seemingly a favourite term of the *Falkirk Herald*) was back on the right wing instead of at inside-right and set up a great goal for centre-forward Brown in the last minute. It was a 'grand finish to a grand game', although rejoicing was somewhat muted at the end with the doleful tidings from the radio that England had beaten Scotland 2–1 at Hampden.

Clyde had now finished their programme and had 44 points. Falkirk had two games to play with 41 points. Two points were allowed for a win, so Falkirk could be Division B champions if they won their two games. Unaccountably, they went to Cowdenbeath on 12 April and lost 0–5. It was indeed inexplicable, but showed up very clearly the manifest weaknesses of this team, for whom 'Delaney was the one forward who looked as if he could score'. The League programme finished on the following Monday with a 3–2 win over Dundee United and Delaney playing at right-half.

Delaney was obviously retained for the following season and was therefore delighted at his age (he would soon be 38) to get another tilt at Celtic, Rangers and particularly Aberdeen, with whom perhaps he felt that he had a more recent point to prove. He resolved to train hard and to enjoy his football. He even finished the season on a high note when, while playing at inside-left in both legs of the Stirlingshire Cup Final, he won a medal, albeit a minor one. He was cheered at the end and he now had the feeling that his football career was far from finished.

Delaney and Falkirk were aware that 1952–53 would be hard. Survival in Division A was important for the long-term future of the club, as manager Bob Shankly kept pointing out. Falkirk would never really be able to compete with the big teams on a long-term basis (although East Fife were showing what could be done), and they would probably stay in the bottom half of the League along with Raith Rovers, Clyde, Queen of the South and other teams of that ilk. But they had a committed set of players, a hard core of support who were loyal and faithful – and they also had Jimmy Delaney.

Unfortunately, for a large part of the early section of the season, Jimmy was troubled yet again by injury. A disappointing defeat at Brockville against Queen of the South robbed the Bairns of their chance of progressing to the League Cup quarter-finals. In the first League game of the season Falkirk found themselves at Parkhead with Delaney on the left wing. He was given his usual warm and genuine reception from the fans, who still loved him and classified him as one of their own, but he sustained an injury near the end as Falkirk went down 3–5 in a high-scoring game. Delaney had in fact been influential in pulling things back to 3–3 after being 0–3 down and it was his injury which tipped the balance in favour of Celtic and allowed them to score two late goals through Charlie Tully and John McPhail.

His subsequent absence from the team coincided with a loss of form for the Bairns. The end of October saw only two points on the board and the team already heading, apparently inexorably, for relegation. He played in a 7–0 thrashing of a team called Deveronvale in an obscure competition called the Dewar Shield in early October, but was clearly not fit enough for Division A duty.

In the middle of October, Shankly signed Jock Weir, another ex-Celt, who was very much a utility player and could play all over the forward line. Clearly, Shankly was backing Weir's experience to save Falkirk. Delaney might have been fit to play against Rangers on 8 November, but Shankly shrewdly reckoned that they were likely to lose to Rangers anyway (they did as it turned out) and that it would be better to keep Delaney for Queen of the South on 15 November. 'Delaney shows the way' chortled the *Falkirk Herald* as the Bairns returned to winning ways by beating the Doonhamers 2–0 with Weir and Delaney scored the goals.

A shocking 2–7 thrashing at Pittodrie (where Jimmy was jeered by the less well-educated section of the home support) followed, but then Falkirk notched up another important victory against Clyde, 2–1 at the end of November. Delaney, now the captain, inspired the team, particularly young goalkeeper McFeat, who had a great game and was visibly overwhelmed at the end by the congratulations of his illustrious captain.

From then on, the team's form improved with wins over Raith Rovers, Partick Thistle, Third Lanark and Dundee to move the team out of the relegation zone. Delaney played most of these games and words like 'inspirational' and 'grand display' were used to describe his performances. A 1–1 draw against Airdrie on 17 January 1953, for example, saw Delaney 'forcing play from the right', and the *Falkirk Herald* is convinced that the Bairns should have had a draw against Celtic the week before Christmas. Sadly, right-half Jimmy Gallacher had been injured, and in those pre-substitute days, he was put on to the right wing. Delaney was thus compelled to take Gallacher's place in midfield, where his usefulness was minimised by the constant attention of Bobby Evans and Charlie Tully.

By the end of January, the town of Falkirk was breathing a little more easily as far as the Scottish League was concerned, but two other things were interesting them. The first was several more experiments in the new concept of floodlight football, which Jimmy liked the sound of but possibly felt, like others of his generation, that it would never catch on. The other was the Scottish Cup.

Falkirk found themselves playing at Blairmount Park, Newton Stewart, in the first round and they came very close to a major embarrassment in a 2–2 draw. The *Falkirk Herald* man was angry at the feckless attack but said, 'if anyone could be exempted from criticism it was certainly veteran Jimmy Delaney who tried valiantly to infuse the lifeless attack with a goalscoring urge'. It was Delaney who scored the two goals at Newton Stewart and it was also Delaney who 'improvised and foraged' for the attack as they won the replay 4–0 at Brockville.

The following week was a League game against Hibernian at Brockville. The conditions were atrocious and it was no disgrace to lose to the strong-going Hibernian, but what was more alarming was the sight of Jimmy limping off the field at the end holding his knee. Such was the ferocity of the wind and the rain that people questioned whether the game should have been played at all, for this was the day (30 January 1953) that 133 people were to lose their lives on the *Princess Victoria* as it sailed from Ireland to Scotland.

Delaney declared himself unfit for the game against Forfar in the next round of the Scottish Cup and reported for treatment at Falkirk infirmary for swelling behind his knee joint. In his absence, the team accounted for Forfar on 7 February but went down badly to St Mirren in the League on 14 February. Delaney was thankfully available for the next round of the Scottish Cup on 21 February. Indeed, he had been determined to make it, for the Scottish Cup draw had brought Celtic to Brockville.

It would be one of the most remarkable games of Delaney's career, even though he was not necessarily the most important player. The game was all-ticket with 23,100 the ground capacity. These tickets were sold within a matter of 24 hours of them going on sale. Celtic were unhappy at the price of the tickets and the small allocation given to Parkhead to sell and their Supporters' Association made a half-hearted effort to organise a boycott. It was a colossal failure as Celtic fans came to Falkirk in midweek to buy tickets after their meagre ration was sold out and the *Falkirk Herald* admits that there was 'more than the odd patch of green' in the crowd. The green would be handkerchiefs and rosettes as well as scarves, for in 1953 supporters' scarves were not yet universal – this would be a phenomenon of the late 1950s and early 1960s.

The shortage of tickets meant that there were many on the train from Glasgow and in the Celtic supporters' buses without them, but thousands were able to clamber over the wall at the Railway End of the ground. The result was that the ground was dangerously overcrowded in the pleasant spring sunshine. On occasion, the crowd spilled over onto the running track and the police had a hard task to shepherd them back. The crowd was closer to 28,000 than 23,000 in the opinion of the writer of the *Falkirk Herald*.

The game was delayed for crowd reasons but began dramatically when Delaney was fouled early on by Celtic's left-back, Frank Meechan. Meechan was spoken to by the referee and earned himself a booing from both sets of fans, especially the Celtic ones. Bringing a winger down was recognised as an essential part of a left-back's trade in the 1950s, but this was Jimmy Delaney. John McPhail was seen to apologise to Delaney on Meechan's behalf. The booing of Meechan continued throughout the first half, for everyone was aware that Delaney had just returned from injury.

Celtic soon had other problems. Falkirk went ahead when Jock Weir ran on to a bouncing ball which Jock Stein and goalkeeper John Bonnar left to each other, and then Delaney beat Meechan, sent over a great cross which found Campbell on the other wing, and Celtic were two down. The Celtic supporters were beginning to turn nasty as a beer bottle or two found its way on to the field. Things could have been even worse for Celtic when Delaney again reached the by-line and crossed, but this time Brown missed from a perfect position.

Half-time thus saw Falkirk two up and in high spirits. But the success was apparent rather than real, for Celtic would be bound to make some sort of a fightback, which their supporters were demanding. In addition, Delaney ('old twinkle toes' as the *Falkirk Herald* called him) was now tired because of his recent injury, the treatment from Meechan and general old age in a game which was played at a blistering pace.

Delaney was also fouled again brutally by Charlie Tully just at the start of the second half. In 1953, the habit at the start of the half was for the centre-forward to slip the ball to his inside-forward, who would then send it back to his defender, who would then either send the ball up the centre of the field or try to find one or other of his wingers. Falkirk would naturally try to find Delaney, but Tully read this move and took Delaney out of the play with a cynical bodycheck before the ball even reached him. It was not one of 'Cheeky Charlie's proudest moments.

A stricter referee might have taken strong action against Tully, perhaps even sent him off. History would have been different if he had done that, for it was Tully who now turned the game. Tully took a corner on the left at the Railway End of the ground early in the second half and scored direct. The crowd erupted and crush barriers buckled. Then, to general consternation, it was seen that the referee was signalling for the corner to be retaken, for the ball had not been properly in the arc. Tully gave the ball to the linesman to place for him, took the corner and scored direct again! This time the crush barriers collapsed and about 20 people were injured as the crowd rushed onto the field, partly to congratulate Tully but partly to escape the crush.

The referee would have been justified in abandoning the game, but after a lengthy delay in which the injured were removed and the crowd pushed back onto the terracing, the game continued. The spirit had now gone from Falkirk, some of whose players were genuinely upset and concerned at the injuries to some of the fans. It was no real surprise when Willie Fernie equalised and John McGrory won the game for Celtic. Falkirk's youngsters were bewildered by it all and, with Delaney limping on the wing, they lacked any real leadership to get back into the game.

Delaney of course was on good terms with all the Celtic players, even Meechan and Tully. His old friend Jimmy McGrory, now manager of Celtic, sought him out at the end and made a few apologetic noises about some of the rough tackles. He then enquired after Delaney, remarking how nice it was to see a 38-year-old playing better than some of the players who were about half his age. It had been an unfortunate game to end Falkirk's Cup run, but one which Delaney had been proud to be part of.

It would be a different story the following week when the team went to Ibrox to lose 0–4. Delaney, in spite of being barracked all game by those who were long on memory if short on education, played some 'intelligent football' but lacked any real support. He had also shone in a friendly on the Tuesday night of 25 February 1953 when Falkirk played their first floodlight game, a friendly with Carlisle which they won 5–2. There had been one or two bounce games before under lights, but this was the first real floodlight game at Brockville. Both Falkirk and Carlisle expressed themselves happy with the possibility of League and Cup games being played under the lights, the idea being that a Wednesday evening would surely attract a larger crowd than a Wednesday afternoon when most people were at work. Delaney was in his 'happiest mood' as the Bairns beat Carlisle 5–2.

All this could not disguise the fact that Falkirk were now, once again, in deep relegation trouble. Delaney scored in a 2–2 draw against Queen of the South at Palmerston, but the team really needed a few victories at this stage. When they lost to Dundee at Dens Park on 14 March, they found themselves at the bottom of the League with only 20 points from 25 games, and only five games left to save themselves. The only good news for Delaney at this point was that the injury to his knee seemed to have cleared up.

It was at this point that manager Bob Shankly called the players together to warn them of the dire consequences of relegation, namely the almost certainty of part-time football at best and the possibility of the cancellation of contracts at worst. Captain Delaney, although no great public speaker, added a few words of encouragement, made a few jokes about having to play against East Stirlingshire or Stenhousemuir next year, but then asked for a mighty effort to preserve the Division A status which they had worked so hard for the previous year. Playing in Division A also meant so much to their fans, who had shown no sign of deserting the colours, however poor recent performances had been.

It was Delaney himself who more or less saved Falkirk, both by his general play and by his inspiring leadership, particularly his ability to coax great performances out of ordinary players. On 21 March, Falkirk beat Clyde 4–1 at Shawfield, a game in which he scored and was 'at his sparking best throughout'. This was followed by a visit to Stark's Park, Kirkcaldy, on 28 March to play fellow strugglers Raith Rovers. The game saw Delaney 'lobbing over perfect crosses' and on two of these occasions, Falkirk's forwards took advantage. In early April an important win was realised at Brockville as his 'cool and studied' play was much in evidence as Falkirk beat Motherwell, the team who would eventually go down with Third Lanark.

Falkirk were now sixth from bottom, but it was still really tight, with Queen of the South, Aberdeen, Raith Rovers, Airdrie, Motherwell and Third Lanark all very close. Falkirk had no game scheduled for 11 April but played a friendly with Dundee United from Division B to keep in shape. Delaney enjoyed himself that day for he scored a hat-trick, but the bad news was that Raith Rovers had won and that Aberdeen had drawn.

It would all be settled on the weekend of Saturday 18 April and Monday 20 April. The Bairns were at home on both occasions to Hearts and Aberdeen. The first game saw Falkirk totally outclassed by a good Hearts team who were now beginning to hint at great things to come for them in the late 1950s. The dressing room radio had mixed tidings for Falkirk. The good news was that Lawrie Reilly had scored in the last minute to equalise for Scotland against England at Wembley, but the bad news was that Motherwell had beaten Aberdeen 4–1 and now had 25 points to Falkirk's 24.

Both teams had one game left. Falkirk were at home to Aberdeen, who were now themselves safe, and Motherwell were at home to a strong Rangers team now playing well and going for the championship. Airdrie were also involved in the relegation struggle, but they had games in hand, as indeed did Third Lanark, but they could not both catch Falkirk if Falkirk won on Monday.

It was complicated, but all Falkirk could do was beat Aberdeen and hope that Motherwell lost to Rangers. If that happened, the Bairns were definitely safe. There were 6,000 at Brockville that Holiday Monday afternoon and they saw Delaney at his vintage best as he scored twice in the 4–1 victory. One was a tap in and the other was a back header which the *Falkirk Herald* described as 'typical', although in fact he had scored very few like that.

It was a fine victory, but then there was an anxious wait to hear the score from Fir Park. As it was a Monday, there was no football programme on the radio, but members of the press were able to phone their offices to find out the score. They then relayed it to the tannoy operator. When it was announced that Rangers had beaten Motherwell 3–0, the roar almost 'lifted the roof from the stand' according to the writer of the *Falkirk Herald*. Delaney would say afterwards that it was his first-ever experience of supporting Rangers! 'I kent my old friends at Ibrox wouldn't let me down!'

Some would say that, in the circumstances, the saving of Falkirk was as good an achievement as any in Delaney's long and glittering career. He was delighted to be awarded another year's contract for season 1953–54, although many people wondered how long he could go on for at this level and at this pace. He certainly was slowing down and increasingly injury prone, but he pointed to his old adversary and good friend Stanley Matthews, who was of a similar vintage and had won the English Cup that year for Blackpool.

He also knew he was doing a great job for the young players and the town of Falkirk, where his popularity knew no bounds. On a cold miserable day more like winter than summer, the young Princess Elizabeth was crowned Queen of Great Britain and its empire on 2 June 1953 (a day after Mount Everest was conquered and one of Delaney's great heroes, the Wembley Wizard, Alec James, died), but it would be doubtful if she was anything like as popular in Falkirk as Jimmy Delaney.

Delaney would have had half an eye and ear on what was going on at Parkhead. On 16 May at Hampden, Jimmy had the rare opportunity to watch two of his old teams in action together. This was in the semi-final of the Coronation Cup, a competition specially arranged between four Scottish teams and four English teams to commemorate the Coronation of the young Queen. Celtic, who had already beaten Arsenal, also beat Manchester United and then, to the delight of their success-starved fans, won the competition itself by beating Hibernian.

The chance to meet Busby and some of his old Manchester United teammates again would have proved irresistible to Jimmy. Carey, Chilton, Rowley and Pearson were still there, but a few young faces like Violett and Byrne were beginning to appear. Celtic beat United 2–1 to the great surprise of everyone, not least their own fans. They had not had a great year in Scotland and had only been invited to join the competition on the strength of their support. Delaney would have been happy for them, for he remained a Celtic supporter, but he would have been distressed by the news in mid-June of the death of Celtic and Falkirk's greatest-ever player, Patsy Gallacher.

Delaney's decline and fall at Falkirk was sudden and dramatic, proving perhaps the old adage that 'you are only as good as your last game', something that is certainly true once you reach the age of 39, as Delaney did on 3 September 1953. To a certain extent, he seems to have been blamed for Falkirk's failure to qualify for the quarter-finals of the League Cup yet again, but this is hardly fair.

The Bairns were up against Hibernian, St Mirren and Queen of the South. In fact they got the better of Queen of the South and St Mirren, but came a cropper against the strong-going Hibernian and their Famous Five forward line. On 8 August, the opening day of the season, Delaney had the misfortune to miss a penalty in the last minute, which would have given Falkirk a 2–1 victory rather than a 1–1 draw. 'Bad show, Jimmy', said the disappointed *Falkirk Herald*. On the other hand, in the game at Palmerston Park, Dumfries, against Queen of the South, Delaney was inspirational in the 4–1 victory. In several other games, Delaney was played all over the forward line but, ominously, is not mentioned at all in a report – a clear sign that a player is having a bad run.

In addition, the usual problems with injuries did not help and he did not play at all in the month of September 1953, other than for the reserves on 26 September. In truth, manager Shankly was experimenting with his forward line, realising perhaps that a younger blend had to be found if continued survival in Division A was to be guaranteed.

The *Falkirk Herald*, however well disposed to Delaney it might have been in the past, now finds itself in reluctant agreement with the manager, commenting: 'Young Sinclair is now a better man for the right wing job' and 'however good

Jimmy may have been in his heyday, there are times when younger men must be called upon'. The pattern of his sporadic appearances for Falkirk's first team that autumn seems to be one of covering for someone who was injured. He was on the left wing on 17 October, missed a game on 24 October, left wing again on 31 October against Hamilton (when he 'looked out of it'), right wing against Clyde on 14 November in a dismal 4–1 thrashing at Shawfield, centre against Queen of the South where he scored in the 5–3 defeat at Palmerston and then the right wing against Dundee on 19 December where he was 'singularly ineffective' as Dundee won 1–0.

He did, however, have one big game and that was when the great Newcastle United with Jackie Milburn and Scotsmen Jimmy Scoular, Ronnie Simpson and Bobby Mitchell came to Brockville to play a game under floodlights on 20 October. Newcastle had a great team, having won the English Cup in 1951 and 1952 and destined to do the same in 1955, but there was a certain amount of awe and respect shown even by these giants of the game to Jimmy Delaney, now quite clearly coming towards the end of his playing career – or was he?

Towards the end of the year, a few phone calls had been made from Londonderry in Northern Ireland concerning the availability of Jimmy Delaney. Delaney himself had clearly been concerned about his lack of impact with Falkirk since the autumn, and was considering hanging up his boots and settling in Ireland, possibly in Waterfoot, County Antrim, from where his wife had come and where they had been left a large house when her parents died. The point was put to him by Mr Shankly that as his usefulness (impressive though it had been) to Falkirk was slowly coming to an end, he might care to think about moving on. Many Scottish Division B clubs would also have been interested, but Derry City had offered £1,500. Shortly after New Year 1954, Jimmy agreed to go.

There were personal and family reasons involved as well. Delaney's son Michael had died in 1944 and, in 1953, Patrick had also become ill. Patrick had developed meningitis and poliomyelitis, both of which had been notorious child killers of the pre-war years. The National Health Service was making strenuous attempts to win the battle against these horrible illnesses, but the victory would not come until the late 1950s when wholesale inoculation had been carried out. In the case of young Patrick Delaney, a drug called streptomycin was deployed but the success was only partial. Jimmy possibly felt that a move to Ireland where the pure mountain air was far better than the filth of industrial central Scotland might be a good idea.

In Waterfoot, there was also the attraction of a house in which to live. The 1950s were of course far removed from the days of mortgages and loans, and houses, both private and council, were hard to come by. This house was a large one and it made sense to move. The Derry City offer came at an opportune moment and Delaney was also encouraged by the suggestion of an old friend of his called Dr Alex McSparran, who happened to be a Celtic shareholder and the doctor in Waterfoot. Healthwise, it is agreeable to record that the move was a success and Pat Delaney grew up healthy enough to enjoy a long and successful career in Scottish professional football with Motherwell, Dunfermline Athletic, Clyde and Airdrie in the 1960s. He might even have joined Celtic if Billy McNeill had moved on as he threatened to do in 1964 before the arrival of Jock Stein.

The writer of the *Falkirk Herald* in early 1954 was disappointed but realistic. He said that Jimmy was a 'sound investment' in 1951, but that now was the time to move on, particularly as 'young Sinclair' was coming on, helped and groomed no doubt by the inspirational presence of Jimmy Delaney. He wished Jimmy all the best, adding presciently that he hoped that 'Derry City would win the Irish Cup this year' with Delaney on board. The writer would have his wishes granted.

Another great episode in the Delaney story had come to an end and an even better one was about to begin.

An autographed picture of Jimmy in his Manchester United days.

James DeCaney.

Jimmy in action for Manchester United.

A fine action photograph of Jimmy (on left) and another Manchester United player giving goalkeeper Sam Bartram of Charlton a hard time.

En route to Wembley for the 1948 English Cup Final – Jimmy's wife Annie is on the left. Beside her is Mrs Chilton, wife of Allenby Chilton.

Jimmy is introduced to King George VI at Wembley before the 1948 English Cup Final, which Manchester United won 4–2.

Manchester United's celebration dinner after winning the English Cup in 1948. Jimmy is sitting on the left-hand side of the third table back.

'If the cap fits, wear it!' Jimmy tries his Scotland cap on his son Patsy.

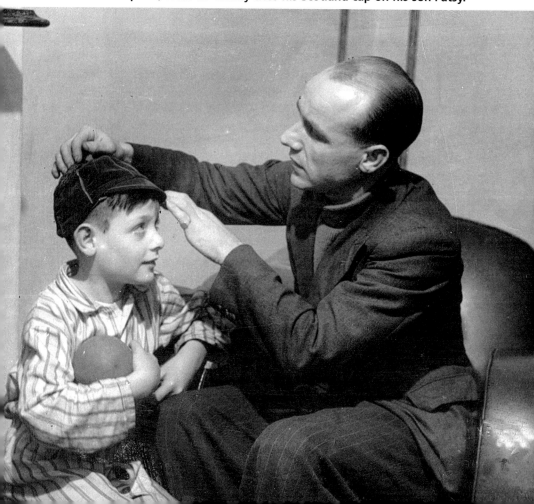

Jimmy playing for Aberdeen in a game against Hibs.

Jimmy on the wing for Aberdeen in a game against Raith Rovers at Stark's Park. Willie McNaught and Harry Colville are the Raith players.

Jimmy in Derry City's colours with the Irish Cup of 1954.

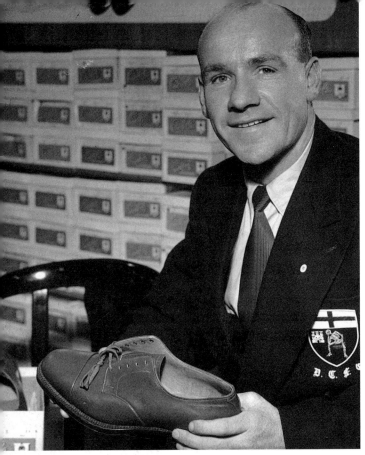

Jimmy in his Derry City days. He didn't always need football boots – he wore ordinary shoes sometimes as well.

Jimmy with Elgin City at Borough Briggs in November 1956. Back row, left to right: Milton, McKenzie, Jenkins, Hector, McLachlan, Gammack. Front row: Delaney, Roe, Davidson, Robertson, MacDonald.

The well-dressed ex-footballer.

Jimmy is second from the right in the front row in this splendid example of Celtic supporters across the ocean.

Jimmy in party mode. Next to him is Jimmy Johnstone.

Jimmy is second from the left of this group, which also includes George McCluskey and John Doyle.

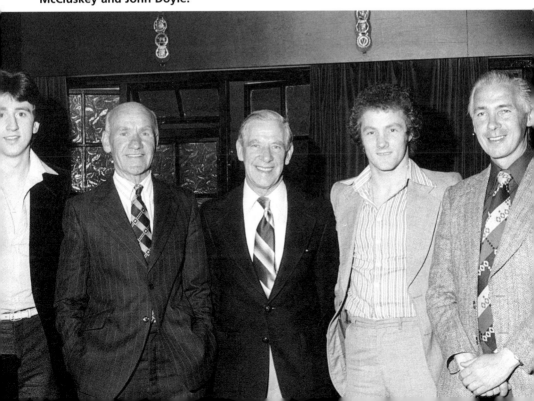

Jimmy holds
the Cup with
red ribbons
and green
ribbons that
was played for
in a testimonial
game for him.

JIMMY DELANEY BENEFIT DINNER

Thursday 22nd October, 1987

MANCHESTER UNITED
EXECUTIVE SUITE

7.30p.m.

The menu for Jimmy's
Benefit Dinner in 1987.

Jimmy shows his four medals to his friend Tommy Lowrie (ex-Manchester City).

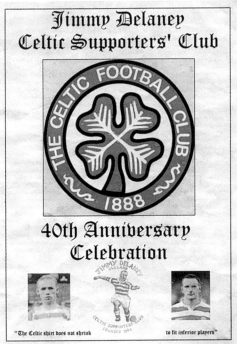

Jimmy Delaney
Celtic Supporters' Club

THE CELTIC FOOTBALL CLUB
1888
FOUNDED 1944

40th Anniversary
Celebration

JIMMY DELANEY
CELLAR
CELTIC SUPPORTERS CLUB
FOUNDED 1944

"The Celtic shirt does not shrink   to fit inferior players"

The programme for the 40th anniversary celebration of the Jimmy Delaney Celtic Supporters' Club in 2005.

BY JOE SULLIVAN

THE name Willie Curran may not be first on the list when Celtic fans recount milestones in the club's long and illustrious history.

But this Derryman, who celebrates his 75th birthday next month, played a crucial part in creating one of those one-off pieces of history that combine to make Celtic unique.

As a 24-year-old he helped Derry City to the second of their three IFA Cup wins when the Candystripes defeated Glentoran 1-0 in the 1953/54 final at Belfast's Windsor Park. They had lifted the trophy in 1949 and would again in 1964, but what made the 1954 victory so special and what was the Celtic connection?

The reason was that between January 12, 1954 and December 21, 1955 Celtic legend Jimmy Delaney – grandfather of current Celt John Kennedy – plied his trade at The Brandywell and managed to create a rather unique piece of history.

In three different decades in three different countries, Delaney clocked up the exceptional treble of FA Cup winners' medals in Scotland, England AND Ireland.

At that time Derry played under the auspices of the IFA in Northern Ireland but in '56 he came within minutes of winning the FAI Cup in the Republic and just lost out by a whisker of winning the national cups of the FOUR different associations.

And when the Jimmy Delaney CSC from the Celtic legend's home patch of Cleland held a special function at the weekend, they invited Delaney's one-time Derry City team-mate Curran.

Willie, who would become City's captain, was just 24 when he helped the Candystripes lift the cup, but even back in 1954, he was amazed at Delaney's engine, which kept him going at his fifth senior club after starting off with Celtic in 1933.

Willie said: "When Jimmy arrived at Brandywell our gates went from a regular 500 up to about 7,000. He was a great personality and motivated the whole place on and off the pitch – he gave us all a lift.

"We were third bottom of the league and Jimmy took us up to fourth and, of course, we reached the cup final.

"There was a crowd of 39,000 at Windsor Park that day and Jimmy played out of his skin. He was running about like a teenager, never mind a man of 39 years!"

In fact, Delaney was just short of his 40th birthday when Derry lifted the cup, but two decades previously, the Scottish Cup win with Celtic not only paved the way for the incredulous personal cup treble, the winger-cum-forward was also part of another historical landmark.

A week earlier, again at Hampden, he helped Scotland beat England 3-1 in front of 149,547 – the British international record – while Celtic's Scottish Cup win over Aberdeen was watched by 146,433, the British club record.

Jimmy left Celtic in 1946 after Matt Busby snapped him up for Manchester United and he lifted the English FA Cup at Wembley in 1948 by beating Blackpool 4-2. Stints at Aberdeen and Falkirk followed but the halcyon days were rekindled when he joined Derry City.

Willie recalled: "Jimmy never once mentioned playing with either Celtic or Manchester United when he played with us and it wasn't until Derry City had won the cup that the story of his unique treble became public knowledge to us.

"But even before we realised that, I remember him opening the medal box just after we had been presented with them.

"He looked at the medal and said, 'I'll treasure this all my days and take great care of it as this is the hardest-earned medal I've ever won in my life'."

Delaney wouldn't retire until just short of his 43rd birthday after nigh on a year with Elgin City, but in between Derry and his stint in the Highlands, he was player/manager of Cork Athletic in the Republic and that's where he nearly racked up the full set of winners' medals.

In 1956 the south coast side met Shamrock Rovers in the FAI Cup Final and with just 13 minutes left on the clock, Delaney's side were leading 2-0.

The Dublin Hoops rallied though and exasperatingly turned the game around to win 3-2 and deny Delaney and even more amazing record.

Willie recalled: "Everyone in Derry was praying Jimmy would win the fourth medal but it wasn't to be."

But here's hoping Jimmy's grandson wins four times as many medals as his granda – and may they ALL be with Celts!

Willie Curran helped Hoops legend Jimmy Delaney create history and was thrilled to join the Celtic family at the weekend

A TASTE OF PARADISE: Willie Curran is pictured at Celtic Park with members of the Jimmy Delaney CSC and was delighted to meet manager Martin O'Neill and big defender John Kennedy – Delaney's grandson – on his visit.

From the *Celtic View* of April 2005. Willie Curran, teammate of Jimmy, at Parkhead with the Cleland Supporters' Club, meeting Martin O'Neill and John Kennedy.

Jimmy's grandson John Kennedy before his ill-fated appearance for Scotland v Romania on 31 March 2004.

Chapter 8

The Irish Years
1954–56

SO, NORTHERN IRELAND was the next stop for Jimmy Delaney's football odyssey. Northern Ireland and football are sometimes strange bedfellows. Even today, an outsider can be amazed and appalled at the behaviour of Ulster crowds. The Northern Ireland national team plays in green jerseys, yet there are sections of their support, dressed in blue and orange, who make it clear that they do not like anyone with connections, past or present, with Glasgow Celtic. In October 2005, John Hartson of Celtic and Wales was singled out for boos and jeers. This was at least understandable, for John was an opponent. It was a lot less easy to explain why Neil Lennon of Celtic and Northern Ireland received similar treatment a few years previously.

In truth it was nothing different to what Anton Rogan in the 1980s and, to a lesser extent, Charlie Tully and Bertie Peacock in the 1950s had suffered. It was in fact Bertie Peacock who hurt the bigots most of all because he was a Protestant – something that mattered not a whit with his devoted fans at Parkhead. But the fact that Bertie became captain of Celtic and led them to their 7–1 League Cup Final win over Rangers in 1957 must have stung those who thought that his religion was important.

For most of the 20th century, Northern Ireland, and in particular the city of Derry, had its troubles. Even its very name seems to be a source of division and tension. The Protestants tend to call this beautiful city on the banks of the Foyle 'Londonderry', to emphasise the British connection, while the Roman Catholics are content to call it Derry. Yet 'we'll guard old Londonderry's walls' does not fit in very well with the tune, so the Orangemen keep it at Derry in this context. One wonders too whether all those who sing that anthem of hate at Ibrox Park and other places realise that in the 21st century (and indeed for most of the 20th century), Roman Catholics were, are and are likely to remain a substantial majority in the city. This is something that has become apparent since the gerrymandering of constituency boundaries, practised shamelessly by the Stormont Government up to 1972, has ceased.

The practice of gerrymandering meant that the constituencies were unfairly divided, so that the Roman Catholics would all live in one huge constituency and elect one MP, whereas the Protestants would live in three or four smaller constituencies and elect more MPs. It was a system that was reminiscent of the 'Pocket Boroughs' or 'Rotten Boroughs' which prevailed in Great Britain before the 1832 Reform Act. When the rest of the world pointed it out as the 1969 troubles started, it caused deep embarrassment to the Harold Wilson Labour Government. Britain was being seen to support a system which persecuted the Catholics – but no one had seemed to care in Whitehall, or even notice. One recalls the Labour Cabinet Minister Richard Crossman saying in a television interview that he saw no objection to a devolved Scotland on the lines of the Northern Ireland system 'which had worked so well'!

There was also the fact that some Protestants were allowed to vote more than once and the existence of a sectarian police force called the B Specials who were there for no other purpose than the maintenance of the Protestant ascendancy, and if this involved brutality and violence, then so be it. Northern Ireland was at peace, one could say, in the 1950s when Delaney played there, but it was a peace based on repression and injustice. One recalls the statement of the British chieftain of the first century AD after the Romans had conquered his country: 'Where they make a desert, they call it peace'. In Ireland, it was the British who were the oppressors, unaware seemingly of what Padraig Pearce had warned them of half a century previously: 'Ireland unfree can never be at peace'.

How one wishes that this lovely city of Derry had been spared the awful things that have happened to it since the Flight of the Earls in medieval times. There is so much more to it than sectarian hatred. Indeed, it has made a positive contribution to Christianity as well. Cecil Frances Alexander, the writer of the Easter hymn *There is a Green Hill Far Away*, composed it in the late 19th century and was influenced by the beauty of Derry. The city has also seen some football.

Derry City FC now play in the Eircom League, the League of the Irish Republic, a competition that they came very close to winning in November 2005, losing heartbreakingly on the last Friday night of the season to Cork. At the time that Jimmy Delaney played for them, they were members of the Northern Irish League. Their history is an interesting one, although ultimately sad and disappointing. The years 1929 to 1972 have been well dealt with in an excellent book, *A History of Derry City Football and Athletic Club*, written by W.H.W. Platt. Fortunately, they have avoided the fate of Belfast Celtic who were forced out of existence in the late 1940s due to hooliganism and sectarian hatred. Their survival is due to an absolute determination to keep going, and to prove that they can keep going, in spite of living in a society which is almost unique in Europe, certainly in Western Europe, in its attitude to what is sometimes simplistically referred to as 'religion'.

The team play at a ground called Brandywell and it was there that Jimmy Delaney arrived from Falkirk in the middle of January 1954. They play in red and white vertical stripes (like those of Sheffield United or Sunderland) and their nickname is, for that reason, the Candystripes. Since their foundation in 1929 until the arrival of Jimmy Delaney, they had not done particularly well, but in 1949 they had achieved their only success to date when they won the Irish Cup, beating Glentoran 3–1 in the final.

The credit for bringing Delaney to Derry is owed to Mr George Sidebottom, one of the directors. He had of course admired the mighty deeds of Jimmy for both Celtic and Manchester United, and felt that although his Falkirk days seemed to be coming to an end, he might still be able to do a job in Irish football. One of his many Scottish contacts alerted him to the possibility that Delaney might be available, for Delaney was now struggling to find a regular first-team place at Falkirk and was considering settling in Ireland. It was certainly Sidebottom who was able to finance the deal, even though £1,500 was a great deal of money, as indeed were Delaney's personal terms for the impoverished Derry City. In fact, Sidebottom had had to advertise for public contributions. Such was the attraction of the name 'Delaney' that £700 was raised very quickly and the run in the Irish Cup would pay for the rest.

It was a big step for the home-loving Jimmy to move his family from Scotland to Ireland, even though his wife was naturally keen on the idea as she came from there, her parents' house was immediately available and the health of young Patrick was a concern. Jimmy felt too that he still had some football left in him, even at the age of 39 and a half. This was an ideal opportunity to continue his career and to keep his wife and family happy at the same time. After two long talks with the Derry City directors, who had travelled to Scotland to discuss the matter, Jimmy decided to add an Irish dimension to his already illustrious career. He signed on Tuesday 12 January 1954. He sailed to Ireland two days later.

Jimmy had still kept himself extremely fit and his advanced years did not really matter too much. The football brain was not affected by age. Centre-half Willie Curran was amazed at the 'engine' that Delaney had, as he joined his fifth senior club. Curran also says that the mere presence of Delaney was enough to lift the crowds from a meagre average of 500 to about 7,000. 'He was a great personality and motivated the whole place on and off the pitch – he gave us all a lift!' It was Delaney's infectious enthusiasm which galvanised all the players. He would happily play anywhere and he 'ran about like a teenager', says Willie

Curran. No wonder the players were inspired by the arrival of this human dynamo, who just happened to be a legend as well.

More important than that, Delaney actually got the whole city of Derry, which until now had been anything other than a football-minded city, talking about football. Derry was the second city of the province but there was no great tradition of the game there at all. It was not unlike Edinburgh in this respect, which has always lagged behind Glasgow as far as football is concerned, but there was more to it than that. Football had tended to be a Protestant game in Ireland and the Catholic population of Ireland had not been all that interested in the sport. Until Jack Charlton came along towards the end of the 20th century, the South preferred horseracing, rugby, hurling and Gaelic football, although it had always exported a few individuals to British football.

There had been polite interest when Derry won the Irish Cup in 1949, but as yet no great groundswell of enthusiasm. The club were certainly down on their luck in 1954. With the arrival of Delaney there was, as it were, an attempt by football to swarm over the walls and capture the city!

Curiously to the outsider, Curran states that Delaney never once mentioned playing for either Celtic or Manchester United. But this is not all that surprising either, for Delaney was a very modest individual but, more than that, he was focused on the job in hand. Celtic and Manchester United were of course very dear to his heart (he would always listen to the radio and read newspapers for the results of Celtic, in particular), as to a lesser extent were Aberdeen and Falkirk, but Derry City was the job in hand. They therefore deserved his undivided attention.

Delaney's house in Waterfoot, County Antrim, was two and a half to three hours away from Derry, a considerable distance for a man who never drove a car. He was technically a part-timer, but such fine distinctions did not matter to a man like Delaney. Whether he was in Waterfoot or the Brandywell did not make a great deal of difference, for Delaney would train and keep himself superbly fit in any case. Underneath the house at Waterfoot, there was a great area which had been the stables at one point. Jimmy used this for his gymnasium. He would also be seen running along the beach, and this stood him in good stead for his readjustment to a new kind of football. But he need not have worried. The standard of Irish football was possibly about the same as what he had found at Falkirk, and he had coped with that.

Delaney's debut was at Brandywell on Saturday 16 January 1954 against Ards. Derry City, third from the bottom of the League, saw a massive increase in their gate that day and a massive improvement on recent pathetic performances as they beat Ards 6–1. Ards' cause was not helped by the injury to their goalkeeper who had to retire hurt early in the game, but even so it was a vintage Delaney performance as he himself scored a hat–trick and assisted centre-forward Young, with whom he had struck up an immediate rapport, for two others. Irish writer Malcolm Brodie wrote of this game: 'I suppose a fiction writer would have had Delaney bursting upon the Derry scene by scoring a goal or two. Reality provided even more and gave a hint of the charisma that followed Jimmy's career... he scored three goals in a 6–1 win.'

Next week saw the return fixture, but this was a victory for Ards even though Delaney scored a penalty kick. He also scored the following week when Derry surprised and delighted their supporters at Brandywell with a fine 4–2 win over Coleraine, last season's defeated Irish Cup finalists.

Supporters of Derry City were delighted with the sprightly veteran. By now he was completely bald (and had been for some time) but still retained a young face. More importantly, he still retained a young man's attitude to the game: the game was there to be won, but hard work was necessary from all the team. Quite clearly the senior statesman of the side – the young and even the less young men looked up to him – he was a kind mentor, imparting wisdom and encouragement where necessary. He could of course get frustrated, as everyone does on the football field from time to time. Anyone not pulling his weight would be liable to receive a mouthful, but it was constructive and never done with any malice or spite.

On 6 February, the quest for the Irish Cup began; a quest which would be ultimately successful, but which would need eight games. Jimmy was well to the fore in the first game, a 1–0 win over Ballymena United. The win was achieved in spite of the loss of goalkeeper Heffron. It was Jimmy who scored the only goal of the game and he also managed to miss a penalty kick. It was, however, a fine win for 10-man Derry City because Ballymena United were top of the League at the time and it showed what a boost the side had received from the arrival of Jimmy Delaney.

It would appear as well that the name did impress and terrify the opposition. Certainly, teams now treated Derry with a great deal of respect, as crowds were visibly increasing to see the bald-headed genius on the right wing. The head looked as if it belonged to anyone other than a footballer, but crowds marvelled at the ball control and speed of this amazingly fit and dedicated man.

Saturday 6 March saw Bangor at Brandywell for the quarter-final of the Irish Cup. A crowd of well over 6,000 saw a fine game in which Delaney starred but failed to find a way through a tight Bangor defence, other than the part he played in the build-up to the goal which O'Neill scored. The game finished 1–1, but the replay at Bangor saw a different game with Derry City winning comfortably.

The semi-final brought Linfield to Derry City's ground. Linfield wore blue and had long been considered the 'establishment' team of Northern Ireland, and certainly were looked upon as the 'Rangers' of Northern Ireland. It would be difficult to find many players of the Roman Catholic religion who had enjoyed playing for Linfield (as it was with Rangers in those days) and it had been Linfield supporters who had been largely responsible for the riot which led to the demise of Belfast Celtic in 1948.

This dreadful and shameful event took place on Boxing Day 1948 at Windsor Park, the home of Linfield. Belfast Celtic's Jimmy Jones was a Protestant, which mattered little to Belfast Celtic's fans, but seemed to be of great significance to the followers of Linfield. Jones was attacked at the end of the game by Linfield fans and had his leg broken as he was thrown to the ground. The Belfast Celtic directors were appalled by this incidence of sectarian violence and decided to close the club down the following summer rather than risk a repetition. This did seem to be a craven decision, but the club has never been resurrected. Ironically, in a friendly in summer 1949 while on tour in the US after they had decided to wind up and leave the Irish League, they beat the Scottish international team.

Linfield, who had defeated Derry City in the League at Windsor Park a couple of weeks earlier, were very confident that they would win at Brandywell on 27 March. This game attracted a huge crowd of 15,000 and included a great deal of Linfield supporters who targeted Delaney for his previous connection with Glasgow Celtic. Such treatment did not affect Jimmy, for he had experienced it before in Scotland, even when playing for Aberdeen and Falkirk. Derry City did well, as they thought, to earn a 2–2 draw and a replay the following midweek, on 31 March at Windsor Park.

The replay was one of the best games in Derry City's history. Delaney was superb as Derry City won 2–1 to reach the final of the Irish Cup. Their opponents were Glentoran, the club that Derry City had beaten in 1949 to record their only success to date, and the date for the final was 24 April 1954. Glentoran, however, were looked upon as the favourites in 1954 simply because they had a better record and appeared to have better players.

Of course, 24 April was an important date in the Delaney scrapbook. Apart from the fact that it was the birthday of his son Patrick in 1940, it was on 24 April 1937 that he won his Scottish Cup medal for Celtic against Aberdeen and on 24 April 1948 that he won his English Cup medal for Manchester United against Blackpool. How appropriate it would be if he could win his Irish Cup medal on the same date of the year. There was an additional element to this bizarre coincidence. On the same day (24 April 1954) the Scottish Cup Final was taking place at Hampden and the teams were Celtic and Aberdeen, the same two who had contested the final exactly 17 years previously when the record attendance was broken and when Delaney was playing for Celtic.

How the world had changed in those 17 years! Millions had lost their lives in military action to rid the world of the evil of Nazism. Hitler, Stalin and

Roosevelt had all played their part on the world stage and had gone. The atomic bomb threatened to demolish mankind in a second. Great Britain had abandoned its *laissez faire* attitude to its population and had embraced the idea of health, welfare and social security for all. Things called televisions were beginning to make their stuttering, flickering appearances in living rooms.

The world had changed and changed utterly, but Jimmy Delaney was still around. He would not have been Jimmy Delaney if he had not been wondering how Celtic were doing against Aberdeen in Scotland, however focused his mind was on Derry City and their Cup Final against Glentoran.

A crowd of 35,000 (huge by Ulster standards and a record for a domestic match) made their way to Windsor Park, Belfast. An estimated 10,000 left Derry that day bedecked in red and white rosettes and favours, in trains, buses and cars. An amateurish slogan, which said more for the enthusiasm that it did for the poetic ability of the author, was written on a banner hanging out of a bus:

> *Come on, Derry, Come on Jimmy, Come on the crew.*
> *We want you to win today – and Celtic too!*

The game turned out to be a slight disappointment for the Derry fans, but most newspapers agreed that Glentoran were worth their draw, even though it was 2–1 to Derry at half-time. Delaney had scored the equaliser to make it 1–1 and had been instrumental in the build-up to what, for a long time, had seemed to be the winning goal. But Derry made the fatal mistake of defending too deep and Glentoran equalised. Near the end both teams missed chances.

The Delaney family would have been disappointed by all this, but would have been cheered by the news from Scotland, for Celtic had beaten Aberdeen 2–1 with an own goal and a tap-in from Irishman Sean Fallon. In 1954, Celtic had thus won the Scottish Cup for the 17th time and had won the double for the first time since before World War One.

Meanwhile, the battle for the Irish Cup continued. The second game was played the following week before a slightly smaller crowd of 30,258 and resulted in a cat-and-mouse match, which finished goalless. The third game was played on Monday 10 May 1954 and guaranteed the immortality of Jimmy Delaney and his three Cup-winners' medals. The Derry City team was: Heffron; Wilson and Houston; Brolly, Curran and Smyth; Brady, Delaney, Forsythe, Toner and O'Neill. Delaney is listed as the inside-right in the excellent *The History of Irish Soccer* by Malcolm Brodie, but this meant little for, according to Willie Curran, he could interchange at will with any of the other forwards, as he had done in the old days with Celtic and Manchester United. He was still fast enough to be the right-winger, he had been a centre-forward with his previous teams and he could even play on the left. Also, in his previous teams he had been famous for taking on a roving commission for himself.

It was left-winger Con O'Neill who scored the only goal just before half-time, but it was Jimmy Delaney who provided the moment of magic for this solitary goal. Harry Smyth lofted a hopeful punt into the penalty area. As two Glentoran defenders, Jimmy Murdough and Flash King, hesitated to go for the high bouncing ball, Jimmy rose between them and headed the ball on into open space for O'Neill to walk the ball past the stranded goalkeeper, who had been caught in no-man's land as his defenders had hesitated. Thus the Candystripes went in at half-time in a high state of euphoria and the onus fell on veteran Delaney to keep their feet on the ground with some solid Scottish common sense, as Lanarkshire words of wisdom like 'Keep the heid!' and 'Get a grip on things, noo!' resounded through the dressing room.

The second half was a long one for the fans of Derry City, as Glentoran piled on the pressure. Fortunately, goalkeeper Charlie Heffron was on form and, like most goalkeepers when they are having a good day, enjoyed a fair share of luck as well. Delaney was compelled to join the defence in the second half for the Glentoran barrage, as the Glens tried to take the game to extra-time and possibly yet another game, but he was still able to break from defence and to 'take the ball for a walk to the corner flag' to waste time and, crucially, to give his defenders a breather. It was a tough struggle, but the referee's final whistle sent the Derry supporters in the 28,000 crowd into ecstasy and brought tears to the eyes of the 39-year-old Delaney.

More than 50 years later, centre-half and captain Willie Curran, who himself had played brilliantly for the club that night and indeed all that season, said:

> Jimmy never once mentioned playing with either Celtic or Manchester United when he played with us and it wasn't until Derry City had won the Cup that the story of his unique treble became public knowledge to us. But even before we realised that, I remember him opening the medal box just after we had been presented with them. He looked at the medal and said, 'I'll treasure this all my days and take great care of it as this is the hardest-earned medal I've ever won in my life'.

Jimmy may have been modest by not boasting about his previous medals, but the press in Scotland and England were very aware of it. In fact, it must have been one of the very few times in history that large sections of Glasgow and Manchester turned on their radios or scanned the following day's newspapers for the result of an Irish football match! Quite rightly, Jimmy's feat was trumpeted as unique and, although one cannot guarantee that it is still unique in world football, it's hard to think of anyone else achieving such greatness in three countries.

In a footnote to this great climax to the season for the hitherto struggling Derry City, the team then won the North West Senior Cup the following Saturday by beating Coleraine 1–0 at Brandywell. Clearly, the Delaney influence had been a great thing for Derry, as indeed had Derry been a great thing for Delaney, whose family were now settled in Ireland. It was no surprise, but it was a great honour nevertheless when Jimmy was named Ulster Player of the Year for 1954.

He returned to Cleland for the summer and it was there on 11 June that a testimonial dinner was held for him. Willie Maley, now well past his 87th birthday, was invited to talk there. He was unable to attend, for reasons of infirmity, but he did send a copy of what he would have said. In a letter to Mr J. Kelly of Cleland from the Bank Restaurant, Maley wishes everyone a very successful evening and passes on his kindest regards to his 'never to be forgotten friend Jamie [sic] Delaney'. What he wrote shows how highly he regarded Delaney. It also says a great deal about Maley himself.

> It is with great regret that I am unable to travel to Cleland to meet my very good friend Jimmy Delaney and his fellow townsmen.
>
> It was in 1934 I think I first saw Delaney when his brother brought him to me by desire after my Scout had seen the Celt to be in his own Junior team and he was a real little laddie that day with a bright cheery face who listened to my questions with great interest. He was of course duly fixed up by me and for years was the life and blood of my beloved team, the Celtic.
>
> He of course won many honours with the Celtic team of those days and was one of Celtic's great team of their life of forty six years. Unfortunately his big run was spoiled by the serious accident he had to his arm which laid him off for a considerable time but he showed no loss of his ever prominent bravery on the field when his arm cured he played with as much dash as ever on the field where his great abilities made him a common mark for rough tackling which he always had to face. Thereafter he left Celtic for Manchester United where he again distinguished himself by winning an English Cup Medal and played for them for years brilliantly. Thereafter he had a turn in Scotland with Aberdeen and Falkirk finishing up with his present team in Derry City where he has made (or at least equalled) a great record gaining an Irish Cup Medal to make him a 'Three Leaved' shamrock winner of the Scottish, English and Irish National Cups, truly a wonderful performance.

To me even in all my years with football I have never had any special favourites in the many heroes of the game I have controlled, but to this clean and dashing player who feared no foe on the field of football I have always had a very sincere liking and after leaving Celtic I followed his career with great interest.

He is now reaching an age when he might fairly 'lay down his gun' and take a rest from the game he loves so well.

Celtic have had many great outside rights such as Neilly McCallum in 1888, followed by Alec Bennett and Jim McColl, but in his outside right place Jamie had no superior wearing for the Green and White whilst his work at times as centre forward won honours for Clubs he played for as well as for Scotland on the International Field. In all the years he has played I have never known him to do a foul action in spite of severe abuse from men who ought to have known better and in respect of his own true sportsmanship.

He has my sincere good wishes for a long life blessed with good health and will carry with him on his retirement the same wish from many thousands of football followers apart from those of the Celtic breed where his name is placed on the same scale as Jamie Quinn, James Kelly, Patsy Gallacher, Alec McNair, John Thomson and many others too numerous to mention but to none of them will memory be so dear as to the man who had the great honour of introducing him to Celtic and football.

The speech, sadly delivered only vicariously, says a great deal about Maley himself. He describes himself as 'The Old Celt of 52 years service' and has his moments of eccentricity, such as when he equates Delaney's three medals with a three-leaved shamrock and when he uses military imagery in 'laying down his gun' (Maley's father had been a soldier).

He also talks bombastically about the 'many heroes of the game I have controlled'. But it is a great example of how highly the grand old man of Celtic rated Jimmy Delaney – in the same breath as Gallacher and Quinn, for example. Yet this was the man who growled at Delaney in 1936, 'Don't let that go to your head' after he scored a hat-trick in the Charity Cup Final against Rangers.

Maley's memory can at times be faulty. Jimmy McColl, for example, was only very seldom an outside-right and Maley may be thinking of Andy McAtee. Hints are given as to how Delaney came to Celtic through the agency of the scout, who seems to have connections with Stoneyburn Juniors, and Delaney's brother seems to have been involved in his joining of the club as well. But Maley's recollections perhaps create more problems than they solve.

Nevertheless, Maley's letter remains an eloquent testimony from a man who did not, as a rule, hand out praise lavishly.

Sadly, on Delaney's return to Ireland, the success for Derry City was not sustained and the following season 1954–55 was an unfortunate one both for Delaney and the club. Shortly after the season started, Delaney celebrated his 40th birthday, a time when most professional football players are considering retirement, if they have not already done so. But Jimmy remained determined to eke out a few more years as a professional football player. He did this by his dedication to training and a continuing and indeed intensifying disdain for nicotine and alcohol which he saw, not without cause, from his observations of other players, as a deleterious influence.

Sadly, the older one gets, the more susceptible one is to injury, or more crucially, the more difficult it becomes to recover from an injury, no matter how fit one has been. This was what happened to Delaney in October 1954 when, after a moderate start to the season, he picked up an injury and found himself sidelined for the rest of the calendar year. Derry City had started the season in an unspectacular fashion and their form was mediocre to say the least.

It was 8 January 1955 that he returned for a game at Brandywell against Portadown. Derry City won 3–0 and the influence of Delaney was immediately apparent for, although he did not himself score, he was responsible for all of the goals. However, a few weeks later at Windsor Park in a game against Linfield, he saw the unacceptable side of Irish football in serious crowd disturbances.

Linfield are the 'Orange' team of Belfast and it is tempting and simplistic to describe what happened at Windsor Park on 5 February 1955 as a sectarian riot, given that Derry City were seen as the 'Fenian' team of Ulster with their refusal to call themselves Londonderry, their support which was predominantly (although not exclusively) Roman Catholic and the presence in their team of the veteran who had made his name playing for Glasgow Celtic.

In truth, there is seldom anything rational in football hooliganism. It is caused by not very bright young men with occasionally severe personality disorders, products of inadequate parenting, housing, culture and education (with perhaps the added element in the case of Rangers and Linfield of bigotry) who need a bit of fun in their otherwise sadly underachieving lives. One cannot really blame religion for, one hopes, both the Roman Catholic and the Protestant Church disown and discourage violence. Perhaps, however, the clerics did not do so as vigorously as they should have in 1950s Belfast.

In this case, it was the Irish Cup, the trophy won so spectacularly by Delaney's Derry the year before. The game itself was a good one, sportingly played and well refereed. Linfield were the better team (they had also beaten Derry the previous week in the League) and won the game 3–2. Delaney had played well and scored one of Derry's goals.

Towards the end of the game the crowd, which was unsegregated, had become agitated and one or two fights had broken out, mainly when Derry City supporters had suffered unprovoked attacks from Linfield fans. Police had settled some of that, but as the players left the field, several Derry players were attacked by fans. Mercifully, no one was seriously injured, but some were kicked and spat upon, including Delaney as he made his way to the dressing room. Then, in a fine example of bathos, but one which nevertheless graphically describes the irrational and illogical nature of football hooliganism in Ulster, Mr Platt's *History of Derry City* says that 'A Protestant Clergyman with the City supporters was spoken to in an insulting manner and left before the game ended'.

The rest of the season fizzled out for both Derry and Delaney, but there was a poignant occasion on 17 May 1955 when Glasgow Celtic appeared at Brandywell and lost 1–2 before 11,000 fans. Sadly, Delaney was injured and did not play, but he must have enjoyed meeting his old friend Jimmy McGrory again, as well as men like Bobby Evans and Jock Stein. Celtic themselves had had an unfortunate season, losing the Scottish League to Aberdeen and then the Scottish Cup to Clyde in a replay after goalkeeper Bonnar had misjudged a corner-kick in the last minute of the first game.

Delaney stayed another half-season at Brandywell. The season 1955–56 got off to a good start as far as Delaney was concerned for he managed to score a hat-trick on Wednesday 24 August in a 5–1 rout of Glentoran. Platt's book describes this game as follows: 'Glentoran crashed in this fixture to Delaney who scored three times'. He also scored a hat-trick when Derry City beat Crusaders in September, but thereafter he rapidly faded into the background as far as Derry City are concerned as repeated injury and old age – he was now 41 – made their mark on him.

Nevertheless, the Delaney story still has a little while to run yet. He was actively contemplating retirement, possibly a return to Scotland and perhaps a job as a coach with a small Scottish team, although he would have loved it if his old friend Jimmy McGrory had offered him a job at Parkhead. It was then that a team called Cork Athletic approached him.

On Saturday 31 December 1955, the *Cork Examiner* broke the news that two Cork Athletic officials, Mr O'Sullivan and Mr Riordan, had travelled to the North to try to persuade the veteran to join them. He needed little persuasion, for he was still eager to try something else, and at this stage of his career, what had he to lose? In addition, the Cork men were able to offer Delaney the captaincy with immediate effect and also the carrot that the Football Association of Ireland Cup was about to begin. How would he like to try to win his fourth Cup medal in four separate countries? Delaney always relished a challenge.

Derry City had no desire to lose Jimmy, but were realistic enough to accept that he wanted to go. He could not, in any case, last forever. He had already pushed the limits of footballing immortality to a level that almost defied credulity and Derry City accepted with grace his desire to win yet another Cup medal. He left with the best wishes of the club and supporters, and with a residue of goodwill that is still remembered yet in the beautiful but tragic city of Derry.

Cork Athletic no longer exist in that form: financial considerations compelled their departure from the game in 1957, only a year after they reached the Football Association of Ireland Cup Final. Cork Hibernians replaced them but they too folded in season 1976–77. At one point there was a Cork Rovers, but the team of the moment is Cork City, a team who, like Derry City, play in the Eircom League. They have had their great moments, and indeed won the Eircom League in November 2005 in breathtaking fashion by beating Derry City on the last day of the season, but sadly they cannot claim to be a big name in any European context.

Association football in the Irish Republic has never been a huge game, though Ireland has of course produced many good players. There has always been a supply of Irishmen playing for English teams from the 1920s onwards. Curiously, Celtic have not been over-endowed with native Irishmen, although one can point to Patsy Gallacher, Charlie Tully, Sean Fallon, Bertie Peacock (the Ulster Protestant who defied the bigots to become captain of Celtic), Paddy Bonner, Neil Lennon and a few others.

The World Cup campaigns of 1990 and 1994 certainly indicate a great deal of Irish talent, but the sad thing about that was they all played their football outside the Emerald Isle, mainly in England. A visit to Dublin, for example, will show many people sporting evidence of the two teams on the British mainland that Irish people support – Manchester United and Glasgow Celtic (the Delaney influence?) – but very few indications, for example, of Shamrock Rovers or St Patrick's support.

There are cultural reasons for this in that association football was the game of the English, of the conquerors, of the oppressors. Ireland had its indigenous Gaelic football, and football never did command the undivided attention of young Irishmen in the way that it did with young Scotsmen, for example. Kevin Barry, who 'gave his young life in the cause of liberty' in 1920, was a sportsman who played various games but not, apparently, association football. In the Easter Rising of 1916, one of the heroes was Padraig Pearse, one of whose famous remarks had been that he wished Ireland to be 'not free merely but Gaelic as well, not Gaelic merely but free as well'. Perhaps this applied to sports as well. After the partition of 1922, there was far more association football played in the North of Ireland than in the South where Gaelic football remained strong.

Delaney's first game was against Waterford in the League at Cork Athletic's beautiful ground called the Mardyke. This ground is still in existence and is owned by University College, Cork. Delaney played at centre-forward and immediately impressed the crowd by combining the 'skill of a veteran with the fitness of a much younger man'. At this stage of his career, Delaney probably had realised that he no longer had the speed of a winger, but that he would be much better as a centre-forward, particularly in the role of leading the line – distributing the ball to both wings and to inside-forwards.

Several things surprised him about Cork Athletic. They were a great bunch of lads, but perhaps carried their Catholicism to extremes by sprinkling themselves with Holy Water before a game, while Delaney, himself a devout but much less flamboyant Catholic, was content merely to meditate and bless himself. On the other hand, the ultra-professional and super-fit Delaney was appalled by their cavalier approach to diet. While Delaney himself would take nothing heavier than a poached egg, the Cork Athletic boys were happy to tuck in to soup, potatoes, cabbage and meat even an hour or so before a game. As captain, Delaney had to put a stop to that.

In round one of the FAI Cup, Cork Athletic had a plum tie at the Mardyke against the Dublin team St Patrick's, who were currently League leaders. A record but unspecified attendance paid the enormous sum of £1,031 on Sunday 19 February to see a five-goal thriller, which Athletic won 3–2. Delaney did not score, the goals coming from Willie Moloney and two from Paddy O'Leary, but once again it was Delaney's influence that was the decisive factor.

Round two saw a local derby against another Cork team called Evergreen on 4 March. This time, 13,553 crammed into the Mardyke ground but were disappointed with a goalless draw. The replay at Turner's Cross, the home of Evergreen, the following Wednesday saw a fine Delaney performance as he scored and fed Collins for the other goal in a 2–0 victory. Cork Athletic's side was: O'Toole; P. Noonan and D. Noonan; J. Moloney, Coughlan and Daly; W. Moloney, Collins, Delaney, Murphy and Wallace.

Cork Athletic were now in the semi-final but, before that happened, there was another happy event in the Delaney family in the arrival of Anne-Marie, his youngest daughter, who would grow up to be the mother of Celtic's John Kennedy. This happened at Waterfoot on 4 April and Delaney was a happy man. Delaney still lived in Waterfoot and only travelled south for important games, although he would sometimes take digs in Cork for a few days between games. Delaney never drove a car and relied on public transport, which in Ireland meant the train.

The semi-final was played on neutral ground at Dalymount Park in Dublin against Waterford on Sunday 8 April 1956. The first game was a draw before 27,000 but the second game on the following Wednesday night saw five goals from the Athletic: two from Jimmy Murphy, two from John Horgan and one from Jimmy Delaney, of whom the headline in the *Cork Examiner* said quite succinctly 'Delaney excels'.

It was back to Dalymount Park for the final against Shamrock Rovers, arguably the most successful team in Ireland (certainly in terms of winning trophies), and one who wore green and white hoops. One recalls a European Cup game at Celtic Park, Glasgow, some 30 years later in 1986 when Shamrock Rovers were the visitors. They were greeted with rapture by the Celtic fans as the game passed in an astonishing and unparalleled atmosphere of mutual love! Back in 1956 the Glasgow green and white hoops had let themselves down badly the previous Saturday by going down 1–3 to Hearts in the Scottish Cup Final – a game that Delaney had been able to listen to on the radio on BBC World Service.

All roads led to Dublin that pleasant Sunday of 29 April 1956 and the crowd was reputed to be in excess of 35,000. All of Ireland, except the lovers of Shamrock Rovers of course, was now supporting Jimmy in his effort to land four Cup medals in four different countries. Delaney himself bundled the goalkeeper over the line in the 33rd minute in a still legal shoulder charge to put Athletic in front and then, just before half-time, Jimmy Murphy headed another to give Athletic a 2–0 lead. Shamrock Rovers now applied pressure in the second half, but John Coughlan at the heart of the defence looked solid until, with only 12 minutes left, Rovers scored through Hamilton. Soon after that, Paddy Noonan had the misfortune to handle in the box and Rovers equalised to take the final to extra-time. Normally, teams seldom recover from such disasters and this game was no exception.

Rovers were indeed the better team and scored early in extra-time through a header from their left-back Ronnie Nolan in the 92nd minute. The 41-year-old Delaney was now simply too exhausted to pull the fat out of the fire. The magic story had not quite managed to deliver the happy ending. The game ended with Delaney dejected but dignified, repeating the much-uttered Scottish gnomic utterance, 'Ah well, that's fitba'. The Shamrock Rovers players felt sorry for him and some of them even said that they would have chaired him round the park if he had won the Cup. As it was, he had to make do with a losers' medal.

Delaney's disappointment was shared by all his many admirers, not least in the heartlands of his previous clubs. Celtic themselves had lost the Scottish Cup Final and had been hoping for some cheer from Delaney, who was still a great favourite. Manchester United were in the process of reaching greatness again, having won the English League with a young side called the Busby Babes. They too were sorry that Delaney had not made it four medals in four different countries and Derry City were all hoping and praying that Delaney could do it, sharing his disappointment when he just missed out.

In the summer of 1956, Britain and Egypt began to square up to each other over the Suez Canal and Jim Laker of Surrey and England took all 10 Australian wickets as he spun England to victory at Old Trafford. The question remained, however, of how long the almost 42-year-old Jimmy Delaney could go on? Jimmy was prepared to give it a go for another season, although he may well have felt that a return to Scotland was now called for. Nevertheless, when Cork Athletic offered him terms for another season, he signed on. He would not be with them for long.

Chapter 9

Elgin City and Retirement 1956–1989

BY 1956, all Jimmy's contemporaries, certainly those who had played when he started in 1933, were long retired, and a dignified retirement for Jimmy would not have been out of the question. But Jimmy was one of these chaps who was 'kinda fond o' fitba' and, although he would have been quite happy to stay in Ireland playing for Cork, when the call came from yet another source, he found it impossible to turn down. This one involved a return to Scotland for it came from the distant field of Borough Briggs, in Elgin, Morayshire – the land of farming, fishing, beautiful scenery, distilleries, couthy inhabitants and the broad Scottish Doric which can be virtually incomprehensible, even to other Scotsmen.

Elgin City are now in the Scottish League and are an asset to it. Even in the days when they were a Highland League team, though, they were considered to be one of the better clubs. Indeed, when Delaney went there in 1956, they had won the Highland League for the previous three years and the North of Scotland Cup for the last two. They had beaten their rivals Buckie Thistle on 12 May to win the Highland League and were determined to retain this much-coveted trophy. Clearly, their enterprising directors, after their indifferent start to the 1956–57 season, believed that the veteran Jimmy Delaney still had a great deal to offer. Jimmy travelled from Ireland to the north of Scotland, liked what he saw and signed for the black and whites of Elgin City on Friday 28 September 1956.

The *Northern Scot*, the local weekly newspaper, chortled with glee. The City management, it says, are 'nothing if not enterprising' and although it concedes that Jimmy is 'getting on in years', he is in the mould of Bert McLachlan, Lachie McMillan and Matt Armstrong who all played for Elgin in their twilight years. Jimmy would have known Matt Armstrong from their encounter in the 1937 Scottish Cup Final and other meetings. Ian Rae, the player-manager, a man who had played for Hamilton Academicals, paid Cork Athletic £150, Delaney himself £100 as a signing-on fee and a weekly wage of £10 per week and £5 travelling expenses.

The travelling expenses were necessary because Delaney, having made up his mind to bring his family back to Scotland, decided against moving them all the way to Elgin and travelled every weekend from Cleland. Indeed, he would frequently be seen getting off the train at Elgin station, then walking down to Borough Briggs with his boots under his arm, wrapped up in brown paper and tied with string. This unpretentious legend of the British game, his bald head making him obvious, would talk to the local kids about the game and nod politely to the locals who had all nudged each other as they saw him coming. 'That's him!' 'That's Delaney!' 'He looks just like an ordinary man.'

In fact, Jimmy arrived in Elgin not a minute too soon, for City were embroiled in one of the early rounds of the Scottish Cup against the Inverness side Clachnacuddin. They had drawn with them the previous Saturday at Borough Briggs and were due to play them at Clachnacuddin's ground, Grant Street Park, on Saturday. Jimmy's debut would therefore be a Scottish Cup-tie, and one with important financial implications for the club: a defeat in the Scottish Cup in September was considered a pecuniary disaster.

It so happened that City did go down to Clachnacuddin 2–3 on 29 September 1956. They were unlucky, though, for Clachnacuddin needed a last-minute goal to win the day. Delaney, however, is absolved from blame. 'But don't blame the old maestro', said the *Northern Scot*. 'He's going to be an asset all right on this form. No, the City's weaknesses were in defence. He [Delaney] can show many players of almost half his age a clean pair of heels.'

About 3,000 (a huge crowd for Elgin) paid their one shilling and sixpence to see Delaney make his home debut for the black and white vertical stripes of Elgin City on 6 October. This was against neighbours Rothes and the visitors were leading 3–2 until late in the game when 'a great goal by Jimmy Delaney turned the tide. He cutely back-flicked a shot which was going wide into the net to level the score at 3–3.' He was then responsible for setting up the winner, something that ensured that the entire crowd 'left smiling'.

Next week, he was in the centre-forward position as the team won 1–0 at Nairn County to return to the top of the League, but they blotted their copybook slightly when they lost 3–4 to the 'Broch', as Fraserburgh are called, on 20 October. A week later, with Elgin having signed a chap from Falkirk by the unlikely name of 'Jarro' Davidson for the centre-forward position, Delaney was returned to the right wing, where he had 'more time to draw breath' as Elgin won 4–1 against Huntly at Borough Briggs.

By this time, the world was in crisis as the Russians brutally crushed a protest in Hungary, and Britain severely imperilled world security by provoking a war between Israel and Egypt and trying to step in the middle of it to take over the Suez Canal. The military intervention was a total flop in the face of opposition at home and abroad, but the *Northern Scot*, as right-wing as most Scottish local newspapers in the 1950s, praises Prime Minister Anthony Eden and berates the socialists in the Labour Party for 'making a bear garden out of the House of Commons' and 'encouraging the Egyptians'.

Jimmy was presumably less concerned with all this than with Celtic's lifting of the Scottish League Cup – for the first time, incredibly, after a decade of striving – on the Wednesday afternoon of 31 October when they beat Partick Thistle in a replay. Three days later, Elgin travelled to Rothes and won 7–0 with Delaney instrumental in the creation of most of them. The *Northern Scot* was exultant: '11 goals in 2 games! Who could ask for more?' However, even in the wake of the now obvious failure of the Suez fiasco, the same newspaper persists in its denial, saying 'Eden has gained in stature' and 'has taken a courageous stand'. All this at the time when Eden was going to Jamaica to recover from a nervous breakdown and the Conservative Party were plotting to rid themselves of him.

Delaney scored in the 2–2 draw against Inverness Caledonian, who 30 years later would amalgamate with Inverness Thistle, join the Scottish League and eventually reach the Scottish Premier League. But then, on 17 November, Delaney sustained one injury too many and the one that would eventually finish his career. This was in the game against Forres Mechanics when he sustained a groin strain as he overstretched himself, limped about to no good purpose for the rest of the game and was out for some time afterwards, missing all of December and the festive fixtures.

By the time that he returned there was a New Year and a new Prime Minister. It was 19 January 1957 and Harold McMillan had taken over from the unfortunate Anthony Eden. Sadly, for Jimmy, in the same way that his first appearance for Elgin saw them exit the Scottish Cup, his reappearance coincided with their exit from the North of Scotland Cup, a trophy that they had won for the last two years.

They went down away to Inverness Caledonian and the *Northern Scot* made a comment which seems to imply that the team had been changed – to its detriment – to allow Jimmy back in: 'The club could not afford to pay Jimmy Delaney, fit again, to hang about the sidelines.' The following week, it goes further. Although the team won 3–2 against Inverness Thistle, they suffered from a 'dead weight, in the shape of Robertson and Delaney, both of whom were sadly off form'.

Very seldom in his career had Jimmy been the subject of such adverse criticism and it was probably about now that the reality was beginning to dawn on him that this would have to be his last football season. It was indeed a long journey every weekend from Cleland to Elgin and it was taking its toll, although, mercifully, the weather was not too bad in winter 1957.

He had a very long journey indeed in early March when Elgin travelled to Wick to play in a competition called the Scottish Supplementary Cup (North). This long trip was justified when he scored with a long-range shot in the 3–0 win. Next week, against local rivals Keith on 9 March, Jimmy scored twice in a 5–1 win. One of these was a penalty, which was interesting in view of the fact that he had refused to take a penalty in one of his early games for the club, in October against Huntly. Jimmy was never the greatest penalty-taker in the world and one can parallel this aspect of his career with many others – like Dixie Deans, Paul McStay, Gareth Southgate and Michel Platini – all brilliant players who have famously missed penalties in their time. Delaney, however, seemed to make a habit out of it and one could say that it was one of the weaknesses of his game, although one that he himself was aware of.

Elgin might have been expected to lift the North Supplementary Cup. The League season had been poor by their standards. Buckie would win the Highland League and Lossiemouth the North of Scotland Cup, something that sat ill with Elgin supporters. Elgin could have brought some sort of a smile to the faces of their fans if they had won the North Supplementary Cup. But even that was beyond them as they managed to lose 1–4 to the amateurs of Aberdeen University at the King's College Grounds in Aberdeen, which thus has the distinction of hosting the last senior game of football played by Jimmy Delaney.

By now the *Northern Scot* was seldom mentioning Delaney in its match reports other than when he scored a goal – a clear sign surely that he was not doing well, but then in its edition of 13 April it stated: 'Jimmy Delaney has paid his way according to the City's Annual Balance Sheet. The drawings at League games are up by £906 at League games.' It then seems to contradict itself by saying that Delaney and Davidson together were responsible for the £1174 increase in wages and then speculates, 'whether Delaney will be at Borough Briggs next season is not disclosed. That's up to the Committee!'

In fact, the committee had no decision to make, for Jimmy approached them after the 2–1 win over Inverness Thistle (in which he did not play) and told them that he was retiring through a combination of family circumstances, repeated injuries and general old age. He thus brought to an end a senior career which had lasted almost 24 years – a remarkable length of time in any case and even more so when one thinks that it included 13 full Scotland caps and many wartime and League internationals, four Cup medals in four different countries (three of them winners' medals in separate decades), a broken arm, many other injuries and a World War. The *Northern Scot* eloquently described Jimmy's retirement:

'The waygoing of Jimmy Delaney creates another gap of top class personalities in the football world. Elgin City can take some reflected glory from the fact that so illustrious a player decided to call a halt to an outstanding career at Borough Briggs. Wherever he went Jimmy drew the crowds, no matter what sphere of football he played in and the Highland League was no exception. Football will be poorer without him.'

Jimmy played 16 competitive games in Northern soccer: 12 Highland League, one Scottish Cup, two North Supplementary Cup and one North of Scotland Cup game. He scored eight goals and, in the 'Delaney season', Elgin finished third in the Highland League.

Just to show that football does move on, however, the same edition of the newspaper that announced Delaney's retirement reported that Elgin on Saturday were to give a trial to a young man from Aberdeen Lads Club by the name of Ron Yeats. Ron would go on to play for Dundee United, Liverpool and Scotland in the 1960s.

Jimmy had liked the people at Elgin but one wonders what his emotions would have been less than three years later when Celtic were drawn at Elgin in the Scottish Cup on 5 March 1960. A crowd of 12,000 packed the small ground and, with only six minutes left, the inexperienced Celtic team were seemingly on their way out of the Cup thanks to a Grant goal. Then John Divers scored to level the score and, as the Highland Leaguers visibly tired, Eric Smith scored a somewhat fortuitous winner for the Glasgow club. Seven years later, Elgin found themselves at Parkhead against a different Celtic team, only three months away from their Lisbon destiny. This time it was 7–0 for Celtic, but Elgin had the compensation of a large cheque. An Elgin stay-at-home fan was reputed to have been told that the score was 7–0. He looked puzzled then said 'Who for?'

Jimmy was not the only ex-Celt to play for Elgin. Jimmy Johnstone had a brief and unhappy time there as well from 1978–79. Elgin City, with a good record of doing well in the Scottish Cup, are now a Scottish League team, and their inhabitants retain their interest in football, supporting either Elgin City or perhaps Aberdeen, although there is a sizeable Celtic faction in the town as well.

Life after football for Jimmy Delaney meant a return to his native village of Cleland. In fact, as soon as they returned from Ireland, the family settled there, for Jimmy would travel up to Elgin every weekend rather than take his family away from the traditional family home. The family lived first of all in Chapel Street with Jimmy's mother (the famously hospitable Bridget Delaney) and then in the flat above Kelly's Bar (where the young Joe Jordan saw him setting off for his work every morning). They moved back to another house in Chapel Street before his final house in Fir Place, where he would eventually die in September 1989.

He did of course retain his interest in football. Many players at the end of their careers take up something else, but not so in the case of Jimmy. When one of his daughters was asked what interests Jimmy had other than football, she shrugged her shoulders and said 'football'. He continued his lifelong love of Glasgow Celtic and was frequently seen at their home games. To a lesser extent, he followed his other old teams, like Manchester United, and he would have suffered a dreadful shock on 6 February 1958.

This was the day in which the triumphant Manchester United team were returning from a European Cup trip to Belgrade. They had stopped at Munich and, after several attempts to take off in the snow, had crashed in a field. It was an appalling disaster with so many young and talented lives lost, and Matt Busby himself teetered on the brink for many weeks. He did at last pull through and indeed returned to being manager of Manchester United, but remained emotionally scarred, one would have thought. The most famous survivor was Bobby Charlton, but the loss of such men as Roger Byrne, Tommy Taylor and the prodigiously talented Duncan Edwards was a blow unparalleled in world football. In fact, had it not been for Munich, the 'Busby Babes' might well have won the European Cup before Celtic did in 1967.

Jimmy retained a tremendous empathy for his old friend and manager, and would have suffered dreadfully in the days immediately after the disaster, worrying about him as well as being genuinely distressed about the loss of life. Some were killed instantly but others, like Duncan Edwards, survived the immediate impact but died some time later. The news of the deaths had to be kept from Busby for a while, lest that imperil his own recovery.

Jimmy had made a reasonably comfortable living out of football, but not so comfortable that he did not need to work. He worked as a general labourer in the Ranko and later the nearby Ravenscraig Steel Works. For a man who had played football all his life, adjustment to a life of manual labour at the age of 43 was not easy, and Jimmy had a few problems to begin with.

He may have dabbled with the idea of a career in football management. He certainly, one felt, would have made an ideal assistant manager or trainer to Jimmy McGrory at Parkhead, but for one reason or another that did not happen. The job of trainer would have been a good one for Delaney. He was himself superbly fit and would have demanded the highest of standards from his charges. He would also have been able to impart the decades of wisdom and experience in the same way that the veteran Jimmy McMenemy did so much to bring on Delaney himself in the late 1930s.

He had been player-manager with Cork Athletic and took on a similar, if unofficial, role as confidant and adviser to Ian Rae at Elgin City in his short time there. But, as he himself was well aware, that was concentrating on nothing other than the football field. A manager must deal with many other problems and Jimmy was simply too shy and too nice to do that. There are times when a manager must be devious, evasive, economical with the truth, hyper-optimistic before a game and cruel to his players in private afterwards. He must know how to kick and how to cuddle and, more importantly, when to do both. He must occasionally be tough and downright nasty. All great managers do have, and indeed must have, that quality. Jimmy simply did not have that in his nature, and it is sadly true that the other Jimmy, Jimmy McGrory, was similarly handicapped. He and the team suffered as a result.

Delaney had few interests other than football – usually going to watch Celtic, where he was frequently seen. Youngsters were told 'That's Delaney ower there' when they were too young to realise who Delaney had been and, in any case, he was just an ordinary man cheering on Celtic like everybody else. He was an Honorary Member of the Glasgow and West of Scotland Celtic Football Club Supporters' Association Social Club. Sometimes he would follow the progress of his son Pat, who played professional football for Motherwell and Dunfermline.

As a supporter he would have seen the best and the worst of Celtic. What must he have thought of the dreadful days of the early 1960s, for those were indeed painful years? How did he feel when the Scottish Cup was thrown away to Dunfermline Athletic in 1961? How did he feel when the support, still massive and raucous, turned nasty, throwing bottles as the only way possible to express their disappointment at the repeatedly sub-standard displays? How did he feel when the talented Pat Crerand was compelled in February 1963 to tread the same path as himself from Celtic to Manchester United largely because of an incompetent and unappreciative management structure? How did he feel when the Celtic End in the 1963 Scottish Cup Final replay emptied in spontaneous and unanimous disgust at their side's inept performance? Yet how great the pay-off was in 1967 when Jock Stein's side became the first-ever British side to bring back the European Cup. Delaney's joy would have been as great the following year when Matt Busby's Manchester United did the same thing.

Scotland, especially with Joe Jordan who happily describes Delaney as his boyhood hero, would also have interested him. Twice in the 1970s, they made it to the World Cup Finals, once to fail honourably in 1974 and once to disgrace themselves before the whole world in Argentina in 1978 by losing feebly to Peru, drawing with Iran and having a player sent home for taking drugs. The man whose two goals 'put Hitler off his tea' in 1936, and who made all Scotland smile in 1946, must have been distressed by that.

Manchester United possibly caused more distress over a longer period of time. Following their European success in 1968, they slid slowly at first but then more obviously and managed to get themselves relegated to Division Two in 1974. Even when they came back, they had clearly lost out to Liverpool, and that state of affairs would continue until well after Jimmy's death in 1989. Their triumphs under Alex Ferguson came in the 1990s after Jimmy had died.

Other than incessant watching and talking about football, one thing that Jimmy did a great deal of was walking. The old habit of keeping himself fit died hard with Jimmy and he would frequently be seen on his walks round Newarthill and Carfin and even as far afield as Motherwell and Wishaw, sometimes with his dog. The dog was called Brandy, which is a strange name for a teetotaller to call his dog, but perhaps it had something to do with the name of Derry City's ground, Brandywell. He was well known and well liked by everyone. He would speak courteously to everyone, but he would hate to have any fuss made over him just because he had been a great footballer.

His fondness for walking became even more pronounced after his hip replacement operation in 1978. He enthused about the operation, telling everyone what a difference it made to his lifestyle. A few years previously he had described himself as a 'helpless cripple forced to hobble with the aid of two sticks because of arthritis', whereas after the operation, in which he had his right hip bone removed and replaced, he was able to walk 10 miles a day with Brandy over the moors. 'Thousands are afraid to take the chance of the operation. I'm glad I did. So are the family. I must have been a sad sight sitting here moping.'

In that same interview, he was quite scathing about modern footballers who do not work hard enough, get ridiculous money and do not enjoy the game as much as he used to. He also said that he was not the best player in that great pre-war Celtic side. 'How could I be with Malky MacDonald in the side?' He denied he was a poacher, but confirmed that 'if there was a 50-50 chance of a goal, I was never far away'.

Jimmy hated being late. If one of his friends, or his son perhaps, was coming round to pick him up to take him to a Celtic game, for example, and the agreed time was 1.30pm and the gentleman concerned was five minutes late, Jimmy would fret and worry.

He was a kind, but strict father. He was himself very regular in his attendances at mass and confession, and encouraged his family to be the same. His obsession with time spilled over into his concern for his daughter's welfare, for 'being home by 11 o'clock' did not include 'five minutes grace'. On one occasion Kathleen, having missed her bus, had to take a taxi, a rare and expensive luxury in the 1960s, lest she risk his wrath.

In April 1989, Jimmy was diagnosed as having bowel and liver cancer. Originally he was given six weeks to live, but such was his desire to keep going and so strong was the love of his family, in particular his wife Annie and his two daughters Kathleen and Anne-Marie, that he lasted another six months, always being cheerful and determined to get the best out of life that he could. The family would soothe him by rubbing his arms, for example, even feeling able to say when they massaged his left arm that they were now massaging a pig's bone!

He had some visitors in his last days to Fir Street, Cleland. The journalist Jack Webster, several of the Celtic players and clerics like his parish priest Father O'Donoghue and even Bishop Joseph Devine. This was befitting for such a humble, religious man who was a prominent figure in his local parish of St Mary's, where he was something of an institution. His family were with him when he died.

Jimmy died on Tuesday 26 September 1989. Curiously, there was no one minute's silence observed for him at Celtic's Cup-winners' Cup game against Partisan Belgrade the following night. The most charitable explanation for this is presumably that it was a European game and the Yugoslavs would not have known who he was. This is of course specious nonsense and says very little for those who were in control of Celtic at that time. In fact, it was a typical attitude from a group of men who would in a few years time lead the club to the brink of extinction. Even more appalling was the lack of commemoration at the Aberdeen v Celtic game the following Saturday – Delaney had played for both these clubs. Once again, it says very little for either club.

Delaney had read stories about all the old Celts like Sandy McMahon, who had had a Celtic jersey draped over their coffins. 'I hope they do the same for me', he would frequently say. They did. His funeral on Friday 29 September was well attended by great Celts like Tommy Gemmell, Paul McStay and Jimmy Johnstone, and it was Celtic's manager in 1989, Billy McNeill, who draped the colours on his coffin. A Manchester United top was also placed on the coffin as it was lowered into the ground at Cambusnethan, near Wishaw.

As often happens in such circumstances after such a long and happy marriage, Jimmy's wife Annie did not long survive him. She died on 1 April 1990, suddenly but peacefully, content in the knowledge that she would soon be united once again with the man that she loved.

Chapter 10

The Delaney Tradition

JIMMY'S DAUGHTER Kathleen has a beautiful quote about her father: 'We didn't realise he was any different from anybody else. He was just our daddy.' Just like Jimmy Quinn of the previous generation and indeed like the Lisbon Lions of later days, Jimmy Delaney was just an ordinary man. The fact that he was one of the greatest footballers of his time meant nothing. He was certainly not bigheaded, nor did he in any way consider himself better than anyone. He was simply a lad from Cleland who had made it good in football in the same way that some chaps are good at bricklaying, hang-gliding or amateur dramatics. The difference, however, is two-fold. One is that he was *very* good at football and the other is that in West Central Scotland, nobody really speaks about anything other than football!

It is unlikely that the name Delaney will ever lose its significance in Scottish football. Those who saw Jimmy play are now few in number, but the legend will live on. There will always be a sparkle associated with the name Delaney which will never fade, both for what Jimmy achieved on the football field and for the sort of man that he was.

It is of course Celtic with whom he will be associated first and foremost. The Celtic Supporters' Club which is based in Cleland calls itself the Jimmy Delaney Supporters' Bus. This is hardly surprising and, indeed, Jimmy's relatives are in the forefront of the club. What he achieved with other clubs and with Scotland is all very impressive, but as he once said himself he would always be known as 'Jimmy Delaney of Celtic. The brand mark is there!'

The Jimmy Delaney Celtic Supporters Club of Cleland was founded in 1964 and recently celebrated its 40th anniversary. When Jimmy played, there does not seem to have been any organised supporters' club or 'brake club', as they had been known in the old days when the transport was horse-drawn. Perhaps this reflects the economic uncertainties of the 1930s, but perhaps it was simply not necessary as the train and the number 44 bus, which went almost from door to door, did the job. In 1951, a Cleland Celtic Supporters' Club was formed, but this organisation suffered badly from the poor displays of the team in the late 1950s and early 1960s, and there was the odd 'fall out' – a fairly endemic condition in Celtic supporters' clubs, it must be said.

But it was not simply Celtic games that they went to. Now and again a double-decker bus went the comparatively short journey to see Falkirk when Jimmy was playing for them between late 1951 and early 1954. In 1954, while most supporters were attending the Scottish Cup Final on 24 April between Celtic and Aberdeen, some had organised a trip across the Irish Sea to see Jimmy play for Derry City in the Irish Cup.

The organisation suffered badly in the late 1950s and seems to have disappeared entirely by the early 1960s as the Celtic team hit all-time depths of fecklessness. But, in 1964, there was a slight improvement in results and, crucially for the area, the local steel industry at Ravenscraig began to flourish, so another attempt was made to form a club. Jimmy, now retired from football, was approached about having the club called after him. He was reluctant at first, but eventually under pressure said 'Aw richt', or words to that effect, and the Jimmy Delaney Celtic Supporters' Club came into being.

There is of course nothing unusual about supporters' clubs being named after individuals. There is, or have been, for example, clubs named after Jock Stein, Henrik Larsson, Davie Hay and others. Famously, in the 1920s there was a horse-drawn brake club named after the goalkeeper Charlie Shaw. The Jimmy Delaney Celtic Supporters' Club is unusual in that it is a club which is still named after a man who played his last game for Celtic 60 years ago. Occasionally, a youngster will notice this bus in the Parkhead Bus Park and say, 'Who was Jimmy Delaney?' to other members of his particular group. It will befall to one of the older members of the club the duty of telling who Jimmy Delaney was.

Jimmy's family tell stories about how, in his later years, they all wondered how on earth he was ever able to play in important games like Old Firm matches, for he found it very difficult to watch a game like that or even to sit at home and listen to Celtic v Rangers games on the radio. Sometimes, he was a coward, unable either to go to the game or follow its progress any other way. He would feign indifference about the result, as many other supporters do, but this fools nobody. Anyone who has ever followed Celtic knows all about the gnawing away at the vitals, the sleeplessness the night before, the worrying about someone's injury, about quirky refereeing decisions, whether someone would freeze on the day, about how irrational and unpredictable the whole thing was. The day itself is usually punctuated by frequent visits to the toilet for what a legendary Celtic supporter once called a 'cathartic experience'.

Jimmy's way of dealing with this endogenous, hereditary and terminal condition called 'being Celtic daft' would sometimes be to go for a walk with his dog and not return home until he had seen a few supporters' buses returning from the game. The demeanour of those on the bus usually indicated very accurately how the game had gone. If they were singing, waving scarves or punching the air, it meant a victory. A defeat was signified by a doleful silence and some punters asleep at the back of the bus – or pretending to be. The weekend was spoiled, irretrievably and permanently.

Supporting Celtic does involve some great moments but some dreadful ones as well, and there is no use anyone saying 'Don't take it so seriously!' or 'It's only a game' or some other such claptrap. Defeat is an awful experience, even for the greatest of players, reaching a depth which outsiders can only wonder at. How would Jimmy Delaney, for example, have coped with Black Sunday of 22 May 2005 when the Scottish Premier League was thrown away in such a devastatingly shattering fashion? Certainly, one of Jimmy's sons described it as the 'worst ever'. There have also been some dreadful Scottish Cup disasters to Inverness (twice) and Clyde. Such things are not easily dealt with.

The Celtic team that Delaney joined in 1933 was by no means a vintage one. There were great players – Jimmy McGrory, Charlie Napier and Jimmy McStay – but death had robbed Celtic of two great players in John Thomson (killed tragically at Ibrox on 5 September 1931) and Peter Scarff (fated to die of tuberculosis or consumption in December 1933) and the team had been unable to mount a strong and consistent challenge to Rangers. The League Championship had last been won in 1926, in the brief and transient heyday of Tommy McInally. In fact, had it not been for Motherwell in 1932, Rangers would have won the League Championship the magical nine seasons in a row long before Jock Stein's side did it in 1974.

However, Maley and his many spies and scouts saw great talent in the few games that the speedy Delaney played for Stoneyburn Juniors. Following a season in the reserves or with junior teams working with Jimmy McMenemy, and after his first season in the full team, Delaney in 1935–36 supplied a great deal of the ammunition for McGrory's 50 goals and restored Celtic to the top of Scottish football. Two years later, Celtic were the best in British football and Delaney, although he himself would never have said so, was the best in that team.

Then came the two catastrophes in 1939 – one personal and one international – an arm so broken as to be shattered and worthy of amputation in the opinion of some medical people, and World War Two. Once Delaney's arm was repaired, it was he who carried a mediocre (and sometimes a sheer bad) Celtic team throughout the war years in which the faithful supporters at home and abroad were thwarted time and time again.

There had been problems for Delaney as well in the shape of having to regain confidence in his arm, the refusal of the Scottish Football Association to play him for Scotland because of insurance problems and finally the worst calamity that can affect anyone; the death of a small child. But he kept going, doing his best for his beloved Celtic in the strange and surreal circumstances of the war, although these years brought little other than disappointment for himself and the fans. Yet he might well have echoed the words of John Divers when it was put to him that World War Two destroyed his career. John said, 'Yes, but it destroyed an awful lot more than that for an awful lot more people than me.'

There was no greater disappointment for supporters than to return home from years of gallant and occasionally glorious military service in February 1946 to find that the timid Celtic board had refused Delaney a justified pay rise and transferred him to Manchester United. The fact that he was playing for another Celt there in Matt Busby hardly helped. It was Celtic that he should have been playing for, but the pill was slightly sugared by what happened in the Victory International of 1946.

By being part of a great forward line – arguably as good a forward line as the Celtic one of 1936 or 1938 – Jimmy brought the hitherto sadly underperforming Manchester United to consistent League glory, including one or two near misses for the Championship itself and the epic English Cup victory of 1948. The post-war years were grim ones, in Manchester no less than anywhere else, but Jimmy lightened them up.

Then there were two teams that he played for on his return to Scotland. He had a good year with Aberdeen and he is still recalled there with pride and pleasure by some veteran Dons fans, even though he never really settled and lasted less than 13 months. But then Falkirk gave him the opportunity to bring some lustre to the twilight (as everyone thought) of his career. He took them up from Division B and then, crucially for the long-term future of the club, kept them in the top division for the following year.

Now nearly 40, he was on his travels again, this time to Ireland where he won an Irish Cup medal with Derry City in the North before almost doing the same in the South with Cork Athletic. He finished his career in Elgin in the Scottish Highland League but wherever he went he brought success, appreciation, admiration and gave them all respect, a feel-good factor (sometimes when that would have been difficult) and the admiring glances of the rest of the footballing world.

And of course there was what he did for Scotland. It is small wonder that the village of Cleland continues to worship his memory. At least three people that have made their mark in Scottish football owe everything to Jimmy Delaney who, in spite of all the efforts to make him into some kind of a demigod, remained, like Jimmy Quinn of a previous generation, just an 'ordinary man'.

One such man is Joe Jordan. The very opening to Joe's book tells about how he saw the great Jimmy Delaney, long after his career had ended, going to his work every morning with an army-type knapsack over his shoulder to carry his piece and his flask of tea. Indeed, like an ordinary man, except that this one had played for Manchester United and Celtic. Joe's father and Jimmy were friends and Joe remains friends with John Delaney, Jimmy's son.

It is not known quite how Jock Stein missed Jordan, but Joe played for Morton, Leeds United, Manchester United and AC Milan, and won 52 caps for Scotland, scoring in each of the 1974, 1978 and 1982 World Cup Finals. But Delaney was always his inspiration, and Joe remained on good terms with his aged mentor. How Jimmy would have winced as he watched the horrors of Argentina unfold on his television!

Jimmy's son Pat, or Patsy, played professional football with Motherwell and Dunfermline. There was a chance that he might have joined Celtic. At one point in Celtic's desperate winter of 1964–65, Billy McNeill might have been tempted to go down south, for Tottenham Hotspur and a few others were certainly interested. If this had happened, the rumour mills had it, Pat Delaney would have been his replacement. As it was, Pat played on for Motherwell, subsequently joined Dunfermline Athletic and earned a deserved reputation as a solid defender.

Then there is John Kennedy, grandson of Jimmy Delaney and the son of his daughter Anne-Marie. John made his debut for Celtic in 2002 and was particularly impressive in season 2003–04 as a tall, commanding defender. He defied Barcelona in particular so well in a UEFA Cup match on 25 March 2004 and then Rangers the following Sunday that he was chosen to play for Scotland against Romania the following midweek. It was a particularly pointless international friendly played by a Scotland team going nowhere under Berti Vogts and John might have been well advised to do what many others do in these circumstances and call off, faking an injury. But it was, and is, an honour to play for one's country – something that his granddad did so well – and he played. Sadly, he lasted only 18 minutes before he was carried off with severe damage to his cruciate ligaments and was out of football for well over a year.

As bad luck goes, this was on a par with the broken arm of his illustrious grandfather in 1939, but the young man has come back. He was seen at the 2005 Scottish Cup Final when Bobo Balde offered him and the other reserves the chance to hold the Scottish Cup and to join the party. He was seen to walk reasonably normally and hopes were expressed that he might be back soon. Unfortunately, there have been quite a few setbacks.

Sportsmanship and fair play is an aspect of the Delaney tradition which is occasionally undervalued. There was Jimmy's famous dictum as he presented the prizes at a school athletics competition that 'It is better to be a champion sport than a sports' champion'. He was seldom in trouble with referees, never suspended by the authorities and seldom booked, even in the tough competitive leagues in which he practised his craft.

He was of course so good a player that he did not need to resort to dirty tactics, but here is what Rangers captain Jock 'Tiger' Shaw says about him. Jock himself was a doughty character and was not called 'Tiger' for nothing.

'I doubt if there was ever a greater sportsman than Jimmy. He was the cleanest player I ever opposed. When you took the ball away from him, you did it with the knowledge that you wouldn't be tripped or pushed. I could have played against Delaney in my bare feet – and finished the game without a scratch, so fair was Jimmy in the tackle.'

Like many great heroes, poems have been written about him. Several have come to light. One of them is entitled simply 'A Tribute to James Delaney':

> *Surely you've heard of many players*
> *And the famous deeds they've done*
> *Of their struggles and their glories*
> *And the games they've fought and won.*
>
> *There's a lad who plays at Parkhead*
> *He's the finest we have seen*
> *Sure his heart is true and faithful*
> *To his jersey white and green.*
>
> *And his name will live forever*
> *Amongst other kings and crowns*
> *Johnny Thomson, James McGrory*
> *And others un-renowned.*
>
> *He's the king of all right-wingers*
> *Aye the daddy of them all*
> *Sure our hopes they are the highest*
> *When Delaney's on the ball.*
>
> *His name is James Delaney*
> *And surely you must agree*
> *Anyone to be his equal*
> *You could never hope to see.*
>
> *You can talk of Stanley Matthews*
> *Or Willie Waddell too*
> *But remember James Delaney*
> *All our hearts go out to you.*

There is also one entitled 'Cleland's Favourite Son':

In the famous village of Cleland
We have a very proud claim
For rearing many fine citizens
And heroes of the game.

Of the footballers so well remembered
One name stands out among the rest
It's peerless James Delaney
Who simply was 'The Best'.

When we think of Celtic legends
Who graced the green and white
Tho' many years have come and gone
His star's still shining bright.

From Celtic on to Manchester
Delaney was destined to go
To continue his career at United
And put his skills on show.

He then journeyed on to Ireland
To Derry City on the Foyle
Helping them win the Northern Cup
Soon after reaching Irish soil.

An amazing football journey
For Delaney, still not complete,
Crossing the Irish border
In Southern Ireland to compete.

Four Cup Final medals
In four countries Jimmy won
So raise a glass to the memory
Of Cleland's Favourite Son.

A poet calling himself Columncille wrote in the late 1940s when Celtic were flirting with relegation and waxed nostalgic about the 'Days of Celtic Glory'. The poem includes the following verse:

Oh to think of it
Oh to dream of it
Fills our hearts with tears.
Oh for the days of Delaney prancing
Down the field with his mates in tune;
Oh for one of those hours of gladness –
Gone, alas, like our youth – too soon.

Jimmy might have been embarrassed by all this acclaim. He always wanted to be a private man, living at home with his Annie and his family, whom he adored and who adored him back. He would have loved to have been an inconsequential, insignificant kind of fellow. Except, of course, he was not. He was Jimmy Delaney, one of Scotland's best ever football players. The stuff of legend.